FROMMER'S

COMPREHENSIVE TRAVEL GUIDE

PRAGUE
1ST EDITION

by Dan Levine

PRENTICE HALL TRAVEL

NEW YORK • LONDON • TORONTO • SYDNEY • TOKYO • SINGAPORE

FROMMER BOOKS

Published by Prentice Hall General Reference
15 Columbus Circle
New York, NY 10023

ISBN 0-671-86798-9
ISSN 1074-4185

Design by Robert Bull Design
Maps by Ortelius Design and Geografix Inc.

Frommer's Editorial Staff

Editorial Director: Marilyn Wood
Editorial Manager/Senior Editor: Alice Fellows
Senior Editors: Sara Hinsey Raveret, Lisa Renaud
Editors: Charlotte Allstrom, Thomas F. Hirsch, Peter Katucki, Theodore
Stavrou
Assistant Editors: Margaret Bowen, Christopher Hollander, Alice
Thompson, Ian Wilker
Editorial Assistants: Gretchen Henderson, Douglas Stallings
Managing Editor: Leanne Coupe

Special Sales

Manufactured in the United States of America

CONTENTS

10 EASY EXCURSIONS FROM PRAGUE 164

APPENDIX 181

INDEX 189

LIST OF MAPS

INVITATION TO THE READERS

In researching this book, I have come across many fine establishments, the best of which I have included here. I am sure that many of you will also come across appealing hotels, restaurants, guesthouses, shops, and attractions. Please don't keep them to yourself. Share your experiences, especially if you want to comment on places that have been included in this edition that have changed for the worse. You can address your letters to:

Dan Levine
Frommer's Prague, 1st Edition
c/o Prentice Hall Travel
15 Columbus Circle
New York, NY 10023

A DISCLAIMER

Readers are advised that prices fluctuate in the course of time, and travel information changes under the impact of the varied and volatile factors that affect the travel industry. Neither the author nor the publisher can be held responsible for the experiences of readers while traveling. Readers are invited to write to the publisher with ideas, comments, and suggestions for future editions.

SAFETY ADVISORY

Whenever you're traveling in an unfamiliar city or country, stay alert. Be aware of your immediate surroundings. Wear a moneybelt and keep a close eye on your possessions. Be particularly careful with cameras, purses, and wallets—all favorite targets of thieves and pickpockets.

CHAPTER 1

INTRODUCING PRAGUE

- **WHAT'S SPECIAL ABOUT PRAGUE**
1. **GEOGRAPHY, HISTORY & POLITICS**
- **DATELINE**
2. **FAMOUS PRAGUERS**
3. **CULTURAL LIFE**
4. **FOOD & DRINK**
5. **RECOMMENDED BOOKS, FILMS & RECORDINGS**

No one ever forgets a visit to Prague, "City of a Thousand Spires." The dreamy images of Prague Castle rising out of the morning mist, or reflecting the last crimson glimmers of sunset are memories that are treasured the world over. The city center's intricately carved sandstone buildings and narrow, winding cobblestone lanes are embodiments of romanticism. Staré Město (Old Town) truly seems magically removed from everyday realities; it's hard to get caught up in the tension and strife of daily life here. Visitors often take circuitous routes to their destinations, just to reexperience the enchantment of Charles Bridge or to watch shadows lengthen around Staroměstské náměstí (Old Town Square).

The entire city center is a museum that has seemingly been untouched over the centuries. But it's actually far from frozen in time. Prague (Praha in Czech) is a dynamic, living, breathing metropolis in the middle of momentous change. The fall in 1989–90 of the Communist regime, which had ruled over Czechoslovakia for some 40 years, opened the city to the most dramatic transformation in its long history.

It has been said that every 35 years or so, a window in time opens for a few short years on a single special place in the world. It was Paris in the 1920s, Haight-Ashbury in the 60s, and in the 90s Prague is the new bohemia. Today, an estimated 20,000 to 30,000 Americans live in Prague. The majority are artists, writers, and musicians in their 20s. For many of these temporary expatriates (known as YAPs, or Young Americans in Prague), the city is just an impermanent playground—a pleasurable place to wait out the slow economy at home. For numerous others, the city represents opportunity—creatively, financially, or both. Paying only $200 or less each month for rent, YAPs can afford to spend time creatively, and expat entrepreneurs are opening businesses there at a swift pace; many are listed throughout

☑ WHAT'S SPECIAL ABOUT PRAGUE

Architecture

☐ Staroměstské náměstí (Old Town Square), one of Europe's most attractive, combining Gothic, Renaissance, baroque, and rococo architecture.

☐ Charles Bridge, Prague's oldest bridge and the symbol of the city.

Castles

☐ Prague Castle (Hrad), dating from Prague's golden age in the 14th century, dominating the west side of the Vltava River.

☐ Karlštejn, 45 minutes from Prague, a well-preserved structure from 1348, built to house the crown jewels of the Holy Roman Empire.

Buildings

☐ Royal Palace, home of Bohemian kings and princes from the 9th to the 16th century.

☐ Old Town Hall, from the 11th century, with its 14th-century tower.

☐ Powder Tower, a 140-foot-tall tower, the only one remaining from Prague's medieval fortifications.

Museums

☐ Šternberk Palace Art Museum, with one of Central Europe's finest collections.

☐ National Museum. The nation's archeological and historical past is displayed in a neo-Renaissance building.

☐ Czech National Gallery, with a major collection of Bohemian painting and sculpture.

☐ St. Agnes Convent, housing within its Gothic halls a gallery of 19th-century Czech art.

Places of Worship

☐ St. Vitus Cathedral, a massive 14th-century Gothic structure containing the tombs of St. Vitus and St. Wenceslas (of Christmas carol fame).

☐ Týn Church, with its twin 260-foot spires, where Jan Hus first heard Reformation sermons.

☐ Old New Synagogue, Europe's oldest remaining Jewish house of worship.

Parks and Gardens

☐ Letná Park, with its Renaissance gardens and Royal Summer Palace.

☐ Waldstein Palace Gardens, surrounding the first baroque palace in Prague.

---

this guidebook. Sure, Prague's environment is polluted, its accommodations are substandard, Czech food can be unhealthy, winters are severe, and telephones don't work very well. But I love Prague. I really

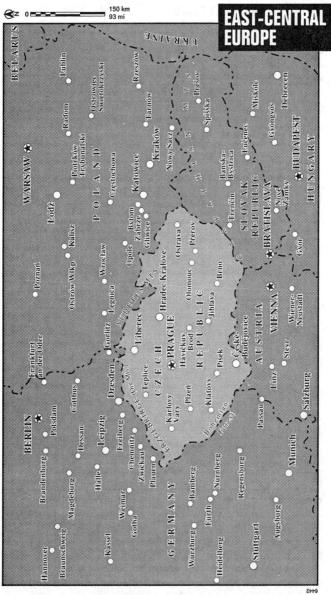

0 ⊨⊨⊨⊨⊨⊨ 150 km
93 mi

do. It's majestically beautiful, historically fascinating, intellectually stimulating, extraordinary fun, and the most amazing place I've ever been.

THE PEOPLE Both self-deprecating and full of black humor, Praguers are most always kind to foreigners—probably because they think that's their lot in life. Czechs have been politically and culturally subjugated by others for such long periods that repression seems to have become a part of the national psyche. It's a special brand of black humor that typifies Czechs. They have a lot to think about, having been subjects of the Habsburgs for some 400 years, suffering in both world wars, and then languishing under Communism for about 40 years. Czech humor magazines, which are quite popular, are packed with cartoons of things happening to blind and crippled people. Typical is the sketch of a man clutching his feet that have just been chopped off by a passing train who says, "Finally, I can bite my toe-nails." It seems that the harsher the misery, the darker the humor. But with the demise of Communism, and the strength of the new Czech state, the traditional black humor may be on the way out.

1. GEOGRAPHY, HISTORY & POLITICS

GEOGRAPHY

The Czech Republic is located in the very heart of Europe. Its neighbors are Austria, Germany, Poland, and Slovakia. Prague, one of Europe's smaller capitals, encompasses a little over 60 square miles on both banks of the Vltava (Moldau) River and has an estimated population of 1.2 million. It is located on the same latitude as Bonn, Cracow, and Winnipeg, and is relatively flat, varying in altitude from 572 to 1,191 feet. (For a map of the country, see page 165.)

The Czech Republic has a total population of about 10.3 million. Some 12% of the country's inhabitants live in Prague. Of that number, only about 2%, or 22,000, live in the very center of the city. The great majority of the population of Prague is ethnically Czech, though Germans, Slovaks, and Poles are widely represented.

To be certain, there are many cultural differences between foreigners and Czechs, as you will discover during your visit. But for all their differences, contemporary Czechs are a lot like the rest of us: Harlequin Romances, first published in the Czech Republic in 1992, are already selling over 7 million copies a year, and *Blesk,* Prague's top-selling daily newspaper, is a trashy tabloid complete with big headlines and pictures of topless women on page three.

IMPRESSIONS

Prague is a golden ship majestically sailing on the Vltava.
—GUILLAUME APOLLINAIRE, French poet (1880–1918)

HISTORY

The earliest known inhabitants of the territory now known as Bohemia were the Boii, a Celtic people who gave their name to this region. The Boii occupied the lands around the Vltava River from as early as 500 B.C. to about 100 B.C., when they were driven from their lands by the seminomadic Germanic Marcomanni people.

Central Europe became a hotbed of contention during the disintegration of the Roman Empire in the 5th century A.D., when two Eastern peoples fought for the same territories. The Huns unsettled the Marcomanni around A.D. 450, only to be defeated themselves by the Avars less than a century later. Around the same time, Slavs crossed the Carpathian Mountains into Europe, and set up a kingdom in Bohemia, where they alternately dominated, and were dominated by, the Avars.

The Avars were expelled from Central Europe in 796 by an alliance of the Slavic Moravians, who established themselves around the River Morava in the 8th century, and the Franks, who were led by Charlemagne. So began the Great Moravian Empire, a kingdom that encompassed Bohemia, Slovakia, and parts of modern Poland and Hungary. The alliance only lasted 100 years—until the Magyar invasion of 896—and marked the first and last time until the 20th century that Czechs and Slovaks were united under a single ruler. After the 9th-century invasion, the Slavs living east of the River Morava swore allegiance to the Magyars, while the Czechs, who lived west of the river, fell under the authority of the Holy Roman Empire.

PŘEMYSLID DYNASTY Bořivoj, the first Přemyslid ruler, reigned in Bohemia according to the will of the Holy Roman Emperor. Prague's first castle was constructed in Hradčany at the end of the 9th century, and in 973 a bishopric was established in Prague, answering to the archbishopric of Mainz. Thus, before the end of the

DATELINE

- **500 B.C.** Celtic people settle in the area of today's Czech Republic.
- **A.D. 450** Huns and other Eastern peoples arrive in Bohemia.
- **870** Bohemia becomes part of Holy Roman Empire. Castle constructed in Hradčany.
- **973** Bishopric founded in Prague.
- **1158** First stone bridge spans the Vltava.
- **1234** Staré Město (Old Town) founded, the first of Prague's historic five towns.
- **1257** Malá Strana (Lesser Town) established by German colonists.
- **1306** Přemyslid dynasty ends following the death of heirless, teenage Václav III.
- **1344** Prague bishopric raised to an archbishopric.
- **1346** Charles IV becomes king and Holy Roman Emperor, as Prague's Golden Age begins.
- **1403** Jan Hus becomes rector of the University of Prague, and launches a crusade for religious reform. *(continues)*

DATELINE

- **1415** Hus burned at the stake, and decades of religious warfare begin.
- **1419** Roman Catholic councilors thrown from the windows of New Town Hall in First Defenestration.
- **1434** Radical Hussites, called Taborites, defeated in the Battle of Lipany, ending religious warfare.
- **1526** Roman Catholic Habsburgs gain control of Bohemia.
- **1584** Prague made seat of the imperial court of Rudolf II.
- **1618** Second Defenestration helps ignite Thirty Years' War.
- **1648** Praguers defend against invading Sweden—the last military action of the Thirty Years' War.
- **1784** Prague's four towns united.
- **1818** National Museum founded.
- **1848** Industrial Revolution begins in Prague, drawing people from countryside and fueling Czech national revival.

(continues)

first millennium, the German influence in Bohemia was firmly established. The Přemyslid dynasty ruled over Bohemia for more than 300 years, during which time Prague became a major commercial area along Central Europe's trade routes. In the 12th century, Prague was known as "Mezihradí," or "between the castles," a term referring to the town's place between Prague Castle and Vyšehrad, a mountain stronghold located a few miles south. A wooden plank bridge stood near where the stone Charles Bridge spans the Vltava today, Václavské náměstí (Wenceslas Square) was a small horse market, and the city's 3,500 residents rarely lived to see their 45th birthday. In 1234, Staré Město (Old Town), the first of Prague's historic five towns, was founded.

Encouraged by Bohemia's rulers, who guaranteed German civic rights to western settlers, Germans established entire towns around Prague, including Malá Strana (Lesser Town), which was founded between the castle and Staré Město in 1257. . The Přemyslid dynasty ended with the death of heirless, teenage Václav III in 1306. After much debate, the throne was offered to John of Luxembourg, husband of Václav III's younger sister.

FIRST GOLDEN AGE & CZECH REFORMATION German by birth and educated in France, John of Luxembourg spent most of his reign participating in foreign wars. Charles IV, also known as Václav, took the thrown in 1346, and almost single-handedly ushered in Prague's first golden age (the second began in the late 16th century). Two years previous, Charles had won an archbishopric for Prague that was independent of Mainz. And when he became king of Bohemia, Charles also became, by election, Holy Roman Emperor. Over the next 30 years of his reign, Prague was transformed into the bustling capital of the Holy Roman Empire and one of the most important cities in Europe. Charles

Bridge and St. Vitus Cathedral were built and Charles University was founded, along with monasteries that also still survive today.

The reign of Charles's son, Václav IV, was marked by serious social upheaval, mostly provoked by rival religious factions. Reformist priest Jan Hus drew large crowds to Prague's Bethlehem Chapel preaching against what he saw as the corrupt tendencies of Prague's bishopric. Hus became widely popular among Czech nationals who rallied behind his crusade against the German-dominated religious and political establishment. Excommunicated in 1412, and charged with heresy two years later, Hus was burned at the stake on July 6, 1415, sparking off widespread riots, and ultimately civil war.

HUSSITE WARS The hostilities began simply enough. Rioting Hussites threw several Roman Catholic councilors to their deaths from the windows of Prague's Novoměstská radnice, a deed popularly known as the First Defenestration. It didn't take long for the pope to declare a crusade against the Czech heretics. The conflict widened into a class struggle, and by 1420 several major battles had been fought between the peasant Hussites and the nobility-backed Catholic crusaders. A schism split the Hussites when a more moderate faction, known as the Utraquists, signed a 1433 peace agreement with Rome at the Council of Basel. The more radical members, known as Taborites, rightly perceived the agreement to be a victory for the nobility, and vowed to continue fighting. But in 1434 the Taborites were decisively defeated at the Battle of Lipany, and for the most part, Bohemia returned to the status quo. Meanwhile, the Utraquists, newly empowered by their agreement with Rome, elected George of Poděbrady as regent, then king, of Bohemia. On George's death, Czech nobles opted in 1471 to be ruled by the Polish Jagiellonian dynasty, a move that in effect gave power to the nobles themselves.

DATELINE

- **1875** Horse-drawn trams operate on Prague's streets.
- **1881** National Theater completed.
- **1883** Franz Kafka is born in Staré Město.
- **1918** Czechoslovak Republic founded.
- **1921** Prague's boundaries expanded to encompass neighboring villages and settlements.
- **1938** Leaders of Germany, Great Britain, Italy, and France meet in Munich and award Czech border territories to Hitler's Third Reich.
- **1939** Hitler absorbs the rest of the Czech lands; puppet Slovak Republic established.
- **1940s** In World War II more than 130,000 Czechs are murdered, including over 80,000 Jews.
- **1944** Prague Uprising fails to liberate capital from Nazi rule.
- **1945–46** Soviet army liberates Prague; 2.5 million Germans expelled; Communist leader Klement Gottwald

(continues)

HABSBURG RULE In less than 60 years the Jagiellonians had been defeated by the Turks and the Czech throne was once again up for grabs. In 1526, Archduke Ferdinand was elected king of Bohemia, marking the beginning of Roman Catholic Habsburg rule, which continued until World War I. Emperor Rudolf II ascended to the throne in 1576 and presided over what was to become known as Prague's second golden age. Rudolf reestablished Prague as the seat of the empire, invited the great astronomers Johannes Kepler and Tycho Brahe to Prague, and endowed the city's museums with some of the best art in Europe.

Continued conflicts between the Catholic Habsburgs and Bohemia's predominantly Protestant nobility came to a head on May 23, 1618, when two Catholic governors were thrown out of the windows of Prague Castle, an event known as the Second Defenestration. This marked the beginning of a string of complex political and religious conflicts known as the Thirty Years' War, during which Bohemia was a battleground for Roman Catholic and Protestant armies. After a Swedish army was defeated on Charles Bridge by a local force that included Prague's Jews and students, the Thirty Years' War came to an end with the Peace of Westphalia. The Catholics won a decisive victory, and the focus of empire shifted back to Vienna. Fresh waves of immigrants practically turned Prague and other towns into German cities. By the end of the 18th century, the Czech language was on the verge of dying out.

The 19th-century Industrial Revolution drew Czechs from the countryside into Prague, where a Czech national revival began. The fall of the French monarchy in 1848 put the Habsburg Empire into crisis, forcing Bohemia's rulers to answer Prague's political demands. As the industrial economy grew, Prague's Czech population increased in number and power, soon overtaking the Germans.

CZECHOSLOVAK REPUBLIC & WORLD WAR II Although they were part of the Austrian Empire, Czechs and Slovaks were united in their aversion to fighting their Slav brothers in World War I. At war's end the two peoples agreed to unite forces and, on Oct. 28, 1918, the Czechoslovak Republic was officially declared in Prague.

DATELINE

1993 Czechoslovakia divides in two: Czech Republic is born as is Slovakia.

The 1930s brought disaster. First, the Great Depression led to much political instability. Then, on Sept. 30, 1938, leaders of Great Britain, Italy, France, and Germany met in Munich and awarded Czech border territories to Hitler's Third Reich without consulting the Czechoslovak government. Britain's Neville Chamberlain returned to London and told a cheering crowd that he had achieved "peace in our time." Within a year, Hitler absorbed the rest of the Czech lands, and installed a puppet government in the Slovak Republic. Over the next six years, more than 130,000 Czechs were systematically murdered, including over 80,000 Jews.

The Russians liberated Prague on May 9, 1945. Some 2.5 million Germans were expelled from Czechoslovakia, and 60% of the country's industries were nationalized. Elections were held in 1946, and Communist leader Klement Gottwald was appointed prime minister after his party won about one third of the vote. By 1948, Communists controlled the government, and little dissent was tolerated. Despite some cultural and economic liberalization in the 1950s, there was much discontent with the Communist regime.

PRAGUE SPRING In January 1968, Alexander Dubček, First Secretary of the Czechoslovak Communist Party, began to create "socialism with a human face," a program of political, economic, and social reform that blossomed into a brief intellectual and artistic renaissance known as the "Prague Spring." Increasingly nervous about what seemed to them as a loss of party control, Communist hard-liners in Prague and other East European capitals conspired with the Soviet Union to overthrow the Czechoslovak government. On Wednesday morning, Aug. 21, 1968, Praguers awoke to find themselves invaded by 200,000 Warsaw Pact soldiers claiming "fraternal assistance." Believing they would be welcomed as liberators, these soldiers from the Soviet Union, Poland, East Germany, Bulgaria, and Hungary were bewildered when angry Czechs confronted them with rocks and flaming torches. The Communist grip tightened, however, and Prague fell deeper into the Soviet sphere of influence.

VELVET REVOLUTION In 1976 the Communist government arrested a popular rock band called the Plastic People of the Universe on charges of disturbing the peace. This motivated a group of

Prague's most prominent artists, writers, and intellectuals, led by playwright Václav Havel, to establish Charter 77, a human-rights-oriented group formed to pressure the government into observing the principles of the Helsinki Accords.

Antigovernment protests erupted in Prague in November 1989, shortly after the demise of the Berlin Wall. Under intense pressure, the Communist government refused to mobilize the military against its people, and instead relinquished power. Because almost no blood was shed, the uprising was dubbed the "Velvet Revolution." In 1990, the first free elections in 44 years were held and the newly formed Civic Forum Party, which includes many Charter 77 members, captured 170 of the Czechoslovak parliament's 300 seats. In 1992, leaders of Czech and Slovak republics reluctantly agreed to a "Velvet Divorce," and on Jan. 1, 1993, the Czech Republic was born, separated from independent Slovakia.

CONTEMPORARY CONDITIONS Splitting from your neighbor and starting a new country is fraught with difficulty. All federally owned property is being split between the Czech and Slovak republics in a 2:1 ratio, based on the countries' respective populations. The former Czechoslovak army is also being divided between the Czech and Slovak republics on a 2:1 ratio. For the time being, the two countries are sharing embassies abroad, until they can arrive at an equitable settlement. Both the Czech and Slovak governments issue separate currencies and, so far there are open borders and no trade restrictions between the two countries.

Throughout Eastern Europe, overt racism appears to be an unwelcome by-product of revolution. The demise of iron-fisted Communist control over the Czech lands, combined with a laggard economy, has resulted in the public expression of long-held racist sentiments. Romany (Gypsies) and Jews are the targets of most attacks. Several serious antiforeigner incidents were reported in 1993 alone. In August, a group of Romany was attacked in northern Bohemia. In June, 300 violent youths shouting "Gypsies to the gas" and carrying racist banners demonstrated in Pardubice, in east Bohemia. In September, the oldest Jewish cemetery in Bohemia was vandalized. For the moment, incidents in Prague have largely been limited to racist graffiti in the housing estates that ring the city.

The fall of Communism has meant some positive changes, and some shocking realities. Crime has risen dramatically, and in February 1993, Prague officials found it necessary to hold the government's first-ever meetings on homelessness. Many observers predict that social problems will increase.

POLITICS

Following the overthrow of the Communist regime in November 1989, Czechoslovakia was ruled by an elected parliament from both

IMPRESSIONS

Your government, my people, has returned to you.
—VÁCLAV HAVEL, 1990.

---

the Czech and Slovak parts of the country. After the country split, on Jan. 1, 1993, when the Czech Republic was born, it was governed by the Czech National Council, an elected representational parliament. When they were first voted into office, Václav Havel's Civic Forum Party won most parliamentary seats.

2. FAMOUS PRAGUERS

Max Brod (1884–1968), writer. Most famous as the editor of many of Franz Kafka's works, published posthumously—against Kafka's wishes. An expressionist writer himself, he published a number of stories including "The Redemption of Tycho Brahe" and "On the Beauty of Ugly Pictures." Brod immigrated to Tel Aviv in 1939.

Alexander Dubček (1921–92), government leader. A Slovak Communist, Dubček became the First Secretary of the Communist Party in January 1968, presiding over the "Prague Spring" reforms.

Antonín Dvořák (1841–1904), composer. Perhaps best known for *From the New World,* a symphony inspired by a lengthy tour of the United States, Dvořák is the most famous of all Czech composers.

Klement Gottwald (1896–1953), government leader. Universally abhorred for his role in the show trials of the 1950s, Gottwald was a leading member of the Communist Party from 1927 to 1953.

Václav Havel (1936–   ), writer and government leader. Absurdist playwright in the 1960s, Havel became a leading spokesperson of Charter 77, and the country's first post-Communist president following the Velvet Revolution.

Jan Hus (1369 or 1370–1415), religious reformer. Hus questioned the authority of the pope and called for a Bohemian National Church before being tried for heresy, and was burned at the stake.

Franz Kafka (1883–1924), writer. Author of *The Trial,* one of the 20th century's most important novels, Kafka was a German-Jewish Praguer who, for much of his life, worked in relative obscurity as a Prague insurance clerk.

Alfons Mucha (1860–1939), Moravian graphic artist. Mucha rose to international fame through his art nouveau posters and artwork for Sarah Bernhardt.

Peter Parler (1330–99), German architect and sculptor. Parler played a major part in the development of Gothic art in Central Europe. In 1353 he was summoned to Prague by Charles IV to continue work on St. Vitus Cathedral. His other accomplishments include All Saints Chapel in the castle, Charles Bridge, and the Old Town Bridge Tower.

Bedřich Smetana (1824–84), composer. After studying piano and musical theory in Prague, Smetana became one of Bohemia's most respected composers, famous for his fierce nationalism.

Franz Werfel (1890–1945), writer. Franz Werfel ranked with Brod, Kafka, and Kisch as one of the great Prague writers of his day. His best-known works include the dramas *The Mirror Man* and *The Last Judgment* and *The Song of Bernadette,* a novel.

3. CULTURAL LIFE

ARCHITECTURE Buildings and monuments from the Middle Ages to the present intermingle with one another throughout Prague. Its earliest extant architectural forms are Romanesque, and date from 1100 to 1250. The long Gothic period spanned about 1250 to 1530, and includes many examples in the Staré Město. And many of Prague's best-known structures are baroque and rococo, enduring styles of the 17th and 18th centuries. The city's most flamboyant buildings are art nouveau. Popular from about 1900 to 1918, this style is characterized by rich ornamentation. The city's most unappealing structures are functionalist designs dating from the late 20th century. No tourist should leave Prague before taking the metro out to Háje, to see the thousands of Communist-era "rabbit house" apartments in which about one quarter of the city's population live. For some reason, when tourists visit Paris or Venice and see dirty, crumbling buildings, they consider them quaint. When they see the same old, dirty, crumbling buildings in Prague, however, they point to the failure of Communism. This is not entirely fair—if you look at photos of Prague around 1900, you'll also see dirty and crumbling buildings. See "For the Architecture Lover" in Chapter 6 for information on specific buildings.

RELIGION After Catholics crushed the Protestant Hussite movement in the 17th century, the Roman Catholic Church became Bohemia's most powerful institution, wielding significant political, social, and economic influence. During the Communist years after 1945, however, religion was discouraged. Churches were portrayed by the Communists as reactionary institutions, churchgoers were pressured not to practice religion. And while practicing Christians, Jews, and others were never threatened physically, they would find themselves overlooked for job promotions or kept from furthering their education.

A public survey undertaken in 1946 concluded that about two thirds of Praguers believed in God. A similar study in 1992 found that only 20% of the people declared themselves believers in God. Organized religion is still largely regarded as something outdated, even dangerous. Despite the liberalizations that came with the revolution of 1989, Czechs have not flocked to places of worship in substantial number. Materialism and Western cultural influences seem to play a more important role in Czech life than religion.

Before the Communists nationalized private real-estate holdings, the Catholic church owned about 1% of the country's land. Czechs are deeply divided as to whether these lands should be returned to the church. Some fear that an economically powerful church will exert disproportionate influence in Czech life.

FOLKLORE Czechs have a legend for every occasion, and myth and folklore are important parts of every student's education. But belief in fables often goes beyond children's stories, as Praguers have a long tradition of believing in the supernatural and mystical. Recent years have been marked by an inordinate number of UFO sightings, and California-style cures using vacuum therapy, crystals, and the like are popular ways of treating physical ailments.

4. FOOD & DRINK

DINING CUSTOMS

For the most part, meals and dining customs are the same in Prague as they are in the United States, but there are some idiosyncracies. Few restaurants employ hosts to greet patrons at the door and seat them. If there is no host, just choose any available table. Many restaurants only offer large tables, seating six or more diners. In these establishments, it is expected that unrelated parties will share the same table. It's customary to ask "Je tady volno?" (Is this spot free?) before joining a large table.

PLACES TO EAT & DRINK

HOSPODA In the Czech Republic, where beer drinking is practically a religion, the hospoda is a veritable temple. Basically a pub, the hospoda, or hostinec, is where the Czech public meet, talk with friends, and drink. There is a kind of rivalry among hospodas, and their related breweries, each vying to serve the best beer in the neighborhood. Some of these pubs are actually quite famous for their beer (and are listed in Chapters 5 and 9). Many hospodas in central Prague serve casual meals of traditional Czech foods.

VINÁRNA Traditionally, the vinárna was an establishment without food that specialized in wine from a particular vineyard. Later, the role of the vinárna changed, and it became a restaurant reserved for special occasions. When eating in a vinárna, always ask about special wines; you'll often get something good.

RESTAURACE Since many hospoda and vinárna double as fine eateries, the term "restaurace" (restaurant) has become a sort of rubric under which several kinds of establishments converge. When it comes to food, the distinctions between hospoda and vinárna have blurred.

PIVNICE Not as traditional as a hospoda, the pivnice is a bar specializing in beer; most offer no food.

CUKRÁRNA A small café serving coffee, tea, and pastries, the cukrárna began as a kind of specialist bakery ("cukr" means sugar).

KAVÁRNA Although not as popular as in Italy or France, the Czech kavárna, or coffee bar, is a mainstay of Czech life. These are usually simple places, where patrons can idle with a newspaper and the morning brew.

THE CUISINE

Czechs are enthusiastic carnivores; most eat meat during every meal. For visitors, it can be a bit difficult getting used to the meat-and-potatoes diet.

The most common Czech meal is roast pork with boiled red cabbage and dumplings (*vepřová pečeně se zelím a knedlíky*). Dumplings, or knedlíky, come in several varieties. Made of potato or bread, they are typically flat, and are sometimes served stuffed with fruit or fried with eggs (usually when left over from the previous night). Duck, chicken, sausage, and trout are also popular menu items, as is potato soup (*bramborové polévka*), another important staple. As you might imagine, vegetarian restaurants in Prague are few and far between, but a couple standouts are included in the listings in Chapter 5.

DRINKS

Beer, soda, and bottled water are popular in Prague, and are sold at small shops and street stands all around the city.

BEER Czech beer has long been world famous. Pilsner Urquell, brewed 55 miles southwest of Prague, in Plzeň, is in both name and deed the original Pilsener. There are at least eight other major breweries in and around Prague: Gambrinus, Budvar (known in German as Budweiser, whence the name of the U.S. brew), Popovicke, Krushvicke, Flekovske, Rakovnik, Staropramen, Branik, and Pragovar. In my opinion, the first three are best. Beware of Master, a nonalcoholic beer with a deceptive label.

Pubs and beer halls are as common in Prague as they are in London and Munich, and as important to Czechs as cafés are to the French. For hundreds of years, Prague's pubs have engaged in a war of pride, each vying to serve the best beer. Although each pub serves only one or two kinds of beer, quality is almost always high.

Several pubs serving both beer and food are listed in Chapter 5, "Prague Dining;" several more are listed in Chapter 9, "Evening Entertainment."

WINE Although Czech wines are relatively unknown abroad, the country has a long history of winemaking. Some very good wines are produced, notably in southern Moravia, where both reds and whites are winning wide reputations. Happily for visitors, the relative obscurity of Czech wines translates into low prices. In stores, very drinkable bottles can be bought for $1 to $2; top vintages cost about $20. Prices triple in restaurants. The most notable white wines are Mopr, Rýnsky Ryzlink, Rulandské, and Tramín. The best reds are Frankovka, Rulandské, and Vavřinecké.

BECHEROVKA Distilled in western Bohemia by a company founded in 1807, Becherovka has long been the national alcoholic drink. Somewhat like the German Jägermeister, it is supposedly made from a secret recipe of 42 herbs infused into local spa water distillate.

WATER No one says that Prague's water is particularly tasty, but there's lots of debate as to whether water from the tap is safe to drink. Many people claim that Prague's water supply is plagued with numerous unmentionables—some even radioactive. So, while Prague tap water may harm you in the long run, personal experience proves that the city's water is free from things that will ruin your trip.

5. RECOMMENDED BOOKS, FILMS & RECORDINGS

BOOKS

FICTION   Iva Pekarková, one of the few top female Czech novelists whose works are translated into English, draws on her experiences as a Bohemian hitchhiker, refugee camp inmate, and New York City cabby. Her first novel, translated as *Truck Stop Rainbows,* was written at age 23. Her second novel is slated for American translation and release in 1994.

Arnošt Lustig, a survivor of Czechoslovakia's Nazi-era Terezín concentration camp and author of many books, including *Street of Lost Brothers,* shared the 1991 Publishers Weekly Award for best literary work with John Updike and Norman Mailer. Ivan Klíma, also a survivor of Terezín, is one of the best-known contemporary Czech novelists. His best work, translated as *Judge on Trial* (Vintage), is about a morally conflicted judge who must hand down a death sentence to a guilty prisoner.

Jaroslav Hašek is best known for *The Good Soldier Švejk,* (Viking Penguin), a classic satire about a soldier who wreaks havoc in the Austro-Hungarian army during World War I.

Bohumil Hrabal scored with two internationally acclaimed hits, *Closely Watched Trains* (Viking Penguin) and *I Served the King of England* (Vintage). The first is a postwar classic that was made into an equally clever film. The second takes place in 1938, and details the deeds and deliberations of a playful antihero.

No Czech reading list would be complete without reference to Franz Kafka, Prague's most famous novelist. *The Collected Novels of Franz Kafka* (Schocken), which includes *The Castle* and *The Trial,* binds most of the writer's claustrophobic works into a single volume.

Milan Kundera is Czechoslovakia's most popular contemporary writer. His political musings in *The Book of Laughter and Forgetting,* provoked the Communists to revoke his citizenship. His most famous work, *The Unbearable Lightness of Being,* is set around the 1968 Warsaw Pact invasion, and was turned into a notable movie some 20 years later. The comic *The Joke,* set in the serious era of Stalinist purges, is widely regarded by Kundera-philes as his best work.

ESSAYS & BIOGRAPHY   Václav Havel is not only the Czech Republic's first leader, he is also a respected author and playwright. His collection of essays, *Living in Truth,* includes one entitled "Power of the Powerless," an indictment of the inactivity of the Czechoslovak masses in the face of Communist "normalization." *Letters to Olga,* is a book of selected letters Havel wrote to his wife while he was in prison in the early 1980s. *Disturbing the Peace* is an autobiographical meditation on childhood, the events of 1968, and Havel's involvement with Charter 77. A recent collection of essays is called *Summer Meditations*.

Heda Margolis Kovlay's *Prague Farewell* (Viking Penguin) is the heartfelt autobiography of a woman who was confined to concentration camps during World War II, then married to a Communist Party hack who was executed in 1952. The book recounts the widespread feelings of fear and paranoia that were brought to bear during the Stalinist era.

Dubček and Czechoslovakia 1918–1990 (Simon & Schuster), by William Shawcross, is one of the best biographies of the most famous figure of the 1968 Prague Spring. It also discusses Dubček's role in the 1989 Velvet Revolution.

FILMS

Filmmaking has a long tradition in Czechoslovakia. Prague's Barrandov studio, founded in the 1940s, is one of the largest in Europe, and FAMU, the city's film school, founded in 1945, is one of the Continent's best. Miloš Forman, the most famous Czech director, is known internationally for his hits *Hair, One Flew Over the Cuckoo's Nest,* and *Amadeus.* He immigrated to the United States in 1968.

Contemporary Czech films, like earlier ones, are usually wrought with dark humor and irony. Today, Vit Olmer is one of the top Czechs in this genre. Banned in the 1970s, along with a host of other creative filmmakers, for failing to bow to government pressure to make socialist-sanctioned films, Olmer produced the first privately made film in Czechoslovakia—an action movie called *Tankový prapor* (Tank Battalion), about obligatory military service in the 1950s. The film made money, but was panned by critics. His latest film *Nahota na prodej* (Nudity for Sale) has garnered high praise.

The father-and-son team of Zdeněk and Jan Svěrák are also widely popular. They were nominated in 1992 for the Best Foreign Film Oscar, for *Obecná škola* (Elementary School), which Jan directed and in which the father starred.

RECORDINGS

Nineteenth-century Czech composers Bedřich Smetana and Antonín Dvořák are the country's most important musical figures. Smetana, composer of the operas *The Bartered Bride* and *The Kiss,* is considered the father of modern Czech music. Dvořák, known for the symphony *From the New World,* is one of the few truly world-class Czech composers. Lesser-known, highly respected 20th-century classical composers include Leoš Janáček (*The House of the Dead* and *The Cunning Little Vixen*) and Bohuslav Martinů (*Thunderbolt*).

Olympic, arguably the most important rock band in Czech history, recorded over a dozen albums during their 30 years together. Though most successful in the 1960s, their best albums are from the 70s and 80s. Look for their compact discs in Czech record stores (see "Shopping A to Z" in Chapter 8).

Petr Muk, one of the Czech Republic's top contemporary pop stars, is a religious convert who packs his shows and persona with Jewish symbolism. In 1992, Muk's band Shalom sold more recordings than any other band.

CHAPTER 2

PLANNING A TRIP TO PRAGUE

Prague is a grand city to visit, but it's not the most visitor-friendly place in the world. Hotel rooms are expensive, and the majority of Prague's restaurants are substandard. Careful pretrip planning will both save you money and enrich your Czech experience. This chapter is designed to help you plan your trip, save time, and get the most out of your Prague stay.

1. INFORMATION, ENTRY REQUIREMENTS & MONEY

INFORMATION

Unfortunately, the Czech Republic has not yet been able to establish a government-run tourist bureau to dispense information and help visitors make arrangements in Prague. **Čedok,** the former Communist government's official travel arm, is now little more than a sluggishly run commercial travel agent. A query to its office for information results in little more than a city map and glossy brochure of expensive all-inclusive tours. See "Tours and Packages," below, for address information.

For a comprehensive list of information sources in Prague, see "Information," in the "Fast Facts" section of Chapter 3.

ENTRY REQUIREMENTS

DOCUMENTS Citizens of the United States, Canada, Great Britain, Australia, and New Zealand need only a valid passport to enter the Czech Republic as tourists. No visas are required. Visitors staying more than three months are supposed to obtain visas, but few do. Health certificates are not required for travel to the Czech Republic. If you have special needs or questions about entry requirements, contact the Czech Embassy in the **United States,** 3900 Linean Ave. NW, Washington, DC 20008 (tel. 202/363-6308). In **Canada,** contact the Consulate General of the Czech Republic, 1305 Pine Ave., West Montréal, Quebec, H3G IB2 (tel. 514/849-4495). In **Great Britain,** contact the Czech Embassy, 26 Kensington Palace Gardens, London W8 4QY (tel. 071/727-4918).

CUSTOMS Czech customs laws are quite lax and poorly enforced. While there may technically be limits on the importation of cigarettes, perfume, and alcohol, "reasonable amounts" is the de facto rule. Officially, items brought into the Czech Republic for personal use during a visit are not liable to import duty. Gifts are taxable if the quantity and value are not in keeping with the reasonable needs of the recipient. Live animals and plants and produce may not be imported.

When returning to the United States, citizens are allowed to bring back $400 worth of merchandise duty free. After that amount, you will be charged a flat 10% tax on the next $1,000 worth of goods. If you do shop in Prague, make sure you retain receipts to show customs officials. See Chapter 8, "Prague Shopping," for more information on the Czech value added tax (VAT), and on sending merchandise home.

Once in Prague, inquiries concerning importing and/or exporting currency, and other customs regulations, should be directed to the Central Customs Authority (tel. 2/232-2270).

MONEY

The basic unit of Czech currency is the *koruna* (plural, *koruny*), or crown, abbreviated *Kč,* which at this writing is worth about U.S. $0.03. U.S. $1 buys 30 Kč; U.K. £1 buys 45 Kč. Each crown is divided into 100 *haléřú* (*h*), or hellers. To make budgeting easier, prices quoted in this book are accompanied by their equivalents in U.S. dollars. Although the Czech crown has been fairly stable against major world currencies, rates can change drastically. The conversions on page 23 should be used only as a guide. See also "Fast Facts: Prague" in Chapter 3 for information on banks and changing money.

The Czech Republic issued new currency in August 1993, and all notes and coins bearing earlier dates became invalid. There are now five banknotes and nine coins. Notes, each of which bears a forgery-resistant metal strip and a prominent watermark, are issued in 100, 200, 500, 1,000, and 5,000 crown denominations. Coins are valued at 10, 20, and 50 hellers and 1, 2, 5, 10, 20, and 50 crowns.

CASH Although it's not safest to travel with too much cash, U.S. dollars do garner a better exchange rate than traveler's checks at Prague's banks. Although the Czech crown is not expected to "float" freely against the world's convertible currencies until 1995, the easing of export laws has all but erased black-market exchange. Today, street rates vary just a hair from official ones, rendering unlawful money not worth the risk. Many tourists have exchanged large sums illegally, only to discover they'd bought invalid notes.

TRAVELER'S CHECKS Foreign-currency traveler's checks can be exchanged at most banks, at **American Express** and **Thomas Cook Travel Services** offices, and at money-change shops all over central Prague. The banks and traveler's-check-issuing companies generally offer the best rates. Traveler's checks are usually not accepted at shops, restaurants, hotels, theaters, and attractions. Some restaurants and hotels—especially the fancier ones—will exchange foreign-currency traveler's checks, but their rates will routinely be worse than bank rates. **Chequepoint** and other private currency-exchange companies maintain offices throughout the city, especially in the most heavily touristed areas. As a rule, they keep long hours, sometimes all night, but their services are deceptively expensive; although an exchange rate may look lucrative, commissions at these places are often as high as 10%.

CREDIT CARDS It is comforting to know that American Express, MasterCard, and VISA are widely accepted in Prague. In addition, many trips to Prague have proved that paying with plastic can be economical. The major credit-card companies bill at a favorable rate of exchange, and save you money by eliminating commissions.

WHAT THINGS COST IN PRAGUE	U.S. $
Taxi from Ruzyně Airport to center city	8.35
Metro, tram, or public bus to anywhere in Prague	0.20
Local telephone call	0.03
Double room at Hotel Pařiž (expensive)	180.00
Double room at Hotel Evropa (moderate)	78.70
Double room at Hotel Juventus (inexpensive)	50.00
Lunch for one at U Kameníka (moderate)	5.00
Lunch for one at most pubs (inexpensive)	2.50
Dinner for one without wine at Parnas (expensive)	22.00
Dinner for one without wine at Restaurant Adria (moderate)	10.50

	U.S. $
Dinner for one without wine at Country Life (inexpensive)	5.00
Pint of beer	0.45
Coca-Cola in a restaurant	0.65
Cup of coffee	0.90
Roll of ASA 100 film, 36 exposures	7.50
Admission to the National Museum	0.70
Movie ticket	0.50 and up
National Theater ticket	1.00–10.00

2. WHEN TO GO — CLIMATE, HOLIDAYS & EVENTS

From most perspectives, May through September is the best time to visit Prague. The weather is warmest, streets are lively, all the restaurants and sights are open long hours, and cultural events like concerts and theater are in full swing.

The off-seasons promise lower rates and fewer crowds. Winters in Prague, however, can be downright dangerous—not because of the cold, but because of air pollution. During some days in winter 1993, air pollution exceeded by eight times the standards set by the World Health Organization. During such days, pollution-emitting heating plants are forced to reduce output and inner-city traffic restrictions are implemented, creating a logistical nightmare. Under city law, only private cars with catalytic converters or vehicles for the handicapped are allowed into the city center when specified pollution levels are reached. Health officials warn senior citizens, children, and pregnant women to stay inside and keep the windows and doors closed.

CLIMATE

The Czech Republic's temperate climate is marked by regular cycles of the four seasons. The average temperature in summer is about 63° Fahrenheit. In winter, the temperature hovers around the freezing mark for the entire season. On the average January, it's sunny and clear only 50 hours for the entire month. During the whole month of February, you can look forward to a total of 72 hours of cloudlessness.

The highest rainfall is in July, the lowest in February.

THE CROWN, THE DOLLAR & THE POUND STERLING

At this writing U.S. $1 equaled approximately 30 Kč (or 1 Kč = 3¢), and this was the rate of exchange used to calculate the dollar values given in this book (rounded to the nearest nickel). At the same time, U.K. £1 equaled about 45 Kč. Note that the rates given here fluctuate from time to time and may not be the same when you travel to the Czech Republic. Therefore this table should be used only as a guide.

Kč	U.S.$	U.K. £	Kč	U.S.$	U.K. £
1	0.03	0.02	150	5.00	3.33
5	0.17	0.11	200	6.67	4.45
10	0.33	0.23	250	8.33	5.55
15	0.50	0.33	500	16.67	11.11
20	0.67	0.45	750	25.00	16.67
25	0.83	0.55	1,000	33.33	22.22
30	1.00	0.67	1,250	41.67	27.78
35	1.17	0.78	1,500	50.00	33.33
40	1.33	0.89	1,750	58.33	38.89
45	1.50	1.00	2,000	66.67	44.45
50	1.67	1.11	2,250	75.00	50.00
75	2.50	1.67	2,500	83.33	55.55
100	3.33	2.22	2,750	91.67	61.11

Prague's Average Daytime Temperature and Monthly Rainfall

	Jan	Feb	Mar	Apr	May	Jun	Jul	Aug	Sep	Oct	Nov	Dec
Temp °F	27	29	37	46	55	61	64	63	57	47	38	31
Rain (in.)	1.7	0.9	1.5	1.5	1.8	2.2	2.3	2.1	1.5	1.7	1.6	1.9

HOLIDAYS

Official holidays in the Czech Republic are observed on January 1 (New Year's Day); Easter Monday; May 1 (May Day); May 8 (Liberation Day); July 5 (Introduction of Christianity); July 6 (Death of Jan Hus); October 28 (Foundation of the Republic); December 24–25 (Christmas); and December 26 (St. Stephen's Day).

PRAGUE CALENDAR OF EVENTS

MARCH

☐ **Prague City of Music Festival.** Contemporary and classical concerts are performed around town throughout the month. Contact Čedok, 10 E. 40th St., New York, NY 10016 (tel. 212/689-9720), or any information/travel agency in Prague (see "Information" in Chapter 3).

MAY

✪ *PRAGUE SPRING FESTIVAL* *The city's biggest music festival is a three-week-long series of classical-music and dance performances held throughout the city. Historically, opening night has always begun with a performance of Bedřich Smetana's Symphonic poem Má Vlast ("My Country"). The country's top performers usually participate.*
   Where: *All around town.* ***When:*** *Last three weeks of May.* ***How:*** *Tickets for concerts range from 200 Kč to 1,500 Kč ($6.70 to $50), and are available in advance from Bohemia Tickets International on Václavské náměstí.*

JUNE

☐ **Concertino Prague.** Another music festival, in which classical music events are staged all around town.

SEPTEMBER

✪ *PRAGUE AUTUMN INTERNATIONAL MUSIC FESTIVAL* *The festival features local orchestras and international soloists performing traditional and new works.*
   Where: *Most of the concerts are performed at Smetana Hall in the Municipal House.* ***When:*** *Usually during the first two weeks of September.* ***How:*** *Tickets can be bought in advance through the Festival Office, Sekaninova 26, Praha 2, Czech Republic (fax 2/242-7564 or 2/692-7650).*

OCTOBER

✪ *PRAGUE MARATHON* *Begun in 1990, this major footrace through the city ends in Staroměstské náměstí.*
   Where: *Citywide.* ***When:*** *Usually during the beginning of the month.* ***How:*** *Entry costs about $35, and registration*

must be done in person at the Obecní Dům, nám.
Republiky 5.

DECEMBER

☐ **Christmas** is a festive time in Prague. The "Good Bishop," the Czech equivalent of Santa Claus, dressed in a white priest's costume, distributes sweets to well-behaved children, and coal and potatoes to poorly behaved ones. Just before the holiday, large barrels of carp are brought into the city, and this traditional Christmas-dinner fish is sold throughout Staré Město.

3. HEALTH, INSURANCE & SAFETY

VACCINATIONS Unless you are arriving from an area known to be suffering from an epidemic, no inoculations or vaccinations are required to enter the Czech Republic. Be sure to carry a doctor's prescription for any medication or controlled substance you require. It's best to bring all the medication you will need on your trip, however, since obtaining the same medicines in the Czech Republic may prove difficult.

INSURANCE Most travel agents sell low-cost health, theft, and trip-cancellation insurance to clients. Compare these rates and services with those offered by local banks as well as by your personal insurance carrier. Flight insurance, against damages suffered in the event of a plane crash, is also available from self-service counters at most major airports. Some credit-card companies also offer free, automatic travel-accident insurance (up to $100,000) when you purchase travel tickets with their cards.

If you fall ill in Prague and wish the services of an English-language doctor, you will probably be required to pay up front for services rendered. Doctors and hospitals can be expensive, so although it is not required of travelers, health insurance is highly recommended. Check to see if you are covered in foreign countries by your insurance carrier before you purchase additional protection.

In addition to medical insurance, you can also protect your travel investment by insuring against lost or damaged baggage and trip cancellation or interruption. These coverages are often combined into a single comprehensive plan and sold by travel agents, credit-card issuers, and the following firms:

Tele-Trip (Mutual of Omaha), 3201 Farnam St., Omaha, NB (tel. 402/345-2400, or toll free 800/228-9792). In addition to selling all types of travel-related insurance, the company offers out-of-country major-medical insurance for $3 per day, with a 10-day minimum.

Travel Guard International, 1100 Center Point Dr., Stevens Point, WI 54481 (tel. toll free 800/826-1300, in Wisconsin 800/634-0644). A seven-day comprehensive insurance package costs $52.

Travel Insurance Pak, Travelers Insurance Co., One Tower Sq., 15NB, Hartford, CT 06183-5040 (tel. 203/277-2318, or toll free 800/243-3174). Travel accident and illness coverage starts at $10 for 6 to 10 days; $500 worth of coverage for lost, damaged, or delayed baggage costs $20 for 6 to 10 days; and trip cancellation costs $5.50 for $100 worth of coverage (up to $2,000).

SAFETY   According to surveys conducted by the Netherlands justice ministry in 1992, the Czech Republic tied with New Zealand for having more burglaries per capita than any other industrialized nation. The republic also suffers from a high rate of sexual assault. See also "Fast Facts: Prague" in Chapter 3.

4. WHAT TO PACK

Prague is usually pleasantly warm in summer, and always freezing cold in winter. It can also be at both these levels on almost any given day in late spring or early fall, making packing for a trip quite difficult.

CLOTHING   If you're traveling to Prague between September and May, be sure to pack your warmest clothes. Even during summer you should pack at least one warm sweater and a light jacket. Any time of the year, an all-weather coat is a good idea, and good walking shoes are also a must if you want to explore the city's many wonderful neighborhoods.

OTHER ITEMS   Few hotels provide hairdryers or electrical current converters. If you bring appliances that need local electricity, you will probably need a converter. In the Czech Republic, electric appliances run on 240 volts and plug into the standardized continental European two-pin socket, different from those used in the United States.

Before you leave home, make two copies of each important document you are carrying—passport (copy the inside page with your photo), airline ticket, driver's license, medical prescriptions, and the like. Leave one set of copies at home, and put the other in your luggage separate from the originals. Should the documents be lost or stolen, you'll have invaluable backup information.

5. TIPS FOR THE DISABLED, SENIORS, FAMILIES & STUDENTS

FOR THE DISABLED The Czechs have made little effort to build special facilities for disabled citizens. There are few elevators or ramps for the wheelchair-bound, no beeping crosswalks for the blind, no TTD telephones for the hearing impaired. Like the Nazis before them, the Communists relocated handicapped people to the outskirts of society, both literally and figuratively. Ghettos for the handicapped were built outside of cities, where they still exist today.

In the cobblestone streets of downtown Prague, wheelchairs are almost unknown. Only a few hotels (like the Praha Penta) offer barrier-free accommodations. Most stores, public transport, theaters, and restaurants are inaccessible to wheelchair users.

Unlike in many other cities, it is not common for Prague's theaters, nightclubs, and attractions to offer discounts to people with disabilities. There are exceptions, however, so always ask before paying full price.

FOR SENIORS Seniors are accorded very few discounts in Prague. Because Communist equality meant that seniors as a group were no worse off financially than younger persons, Czechs have little experience offering special discounts to retirees. Older travelers should always ask if there's a senior discount, especially at hotels and shops. You might receive an unexpected markdown.

Older travelers are particularly encouraged to purchase travel insurance (see "Insurance," above). If you're carrying your own bags, you'd be well advised to be very frugal when it comes to packing.

When making airline reservations, ask about a senior discount (usually 10%), but find out if there is a cheaper promotional fare before committing.

In addition to organizing tours, The **American Association of Retired Persons (AARP)** Travel Service (tel. toll free 800/927-0111) provides a list of travel suppliers who offer discounts to members.

Travel Companion Exchange, P.O. Box 833-F, Amityville, NY 11701 (tel. 516/454-0880), provides listings of people interested in finding partners in travel. Matches are made by computer, which groups travelers into categories based on interests, education, age, and location. The service costs $36 for six months and boasts over 2,000 active participants.

FOR FAMILIES Children add joys and another level of experience to travel. They help you see things in a different way, and sometimes draw reticent local people like a magnet, which would probably not happen were you alone. Taking kids to Prague also means additional planning. All children, even infants, are required to have a passport. On airplanes, order special children's meals as far in advance as possible. Most airlines don't carry baby food, but they will be glad to heat up any you've brought with you. Pack first-aid supplies, such as a thermometer, Band-Aids, cough drops, and children's aspirin, and always carry snacks like raisins, crackers, fruit, water, or juice.

Because facilities are not as good and service less attentive than in most American and western European cities, Prague is not the easiest place to travel with kids. Then again, Praguers have been bringing up children here for quite some time. Baby food, diapers, and other childrens' needs are readily available in food stores around town, and the city is full of sightseeing opportunities and special activities that older children will enjoy.

FOR STUDENTS Students in Prague regularly enjoy discounts on travel, theater, and museum tickets.

The **International Student Identity Card (ISIC)** is the most readily accepted proof of student status, and is available from most university travel agents and from the **Council on International Educational Exchange,** 205 E. 42nd St., New York, NY 10017 (tel. 212/661-1414). To be eligible for the card, you must be enrolled in a degree program. The application must include proof of student status via an official letter from the school registrar or high school principal, a $10 registration fee, and one passport-size photo. The card should be purchased before you leave home, but if you've arrived in Prague without one and are a good enough talker (or just happen to be carrying a registrar-stamped and -signed copy of your current school transcript), you can obtain one for 100 Kč ($3.35) from **ČKM Agency,** Jindřišská 28 (tel. 26-85-07), near Václavské náměstí. The office is open Monday through Friday from 9am to 5pm and Saturday from 10am to 4pm.

Prague's hostels are not only some of the cheapest places to stay, they are also great for meeting other student travelers. You don't have to be a card-carrying member of the International Youth Hostel Federation (IYHF) to lodge at any of them, since none are affiliated with that organization. If you still want to buy an IYHF card, purchasing it in Prague will save you a good deal of money. In the United States, **American Youth Hostels, Inc.,** P.O. Box 37613, Washington, DC 20013-7613 (tel. 202/783-6161), charges 750 Kč

($25) a year for the same card that Prague's ČKM Agency (see address above) sells for 100 Kč ($3.35).

6. GETTING THERE

Go to a travel agent and buy your ticket, right? You can, but it may not be the cheapest nor most interesting way to travel. Prague is easy to reach, but be warned: Not all transportation options are equal. There are many exciting travel alternatives, so it may well pay to look beyond the obvious choices.

BY PLANE

MAJOR AIRLINES About two dozen international airlines offer regularly scheduled service into Prague's Ruzyně Airport. **Delta** (tel. toll free 800/221-1212), the principal U.S. carrier making the trip, connects via Frankfurt, Germany, with gateways at Atlanta, Cincinnati, Los Angeles, New York, Orlando, San Francisco, and Washington, D.C. Following are other major carriers serving the Czech Republic, along with their U.S. toll-free telephone numbers: **Air France** (800/237-2747); **Alitalia** (800/223-5730); **Austrian Airlines** (800/843-0002); **British Airways** (800/247-9297); **ČSA Czech Airlines** (800/223-2365); **Finnair** (800/950-5000); **KLM Royal Dutch Airlines** (800/777-5553); **Lufthansa** (800/645-3880); **SAS** (800/221-2350); and **Swissair** (800/221-4750).

REGULAR AIRFARES Prices to Prague vary by airline. Check newspapers for advertisements, and call a few of the major carriers before committing.

The lowest economy-class fares usually come with serious restrictions and steep penalties for altering dates and itineraries. When purchasing these tickets, it is often best not to use terms like "APEX," "excursion," or other airline jargon, but just to ask for the lowest fare. If you are flexible with dates and times, say so. Ask if you can obtain a cheaper fare by staying extra time, flying during midweek, or by purchasing the ticket in advance. Most airlines won't volunteer this information.

Airlines observe three pricing seasons to Prague: low (during winter), high (during summer), and shoulder (during spring and fall). At presstime, the lowest published round-trip summer fare from New York was $778; from Chicago, $793; and from Los Angeles, $878. During winter, the fare from New York was $558; from Chicago, $598; and from Los Angeles, $659. You may well find cheaper fares. Business-class seats can cost more than twice the price of coach.

Expect to pay about $2,720 from New York, $2,900 from Chicago, and over $3,000 from Los Angeles. Airlines sometimes offer free business-class upgrades to passengers who purchase an unrestricted coach-class ticket. Unrestricted fares are the most expensive, but may still be less than a business-class seat. Ask about this when purchasing your ticket.

Most airlines offer only a handful of expensive first-class seats on Prague flights. The published first-class airfare from New York is about $5,500; from Chicago, about $5,800; and from Los Angeles about $6,000. Before buying, see if your airline offers a first-class upgrade with a full-fare business-class ticket.

DISCOUNTED AIRFARES   Alternatives to traditional tickets have advantages (usually price) and drawbacks (usually lack of flexibility).

By negotiating directly with airlines, **consolidators,** or **bucket shops,** can sell tickets on major scheduled carriers at deeply discounted rates—often 20% to 30% lower. Such fares are often the least-expensive means of traveling to Europe, lower in most instances than charter-flight fares. For example, in winter from New York, you can buy bucket-shop tickets to Prague on well-known international airlines for as little as $250 each way; the prices rise to about $350 in summer. Flying to other, more popular European cities (like London and Amsterdam) is slightly less expensive. There are drawbacks, however. The tickets are restrictive, valid only for a particular date or flight, nontransferable, and nonrefundable except directly from the consolidator. Also, such outfits usually don't offer travel counseling nor book hotels or rental cars. On the plus side, their tickets rarely carry advance-purchase requirements; if space is available, you can buy your ticket just days before departure.

The lowest-priced bucket shops are typically local operations with low profiles and overheads. Look for their advertisements in the travel or classified section of your newspaper. Their ads typically are small, usually a single column in width and a few lines deep. They contain a list of cities and corresponding ticket prices.

While prices for flights available through bucket shops are low, at times they may be eclipsed by special offers by the airlines. As usual, compare prices before you buy.

Nationally advertised consolidators are usually not as competitive as smaller local operations, but they have toll-free telephone numbers and are easily accessible. Such consolidators include **Access International, Inc.,** 101 W. 31st St., Suite 1104, New York, NY 10107 (tel. 212/333-7280, or toll free 800/827-3633); **Sunline Express Holidays, Inc.,** 607 Market St., San Francisco, CA 94105 (tel. 415/541-7800, or toll free 800/877-2111); and **Euro-Asia, Inc.,** 4203 E. Indian School Rd., Suite 210, Phoenix, AZ 85018 (tel. 602/955-2742, or toll free 800/525-3876).

Charter operators mostly sell seats through travel agents, making these local professionals your best source of information. Two well-known operators that sell tickets directly to passengers include **Travac,** 989 Sixth Ave., New York, NY 10018 (tel. 212/563-3303, or toll free 800/872-8800), and **Council Charters,** 205 E. 42nd St., New York, NY 10017 (tel. 212/661-0311, or toll free 800/223-7402). Look for round-trip fares from New York as low as $550 (midwinter) and $700 (summer).

Before deciding to take a charter, check the restrictions on the ticket. You may be asked to purchase a tour package, pay far in advance of the flight, be amenable if the day of departure or the destination is changed, pay a service charge, fly on an unfamiliar airline, pay a harsh penalty if you cancel, or be understanding if the charter does not fill and is canceled up to 10 days before departure. Summer charters fill more quickly than others and are almost sure to fly, but if you decide on a charter flight, seriously consider purchasing cancellation insurance.

Standbys provide another inexpensive means of crossing the Atlantic. In order to fill seats that would otherwise go unsold, airlines offer discounted fares to last-minute ticket purchasers. Standby is usually offered from April to November only. You can save about $50.

You can also travel to Europe as a **courier.** Companies transporting time-sensitive materials, such as film, blood, or documents for banks and insurance firms, regularly hire couriers. Travelers who wear two caps, that of airline passenger and that of courier, stand to save a lot of money crossing the Atlantic. It's not difficult, as the courier company handles the check-in and pickup of packages at each airport. All you have to do is give up your checked-baggage allowance and make do with carry-on. Expect to meet a courier service representative at the airport before departure to get the manifest of the checked items. Upon arrival, you deliver the baggage-claim tag to a waiting agent. Flights are often offered at the last minute, and you may have to arrange a pretrip interview to make sure you're right for the job.

One drawback, besides restricted baggage, is that you have to travel alone, since only one person can take advantage of any given flight. If there are two of you, try to arrange your departures on two consecutive days; the first to arrive can secure the hotel room and learn the lay of the land. **Now Voyager, Inc.,** 74 Varick St., Suite 307, New York, NY 10013 (tel. 212/431-1616 from 11:30am to 6pm) is one of the best-known courier companies. Most flights depart from New York. Prices change all the time, from low to very low. If a company needs emergency courier service and you can fly immediately, you could travel free or for next to nothing—say, $50 round-trip. Flights are booked on a round-trip basis exclusively, though there is often nothing to carry on the way home.

INTRA-EUROPEAN FLIGHTS   For the most part, air transport

**Ⓕ FROMMER'S SMART TRAVELER:
AIRFARES**

1. Shop all the airlines that fly to your destination.
2. Always ask for the lowest fare, not "discount," "APEX," or "excursion."
3. Keep calling the airline—availability of cheap seats changes daily.
4. Seek out budget alternatives. Phone "bucket shops," charter companies, and discount travel agents.
5. Plan to travel midweek, when rates are usually lower.

---

within Europe remains in the realm of the business traveler and not the budget tourist. The cost is usually prohibitively high for budget travelers. Some airlines offer **special promotions,** however, as well as 7- and 14-day advance-purchase fares. For instance, British Airways has offered a $228 round-trip fare from London to Prague with 14-day advance purchase. Unlike domestic air travel in the U.S., lower-priced airfares are available throughout Europe on **charter flights** rather than regularly scheduled ones. Look in local newspapers or visit a European travel agent to find out about them.

BY TRAIN

European train fares are lower than those in the United States— Czech tickets are particularly inexpensive. Because European countries are relatively compact, it often takes less time to travel from one city center to another by train than by plane.

The cost of a train ride from London to Prague is about $320 in first class, or $220 in second class. The difference between the classes is relatively small, a matter of one or two inches of padding on the seats and slightly more legroom.

Following is a list of European rail passes, along with 1994 prices. **Note:** These passes are *not* valid in the Czech Republic.

Eurailpass: 15 days, $498; 21 days, $648; one month, $798; two months, $998; three months, $1,098. First class only, with access to many ferries, steamers, and buses free or at a discount.

Eurail Saverpass: For two or more people traveling together October through March, or for three people traveling together April through September: 15 days, $430 per person; 21 days, $550 per person; one month, $678 per person. First class only; same privileges as Eurailpass.

Eurail Flexipass: Any five days within two months, $348; any 10 days within two months, $560; any 15 days within two months, $740. First class only; same privileges as Eurailpass.

Eurail Youthpass: 15 days, $398; one month, $578; two months, $768. For travelers under 26 years of age. Second class only; same privileges as Eurailpass.

EurailDrive Pass: Any 7 days (4 rail, 3 car) for use within 21 days, $269. Additional rail days are available for $40 per person per day; additional car days for $50 per car per day. A single traveler pays $439 for seven days.

Children under 12 travel for half fare, and under 4 for free, when with a parent with a Eurailpass, Eurail Saverpass, and Eurail Flexipass.

BY BUS

Bus transportation is readily available throughout Europe. It sometimes is less expensive than rail travel, and covers a more extensive area. European buses generally outshine U.S. counterparts. In the Czech Republic, buses cost significantly less than trains, and often offer more direct routes to the places you want to visit. **Europabus,** c/o DER Tours/German Rail, 11933 Wilshire Blvd., Los Angeles, CA 90025 (tel. 310/479-4140, or toll free 800/782-2424), provides information on regular coach service as well as 17 different bus tours in eight European countries from 2 to 14 days long. The buses are all no-smoking, and about 30% of the passengers come from North America. **Cosmos,** a British operator, specializes in economical bus tours of Europe that can be booked through travel agents in the U.S. It will match single travelers who want to share a room to avoid paying a supplement.

BY CAR

Low-cost travel and rental cars do not usually go hand in hand, and you definitely do not need to rent a car to explore Prague. But if you want to see the countryside, driving can be a fun way to travel. In addition, a car will lend added mobility to find a budget hotel or a comfortable spot to camp.

Rental cars are not only pricey in Prague, but gasoline costs much more than Americans are accustomed to paying—about $3.50 per gallon. Expect a standard-shift vehicle unless you specifically ask for an automatic. Find out all the charges you are likely to incur from the car-rental company; besides the daily or weekly rental charge, consider a mileage charge, insurance, the cost of fuel, and tax on the total rental bill (23% in Prague). In addition, you will be paying for parking and tolls along the way. If you already have collision coverage on your own automobile insurance, you're most likely covered when you are behind the wheel of a rental car; check with your insurance carrier. If you decide on European insurance, be sure it doesn't come with a $1,000 deductible.

A collision-damage waiver (CDW) costs a hefty $7 to $13 per day.

Some credit-card companies, including American Express, automatically insure cardholders against collision damage at no additional charge when they rent a car using their card. Also, Travel Guard International (see "Insurance," above) sells low-cost auto insurance at rates that are more attractive than those offered by car-rental firms.

Car rates can be negotiable. Try to obtain the best possible deal with the rental company by asking about special discounts. Special rates are sometimes offered for keeping the car longer, for unlimited mileage (or at least some miles thrown in free), or for a bigger car at a lower price. You can usually get some sort of discount for a company or association affiliation. Check before you leave home and take a member-identification card with you.

To begin the shopping-around process, contact some of the American car-rental companies with international branches: **Avis** (tel. toll free 800/331-1084); **Budget** (tel. toll free 800/527-0700); **Dollar Rent a Car** or **InterRent** (tel. toll free 800/421-6878); **Hertz** (tel. toll free 800/654-3001); and **National** or **Europcar** (tel. toll free 800/227-3876).

U.S.-based companies specializing in European car rentals include **Auto-Europe** (tel. toll free 800/223-5555); **Europe by Car** (tel. toll free 800/223-1516); and **Kemwel** (tel. toll free 800/678-0678).

See "Getting Around" in Chapter 3 for information on inexpensive Prague car-rental firms.

TOURS & PACKAGES

Tours and packages are offered by tour operators, airlines, hotels, and transportation companies. A **tour** usually refers to an escorted group, and often includes transportation, meals, and accommodations. The entire group travels together and shares the same preplanned activities.

A **package,** on the other hand, can include any or all of the above components, but travelers are usually unescorted and free to make their own itinerary. Many travelers who purchase airfare, hotel, and theater tickets from travel agents may not even be aware of the fact that they are buying a tour operator's package.

Even if you are an independent traveler, don't shy away from a package; it can be a very good value. Packagers buy in bulk, which sometimes allows them to sell their services at a discount.

For the latest in what's available in tours and packages today, check the ads in the travel section of your newspaper. Tours and packages are most often put together by airlines, charter companies, hotels, and tour operators and sold through travel agents.

Before signing up for a tour or package, read the fine print carefully and obtain answers to key questions like the following.

How reputable is the operator? Ask for references of people who have participated in tours run by the same company. Call travel agents and the local Better Business Bureau, and check with the consumer department of the **U.S. Tour Operators Association,** 212 E. 51st St., Suite 12B, New York, NY 10022 (tel. 212/944-5727). Be leery of any outfit that does not give you details of the itinerary before demanding payment.

What is the size of the tour? Decide whether you can handle an experience shared by 40 other people or if your limit is 20. A smaller tour usually is a better-quality tour.

What kind of hotels will be used, and where are they located? Get the names of the hotels and then look them up in guidebooks or in your travel agent's hotel guide. If you sense that the hotels provide only minimal essentials, so might the entire tour. If the hotel is not conveniently located, you may feel isolated or unsafe and you'll probably spend extra money and time getting to and from attractions and nightspots.

If meals are included, how elaborate are they? Is breakfast continental, English, or buffet? Is the menu for the group limited to a few items?

How extensive is the sightseeing? You may have the chance to get off the bus many times to explore attractions or you may see most only from the bus window. If you like to explore, pick an attraction you are interested in and ask the operator precisely how much time you can expect to spend there. Also, find out if admissions are included in the price of the tour.

Are optional activities offered at an additional price? This is usually the case, so make sure the activities that particularly interest you are included in the tour price.

What is the refund policy should you cancel?

How is the price paid? If a charter flight is involved, make sure that you can pay into an escrow account to ensure proper use of the funds or their return in case the operator cancels the trip.

Most airlines listed above offer both escorted tours and on-your-own packages. Dozens of other companies also compete for this lucrative business. Czech tour operators include **Čedok,** 10 E. 40th St., Suite 1902, New York, NY 10016 (tel. 212/689-9720), and **General Tours,** 139 Main St., Cambridge, MA 02142 (tel. toll free 800/221-2216).

7. FOR BRITISH TRAVELERS

GETTING TO CONTINENTAL EUROPE

BY PLANE   There are no hard and fast rules about where to obtain the best deals for flights to the continent, but bear the following points in mind. (1) Daily newspapers often carry advertisements for companies offering cheap flights. **Trailfinders** (tel. 071/937-5400), which sells discounted fares to Prague on a variety of airlines, is a highly recommended company. (2) In London, there are many consolidators, or bucket shops, in the neighborhood of Earl's Court offering cheap fares. For your own protection, make sure that the company you deal with is a member of the IATA, ABTA, or ATOL. (3) Travel agents often sell package holidays that include airfare, and offer very good value. Don't overlook the opportunity to purchase your transportation and accommodations at the same time.

BY TRAIN Many rail passes are available in the U.K. for travel in Britain and Europe. Unfortunately, one of the most widely used of these passes, the InterRail card, is not valid for travel in the Czech Republic. The cost of a train ride from London to Prague is about £215 in first class, and £150 in second class. For information on routes and seat availability, visit the **International Rail Centre** in London's Victoria Station (tel. 071/834-2345).

Passengers under age 26 with lots of holiday time sometimes opt for a EuroYouth ticket, which allows unlimited stopovers en route between London and the Czech border, after which it costs the equivalent of £10 to £20 to reach Prague.

You can purchase rail tickets to Prague from any "international" ticket window in London's Victoria Station. If you need some help planning your rail trip, visit **Wasteels, Ltd.** (tel. 071/834-7066), located opposite Victoria Station's platform 2. This company is an especially convenient outlet for buying railway tickets to virtually anywhere in Europe. In addition to ticket sales, they provide railway-related services, discuss the various types of fares and rail passes and their various drawbacks, and its staff will probably spend a bit more time with a client during the planning of an itinerary. Depending on circumstances, Wasteels sometimes charges a £5 fee for its services, but it's money well spent.

BY COACH & FERRY Since the advent of the automobile age, coach travel has competed aggressively with rail travel throughout Europe. **Eurolines,** 52 Grosvenor Gardens, London SW1 W OAU (tel. 071/730-0202), runs regular bus service from London to Prague costing about £95 for a round-trip. Coaches are equipped with toilets and reclining seats, and take about 30 hours. By law, drivers are required to stop at regular intervals for rest and refreshment.

BY CAR & FERRY Taking your own car abroad avoids spending on car rentals and gives you maximum flexibility in setting your own pace and itinerary. **P & O Ferries** (tel. 081/575-8555 or 0304/203-388) is one of the U.K.'s largest drive-on ferryboat operators, carrying cars, passengers, and freight. The company offers daily crossings of the English Channel from Dover to Calais, France, and from Folkestone to Zeebrugge, Belgium.

Brittany Ferries (tel. 0752/221-321), P & O's largest competitor, offers regular ferry service from Portsmouth to St-Malo and Caen, in France.

BY SEACAT   Traveling by SeaCat (a form of high-speed motorized catamaran) cuts your journey time from the U.K. to the Continent. A SeaCat trip can be a fun adventure, especially for first-timers and children, as the vessel is technically "flying" above the surface of the water. A SeaCat crossing from Folkestone to Boulogne, France, is longer in miles but more timesaving to passengers that the Dover to Calais route used by conventional ferryboats. For reservations and information, call **HoverSpeed** at 0304/240-241.

VIA THE CHANNEL TUNNEL   Scheduled to open in 1994, the "Chunnel" runs between Folkestone and Calais, France. It will reduce the train travel time between England and France to a brief 30 minutes. Train passengers can use the tunnel on direct routes to Paris from London's Waterloo Station. If you opt to take a car with you, you'll drive it into a railway compartment in preparation for the crossing, and drive it away from the rail yard once you reach France. For up-to-the-minute information, call **Brit Rail** at 071/928-5100.

GETTING TO KNOW PRAGUE

1. ORIENTATION
2. GETTING AROUND
• FAST FACTS:
 PRAGUE
3. NETWORKS &
 RESOURCES

Reaching Prague has never been easier. Once there, you will find that negotiating your way around the city is relatively straightforward, but, like all unfamiliar territory, this metropolis will take a little time to master. This chapter will familiarize you with the major parts of the city.

---

1. ORIENTATION

ARRIVING

BY PLANE   Prague's **Ruzyně Airport** (tel. 36-77-60 or 36-78-14), located 12 miles west of center city, is pleasingly small and terrifically convenient, making transit to and from Prague a relative breeze. Although the airport lacks conveniences that are common in other international gateways (such as duty-free shopping, left-luggage, and postal facilities), there is a bank for changing money (usually open 7am to 11pm), several car-rental offices (see "Getting Around By Car," below), and telephones that work.

Travel time to the downtown area is about 30 to 45 minutes. There are several ways of making your way from airport to hotel.

Taxis are plentiful, and line up in front of the airport. Eager taxi drivers probably will approach as you exit the customs area. Warning: Many Prague taxi drivers are not too honest; obtaining a properly metered ride from the airport is next to impossible (see "Getting Around," below). If you do let a driver convince you to use his or her services, negotiate the fare in advance; it should cost no more than 250 Kč ($8.35) to Václavské náměstí (Wenceslas Square) but be prepared to pay twice this amount or more.

Since most tourists who land at the airport are headed in the same direction, it makes sense for solo travelers to look for others to share the expense of a taxi.

ČSA, the Czech national airline, operates an **airport shuttle** to and from their main office in downtown Prague. It leaves every 30 minutes or so from 7:30am to 7:30pm. The ČSA main office is at Revoluční 25, about five blocks from náměstí Republiky metro station. The shuttle costs just 20 Kč (65¢) per person.

Even cheaper is **city bus 119,** which delivers passengers from the airport to Dejvická metro station (line A). The bus/subway combination into center city costs only 12 Kč (36¢).

Airlines   For information on flight arrivals and departures, or to make reservations or changes, contact the following airlines at their Prague city offices: **Air France,** Václavské nám. 10, Praha 1 (tel. 26-01-55); **Alitalia,** Revoluční 5, Praha 1 (tel. 2331-0535); **Austrian Airlines,** Revoluční 15, Praha 1 (tel. 231-3378 or 231-1872); **British Airways,** Staroměstské nám. 10, Praha 1 (tel. 232-9020 or 232-9040); **Canadian Airlines International,** Thámova 23, Praha 8 (tel. 229-9221); **ČSA Czech Airlines,** Revoluční 1 (tel. 235-2785); **Delta,** Národní 32, Praha 1 (tel. 26-71-41); **Finnair,** Španělská 2, Praha 2 (tel. 22-30-62 or 22-64-89); **KLM Royal Dutch Airlines,** Václavské nám. 37, Praha 1 (tel. 26-43-62); **Lufthansa,** Pařížská 28, Praha 1 (tel. 231-7551); **SAS,** Štěpánská 61, Praha 1 (tel. 22-81-41); and **Swissair,** Pařížská 11, Praha 1 (tel. 232-4707).

BY TRAIN   Passengers traveling to Prague by train (see "Getting There" in Chapter 2) typically arrive at one of two centrally located train stations—Hlavní Nádraží (Main Station) or Nádraží Holešovice (Holešovice Station). Both are on line C of the metro system, and both offer a number of visitor services, including money-changing, a post office, and left-luggage. **AVE Ltd.** (tel. 236-2560 or 80-75-05), an accommodations agency that arranges beds in hostels as well as rooms in hotels and apartments, is at both rail terminals. They're open 24 hours from June to September, and from 6am to midnight the rest of the year. If you've arrived without room reservations, this agency is definitely worth a visit.

Hlavní Nádraží, Wilsonova třída, Praha 2 (tel. 235-3836 or 26-49-30), is both the grander and more popular of Prague's two primary train stations. It's also seedier. Built in 1909, this beautiful, four-story, art nouveau structure was certainly one of the city's most beloved architectural gems, before it was connected to a functionalist-style dispatch hall in the mid-1970s. From the train platform, you'll walk down a flight of stairs and through a tunnel before arriving in the station's ground-level main hall, which contains ticket windows, a marginally useful **Prague Information Service (PIS)** office that sells city maps and dispenses information (sometimes inaccurate), and filthy restrooms. The station's basement holds a left-luggage counter, which is open 24 hours and charges 10 Kč (35¢) per bag per day. Though cheaper, the nearby lockers are not secure and should be avoided. Surprisingly clean public-showering facilities are also located beneath the station's main hall. They are a good place for travelers to refresh, and cost just 30 Kč ($1). The showers are open Monday through Friday from 6am to 8pm,

Saturday from 7am to 7pm, and Sunday from 8am to 4pm. On the station's second floor you'll find the train information office (marked by a lowercase "i"), open daily 6am to 10pm. On the top floor is a tattered restaurant that is recommendable only to the most famished.

The train station is a five-minute stroll to the "top" end of Václavské náměstí and 15 minutes by foot to Staroměstské náměstí. Metro line C connects the station to the rest of the city. Metro trains depart from the lower level, and tickets, which cost 6 Kč (18¢), are available from the newsstand near the metro entrance. Taxis line up just outside the station, and are plentiful enough throughout the day and night.

Nádraží Holešovice, Prague's second train station, is usually the terminus for trains from Berlin and other points north. Although it is not as centrally located as the main station, its more manageable size and location at the end of metro line C make it almost as convenient.

Prague contains two smaller rail stations. **Masaryk Station,** Hybernská ulice, is primarily for travelers arriving on trains originating from other Bohemian cities or from Brno or Bratislava. Situated about 10 minutes by foot from the main train station, Masaryk is located near Staré Město, just a stone's throw from náměstí Republiky metro station. **Smíchov Station,** Nádražní ulice, is the terminus for commuter trains from western and southern Bohemia, though an occasional international train pulls in here too. The station contains a 24-hour baggage-check and is serviced by metro line B.

For more information on traveling on České dráhy (Czech Railways), see Chapter 10, "Easy Excursions From Prague."

BY BUS   Central Bus Station Praha—Florenc, Křižíkova 5, Praha 8 (tel. 22-14-45 or 22-14-40), is located a few blocks north of the main railroad station. Most local and long-distance buses arrive at this terminal, situated just beside the Florenc metro station, on both metro lines B and C. Smaller bus depots are located at **Želivského** (metro line A), **Smíchovské nádraží** (metro line B), and **nádraží Holešovice** (metro line C).

Fares on Czech buses typically are half those of trains. Reservations should be made as far in advance as possible. See Chapter 10, "Easy Excursions From Prague," for more information on departing Prague by bus.

BY CAR   Travelers approaching Prague from the west drive through Nürnberg, Germany, before entering the Czech Republic at the Waidhaus/Rozvadov border crossing. Drivers from the northwest motor through Chemnitz (formerly Karl-Marx-Stadt), Germany, before entering the Czech Republic at the Reitzenhain/Pohraniční border crossing. From the south Linz, Austria, is a gateway to the Czech Republic, and from the east, Zilina, Slovakia, is a gateway.

For information on driving in and around the city, see "Getting Around," below.

TOURIST INFORMATION

Despite tourism's terrific importance to the nascent capitalist Czech economy, the country's politicians haven't yet gotten around to funding an official visitor agency. For the moment, prospective visitors to Prague are on their own when it comes to collecting accurate travel information. **Čedok,** located at Na příkopě 18 and at Václavské náměstí 24 (tel. 212-7512), once the country's official state-owned visitors bureau, is now just a traditional semiprivate travel agency. Like others in town, it prefers selling tickets and tours to dispensing free information.

The **American Hospitality Center,** Na Můstku 7, Praha 1 (tel. 2422-9961 or 2423-0467) is, well . . . hospitable, and the best place to obtain brochures, guidebooks, advice, and information on events citywide. Opened by two American businessmen of Czech ancestry, at the behest of the mayor of Prague, the center is staffed almost exclusively with bilingual Czechs, who are as happy to dispense advice as they are to sell tickets and tours. They also make hotel reservations. The center is open seven days a week from 8am to 8pm.

Prague Information Service (PIS), Na příkopě 20 (tel. 54-44-44), located between Václavské náměstí and náměstí Republiky, is one of the city's largest Czech-owned tourist offices, offering brochures on upcoming cultural events as well as tickets to sightseeing tours and concerts. In summer, they're usually open Monday through Friday from 8am to 7pm, and on Saturday and Sunday from 9am to 3pm. In winter, hours are slightly shorter. A second PIS office is located inside the main railway station (see "Arriving," above).

Literally dozens of other tour-and-ticket sellers disguised as information agencies are located throughout Prague's tourist center. While all are primarily interested in sales, most are also willing to answer simple questions. Many can also help you find accommodations.

When entering Prague via Ruzyně Airport, you might try your luck for information at the Čedok office in the main terminal. They might even give you a city map if they have one. The office is usually open daily from 9am to 6pm. Those arriving via train, into either of Prague's two primary stations, will find the greatest success obtaining information from AVE Ltd. (tel. 236-2560 or 80-75-05), an accommodations agency that also distributes a limited amount of printed information. They're open 24 hours from June to September, and from 6am to midnight the rest of the year.

For information about travel by train, visit the train information window (marked with a lowercase "i") in the main train station (Hlavní Nádraží). The American Hospitality Center (see above) is your best bet for coherent English-language information on bus, metro, streetcar, and other transportation options.

CITY LAYOUT

The Vltava (Moldau) River bisects Prague. Staré Město (Old Town) and Nové Město (New Town) are located on the east (or right) side of the river, while Hradčany (Castle District) and Malá Strana (Lesser Town) are situated on the river's west (or left) bank.

MAIN ARTERIES & STREETS Bridges and squares are Prague's most prominent landmarks. Charles Bridge, the oldest and most famous of the 15 that span the Vltava, is right in the middle of the city. Staroměstské náměstí (Old Town Square), a few winding blocks east of Charles Bridge, is, appropriately enough, the center of Staré Město. Several important streets radiate from this hub, including fashionable Pařížská to the northwest, historic Celetná to the east, and Melantrichova, which connects to Václavské náměstí (Wenceslas Square) to the southeast.

On the west side of Charles Bridge is Mosteká, a three-block-long thoroughfare that runs into Malostranské náměstí, Malá Strana's main square. Hradčany, the Castle District, sits just northwest of the square, while a second hill, Petřín, is located just southwest of the square.

FINDING AN ADDRESS At one time or another you'll probably get lost in Prague. To the chagrin of tourists and postal workers alike, the city's tangle of streets follows no discernible pattern. There are a couple of consoling factors, however. One is excellent street signing; signs are usually posted on the sides of buildings. The other is dependable house signing, with numbers that usually increase as one moves away from the Vltava. Note that on signs and literature in Prague, as well as in this book, street names always precede the numbers. Also, in contemporary Czech signage, the word for street (*ulice*) is either abbreviated to *ul.* or usually simply omitted altogether—Pařížská ulice, for instance, is best known as Pařížká. *Třída* (avenue) and *náměstí* (square) are also routinely abbreviated to *tř.* and *nám.,* respectively.

Greater Prague is divided into 10 postal districts, each encompassing from 2 to 22 neighborhoods. While the postal districts are too large to effectively help you locate a particular restaurant or hotel, district numbers are routinely included in addresses, and are therefore listed below with their corresponding neighborhoods.

Praha 1 Hradčany, Malá Strana, Staré Město, Josefov, northern Nové Město.

Praha 2 Southern Nové Město, Vyšehrad, western Vinohrady.

Praha 3   Eastern Vinohrady Žižkov.

Praha 4   Nusle, Michle, Podolí, Braník, Krč, Chodov, Háje, Hodkovicvky, Lhotka, Kunratice, Šeberov, Újezd, Modřany, Libuš, Komořany, Cholupice, Točná, Písnice.

Praha 5   Smíchov, Motol, Košíře, Radice, Jinonice, Stodůlky, Zličín, Sobín, Hlubočepy, Malá Chuchle, Slivenec, Holyné, Řeporyje, Velká Chuchle, Lochkov, Zadní Kopanina, Lahovice, Radotín, Zbraslav, Lipence.

Praha 6   Western Bubeneč, Dejvice, Vodovice, Střešovice, Břenov, Veleslavín, Liboc, Ruzyné, Řepy Nubušice, Lysolaje, Sedlec, Suchdol.

Praha 7   Eastern Bubeneč, Holešovice, Troja.

Praha 8   Karlín, Libeň, Kobylisy, western Střížkov, Bohnice, Čimice, Dáblice, Dolní Chabry, Březiněves.

Praha 9   Vysočany, Hloubětín, Hrdlořezy, Kyje, Hostavice, Černý most, Prosek, eastern Střížkov, Letňany, Kbely, Satalice, Dolní Počernice, Horní Počernice, Klánovice, Béchovice, Kolodéhe, Újezd and Lesy.

Praha 10   Vršovice, Stašnice, Malešice, Štěrboholy, Dubeč, Hájek, Královice, Uhříněves, Dolní and Horní Měcholupy, Záběhlice, Hostivař, Petrovice, Křeslice, Pitkovice, Benice, Kolovraty, Lipany, Nedvězí.

NEIGHBORHOODS IN BRIEF

The invisible lines that divide local communities were drawn up long ago. Originally developed as four adjacent, self-governing boroughs, plus a walled Jewish ghetto, central Prague's neighborhoods have maintained their individual identities along with their medieval street plans.

STARÉ MĚSTO [Old Town]   Staré Město was established in 1234 as a result of Prague's growing importance on central European trade routes. Its ancient streets, most of which meander haphazardly around Staroměstské náměstí (Old Town Square), are still the city's biggest draws. Many of Prague's most important buildings and churches are located here, as are the city's best shops and theaters.

JOSEFOV [Jew's Town]   Prague's celebrated Jewish ghetto, located entirely within Staré Město, was once surrounded by a wall, before it was almost all destroyed to make way for more modern 19th-century structures. Prague is considered one of Europe's great historic Jewish cities, and a tour of this remarkable area will make clear why. See Chapter 7, "Strolling Around Prague," for an informative walking tour.

NOVÉ MĚSTO [New Town]   Draped like a crescent around Staré Město, Nové Město (New Town) is home to Václavské náměstí (Wenceslas Square), the National Theater, and many of the city's business-oriented buildings that are often overlooked by casual tourists. When it was founded by Emperor Charles IV in 1348, Staré Město was the largest wholly planned municipal development in Europe. The street layout remains largely unchanged since the 14th century, but most of Staré Město's structures were razed in the late 19th century and replaced with the offices and apartment buildings that stand today.

HRADČANY   Literally "Castle District," this part of central Prague contains little more than the castle itself.

MALÁ STRANA [Lesser Town]   Prague's "Lesser Town" was founded in 1257 by German settlers who were enticed here by the region's Přemyslid rulers. Nestled between Prague Castle and the Vltava River, Malá Strana is relatively compact. It's winding lanes are some of the city's prettiest, especially those surrounding Kampa park, situated along the river, just south of Charles Bridge. Many embassies are located here, as are old palaces and gardens that once belonged to the city's richest families.

STREET MAPS

A Prague street map is essential, especially if you want to venture off the main tourist streets without getting too lost. Bookstores, souvenir shops, and many sidewalk newsagents sell local maps. Expect to pay about 50 Kč ($1.65). For an in-depth look at Prague's web of streets, buy a comprehensive accordion-style foldout map, available in Prague for about 100 Kč ($3.35). The best map for exploring roads outside of Prague is the Velký Autoatlas Československa, an exhaustive street guide covering the country's maze of backroads.

2. GETTING AROUND

BY PUBLIC TRANSPORTATION

Prague's public transportation network is both vast and efficient— one of the few reliable Communist-era legacies. In central Prague, metro (subway) stations abound. Above ground, punctual trams and buses traverse the city in all directions. The city's metros, trams, and buses all share the same price structure and ticket system. As of this writing, tickets on all cost 6 Kč (20¢) each for adults and 3 Kč (10¢) for children aged 10 to 16. Rides are free for those aged under 10 and over 70. The same tickets are valid on the city's entire public transportation network, and can be purchased from orange coin-operated machines in metro stations or at most newsstands. Ticket prices do not vary with the length of your ride. Hold onto your ticket throughout your ride; you'll need it to prove you've paid if asked by a ticket collector. If caught without a valid ticket, you will be told to pay a 200 Kč ($6.70) fine on the spot. You can transfer free from metro to bus or tram within one hour of validating a ticket.

A money-saving booklet of 25 tickets (called *ekologicke jízdenky*) costs 125 Kč ($4.15). If you're planning on staying for a couple of weeks or more, it makes financial sense to buy a one-month or three-month pass (*měsíčni jízdenka*), which cost 300 Kč ($10.00) and 750 Kč ($25), respectively. These can be purchased at the "DP" windows at any metro station. After the first week of the month, passes are only available at the Dopravní podnik (transport department) office on Na bojišti, near the I.P. Pavlova metro station.

METRO [Subway] Opened in 1974, Prague's metro trains are smooth, fast, and efficient. They operate daily from about 5am to midnight, and run every two to six minutes or so. There are three lines—called A, B, and C—which intersect with each other at various points around the city. The most convenient central Prague stations are Můstek, located at the foot of Václavské náměstí (Wenceslas Square); Staroměstská, for Staroměstské náměstí (Old Town Square) and Charles Bridge; and Malostranská, serving Malá Strana and Hradčany (Castle District).

Validate your ticket by inserting it into the date-stamping machine before descending on the escalator to the train platform.

TRAM Even if you usually shy away from public transport in foreign cities, use Prague's trams. The city's 26 electric streetcar lines run practically everywhere, they run regularly, and they're actually a lot of fun. You can never get too lost, because no matter how far from the center you travel, there's always another tram with the same number traveling back to where you started. Trams, like trains, automatically make every stop. Schedules are posted at each stop, and trams are usually on time. The tram network is intelligently coordinated with the metro; an "M" on the tram schedule means that the stop is at a metro station.

The most popular tram, number 22 (dubbed "the tourist tram" or "the pickpocket express"), runs past top sights like the National

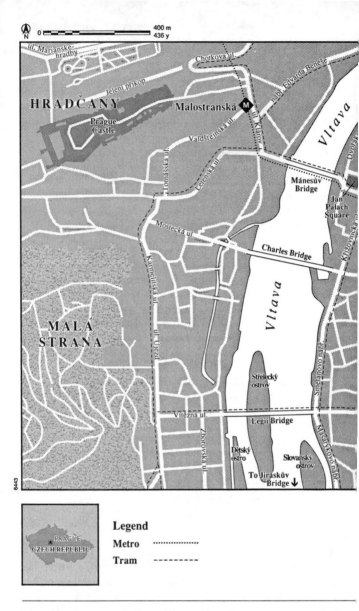

Legend

Metro ··················

Tram - - - - - - - - -

Theater and Prague Castle. In winter, when the temperature routinely hovers around freezing, the individually heated seats on the trams are some of the warmest places in town.

Immediately after boarding, stamp your ticket in the machine on the tram. Face the side of the ticket with the numbers toward you, slide it into the ticket box, and pull the black lever forward.

BUS Bus riders must purchase tickets in advance, from either a

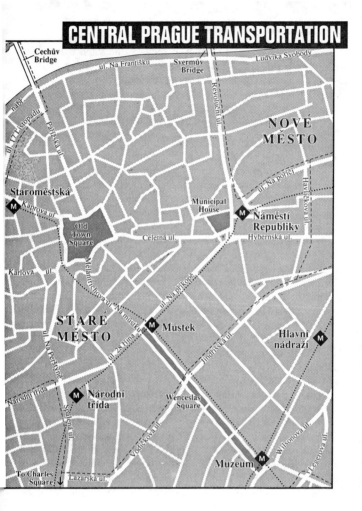

newsstand or a metro station machine, and validate them upon boarding. Regular bus service stops at midnight, after which selected routes run reduced schedules (usually only once per hour).

FUNICULAR The funicular, a kind of cable car on a track, dashes up and down Petřín Hill every 10 minutes or so from 9:15am to 8:45pm (see Chapter 6). The incline tram only makes two stops—one of which is at Nebozízek Restaurant in the middle of the hill (see

Chapter 5, "Prague Dining")—and requires the same 6 Kč (20¢) ticket as other means of public transport. The funicular departs from a small house in the park just above the middle of Újezd in Malá Strana.

BY TAXI

Taxis can be hailed in the streets or found in front of train stations, large hotels, and popular tourist attractions. Be warned: The great majority of cab drivers routinely rip off unsuspecting tourists. Taxi horror stories abound. You will likely see a Christmas tree–shaped "odor-eater" or other ornament hanging in front of the taxi meter. Ask the driver to remove it so you can see the meter.

When entering a taxi, the meter should start no higher than 10 Kč (35¢). When riding within the city center, the meter should then climb at a rate of 12 Kč (40¢) per kilometer. You will see two numbers on the taxi meter. The one on the left that keeps climbing is the fare. The one on the right will read either 1, 2, 3, or 4. The higher the number, the faster the meter runs. When riding in the city center, if the rate window doesn't read 1, you're getting ripped off. You still might be getting ripped off, as some drivers have rigged their meters to show 1 but run at a higher rate. Keep your eye on the meter, as drivers will often start the trip with the meter on 1, then raise the number stealthfully while shifting gears. Be prepared to tell the driver to stop if you spot cheating. Writing down the cab's license number is a good way to persuade drivers to charge you the correct fare.

If you phone for a taxi, chances are pretty good that you'll be charged the official rate, as your trip is logged in an office and is a matter of public record. Taxis are allowed to start the meter when they get the call, however, so by the time the cab arrives, it will already have crowns on its meter. Larger taxi companies with English-speaking dispatchers include **AAA Taxi** (tel. 34-24-10 or 32-24-44); **RONY Taxi** (tel. 692-1958 or 43-04-03); and **SEDOP Taxi** (tel. 75-21-10 or 72-08-34).

A final warning: Only the foolish hail cabs in Václavské náměstí, Malostranské náměstí, or at the foot of Charles Bridge. In general, these tourist-oriented drivers are the worst offenders.

BY CAR

My advice is simple: If you're staying in central Prague, don't drive. Fraught with adventure, driving in the city center is only for the iron-nerved. A maze of narrow streets, pedestrian-only thoroughfares, one-way roads, and a plethora of restrictions designed to discourage cars from the center make driving a poor choice for visitors. If you are staying on the outskirts of the city, and need a car for trips into the countryside, that's another matter entirely. Driving around the Czech Republic is relatively straightforward. Car-rental rates are low compared to some western European cities.

RENTALS The big American car-rental firms are the most expensive. Rates vary, but expect to pay about 21,000 Kčs ($700) per week, depending on the season.

Europcar, Pařížská 26 (tel. 231-3405), rents cars for 1,637 Kč to 4,437 Kč ($55 to $148) per day with unlimited mileage and full insurance. They're open daily from 8am to 7pm. A second Europcar office is located at Ruzyně Airport (tel. 316-7849), and is open daily from 8am to 10pm. **Hertz,** Karlovo nám. 28, Praha 2 (tel. 29-78-36), charges 2,837 Kč to 5,655 Kč ($95 to $189), including VAT (value-added tax), per day with unlimited mileage. **Budget,** at Ruzyně Airport (tel. 316-5214) and in the Hotel Inter-Continental, náměstí Curieových, Praha 1 (tel. 280-0995), charges similar rates. **Avis** has four different locations in Prague: Opletalova 33, Praha 1 (tel. 22-23-24); Ruzyně Airport, Praha 6 (tel. 36-78-07); Hotel Atrium, Pobřeží 1, Praha 8 (tel. 284-2043); and Hotel Forum, Kongresová 1, Praha 4 (tel. 419-0215).

Local Czech car-rental companies sometimes offer lower rates. Compare **Prague Car Rent,** Malá Štěpánská 7, Praha 1 (tel. 691-0323 or 29-58-57); **Pragocar,** Milevská 2, Praha 1 (tel. 692-2875 or 692-2599); **Avanti Car,** Evropská 178, Praha 6 (tel. 316-5204; fax 23-16-41); and **Dancar,** Bělohorská 186, Praha 6 (tel. 35-77-39).

Make sure the rate you pay includes unlimited mileage, all taxes, and the collision-damage waiver (CDW), as extras can send prices into the stratosphere.

PARKING Finding a parking spot in Prague can sometimes be more of a challenge than driving in this maze of a city. Fines for illegal parking can be stiff, but worse are "Denver Boots," which immobilize cars until a fine is paid. If you find your car booted, you must pay a several-hundred-crown fine at police headquarters, Kongresová 2, Praha 4 (metro: Vyšehrad), the large building just south of the Forum Hotel, then return to your car and wait for the clamp removers.

DRIVING Seat belts are required, you may not legally make a right turn when a traffic light is red, and automobiles must stop when a pedestrian steps into a crosswalk. Gasoline is expensive; about 100 Kč ($3.35) per gallon, and filling stations can be difficult to find. Stations open 24 hours in center city are located in Praha 3 on Olšanská; in Praha 4 on Újezd; and in Praha 7 on Argentinská.

BY BICYCLE

Although there are no bike lanes, and smooth streets are unheard of, Prague is a particularly wonderful city to bike in. Vehicular traffic is limited in the city center, where small winding streets seem especially suited to two-wheeled vehicles. Surprisingly, few people take advantage of this opportunity; cyclists are largely limited to the few foreigners who have imported their own bikes. The city's ubiquitous cobblestones make mountain bikes the natural choice for cyclists, and there are two shops in the city that rent them on a daily basis. **Cyklocentrum,** Karlovo nám. 29, Praha 2 (tel. 20-54-51), and **Rent-A-Bike,** Školská 12, Praha 1 (tel. 22-10-63). Both rent sturdy American-made 18-speeders for about 300 Kč ($10) per day and 1,500 Kč ($50) per week. They are open daily from about 9am to 8pm; phone for exact hours. A security deposit of 10,000 Kč ($333.35) or your passport is required.

ON FOOT

Prague can be a difficult city to negotiate on foot, but in the winding streets of Staré Město and in the little lanes of Malá Strana, there is no better way to go. The city's tangle of streets is confusing. It seems as though no two streets run parallel, and even some locals regularly consult maps. Like wandering through Venice, a stroll through Prague often means getting wonderfully lost. And like Venice, Prague's jumbled center is so small, you can always extradite yourself from a seemingly hopeless situation with just the slightest amount of effort.

FAST FACTS PRAGUE

Airport   See "Orientation," earlier in this chapter.

American Express   For travel arrangements, traveler's checks, currency exchange, and other member services, visit the city's sole American Express office, located at Václavské nám. (Wenceslas Square) 56, Praha 1 (tel. 22-94-87; fax 26-15-04). It's open Monday through Friday from 9am to 7pm, and Saturday from 9am to 3pm. The office sometimes closes for lunch from 1:30 to 2pm. To report lost or stolen Amex cards, call American Express collect in the United States (tel. 202/554-2639) at any time.

Auto Rentals   See "Getting Around," earlier in this chapter.

Babysitters   If your hotel can't recommend a sitter, phone **Affordable Luxuries,** Sarajevská 23, Praha 2 (tel. 691-1147), which provides various child-minding services. Make reservations far in advance.

Bookstores   There are several shops around the city selling English-language books; see Chapter 8.

Business Hours   Most **banks** are open Monday through Friday from 9:30am to 3:30pm. Some also open Saturday from 9:30 until noon. Business **offices** are generally open Monday through Friday from 8am until 4pm. **Pubs** are usually open daily 11am to midnight. Most **restaurants** open for lunch from noon to 3pm and for dinner from 6 to 11pm. A very few stay open later. **Stores** are typically open Monday through Saturday from 10am to 6pm, but those in the tourist center keep longer hours and open on Sunday as well. Note: Many small food shops that keep long hours charge up to 20% more for all their goods after 8pm or so.

Climate   See "When to Go" in Chapter 2.

Currency   See "Information, Entry Requirements, and Money" in Chapter 2.

Currency Exchange   When changing money at an exchange office, you will get a better rate for cash than you will for traveler's checks. **Banks** generally offer the best exchange rates, but **American Express** and **Thomas Cook** are competitive and do not charge commission for cashing traveler's checks, regardless of the issuer. Don't hesitate to use a credit card. I have found that card exchange rates are regularly to my advantage. There is one American Express office in Prague (see above). Thomas Cook is located directly across Wenceslas Square at Václavské nám. 56 (tel. 235-2468). It's open Monday through Friday from 9am to 5pm, and Saturday from 9am to noon.

Komerční Banka has three Praha 1 locations: Na příkopě 28, Na příkopě 3–5, and Václavské nám. 42. The exchange offices are open Monday through Friday from 8am to 6:30pm.

Živnostenská Banka has two Praha 1 locations: Na příkopé 20 (open Monday to Friday from 8am to 6pm, Saturday from 8am to noon) and Celetná 3 (open Monday to Friday from 1 to 6pm, Saturday from 9am to 1pm).

Čekobanka Chequepoint keeps the longest hours, but offers the worst exchange rates. Central Prague locations include Řijna 13 and Staroměstské nám. 21. (both open 24 hours); Staroměstské nám. 27 (open daily 8am to 11:30pm); and Václavské nám. 1 (open daily 8am to 11pm).

Automatic Teller Machines (ATMs) are located throughout the city center, and many accept foreign cards linked to the Cirrus network. Some of the most convenient Praha 1 locations include Na příkopě 5; Václavské nám. (Wenceslas Square) 42; and nám. Republiky 8, near the Kotva department store. ATMs at the above locations are all open 24 hours.

Doctors and Dentists   If you need a physician or dentist, and your condition is not life-threatening, visit the **First Medical Clinic of Prague Ltd.,** Vyšehradská 33, Praha 2 (tel. 29-22-86). The clinic provides 24-hour emergency health care as well as EKGs, diagnostics, ophthalmology, house calls, and referrals to specialists. The **Diplomatic Health Center for Foreigners,** Na homoice 724, Praha 5 (tel. 5292-2146 weekdays; 5292-1111 evenings and weekends), is another safe bet for 24-hour emergency medical and dental services. There is a 1,000 Kč ($33.35) examination deposit, which may be returned depending on services rendered.

For **emergency medical aid** call 29-93-81.

Driving Rules See "Getting Around," earlier in this chapter.

Drugstores An emergency pharmacy is located at Na příkopě 7 (tel. 22-00-81).

Electricity Czech appliances operate on 220 volts, and plug into two-pronged outlets that differ from those in America and in Great Britain. Appliances designed for the U.S. or U.K. markets must use an adapter and transformer. Do not attempt to plug an American appliance directly into a European electrical outlet without a transformer; you will ruin your appliance and possibly start a fire.

Embassies The **U.S. Embassy,** Tržiště 15, Malá Strana, Praha 1 (tel. 53-66-41 or 53-66-49), is open Monday through Friday from 8am to 4pm. The **Canadian Embassy,** Mickiewiczova 6, Hradčany, Praha 6 (tel. 2431-1112), is open Monday through Friday from 9am to 9pm. The **U.K. Embassy,** Thunovská 14, Praha 1 (tel. 53-33-47), is open Monday through Friday from 9am to 1pm. The **Australian Embassy,** Činská 4, Bubeneč, Praha 6 (tel. 311-0641), is open Monday through Thursday from 9am to noon, and 1 to 4pm, and Friday from 9am to 1:30pm.

Emergencies Prague's police and fire services can be reached by dialing **158** from any phone. To call an ambulance, dial **155.**

Eyeglasses A number of spectacle shops are located on Na příkopě and Václavské náměstí. Even if you forgot to bring along your prescription, **Lunettes Optika,** Václavské nám. 51, Praha 1 (tel. 26-47-74), can fit prescription glasses in about one hour. They're open Monday to Friday from 9am to 7pm, Saturday from 9am to 5pm. Alternatively, try **Optika V Celetné,** Celetná 32, Praha 1 (tel. 22-26-20). It's open Monday through Friday from 9am until 7pm and Saturday from 10am until 7pm; AE, DC, and V are accepted.

Hairdressers and Barbers Prague is hardly one of the style capitals of the world. If you just need to get your hair done here, visit a salon in the Forum, Diplomat, or Atrium hotel.

Holidays See "When to Go" in Chapter 2.

Hospitals **University Hospital Motol,** V úvalu 84 (Motol), Praha 5 (tel. 5295-1070), is particularly welcoming to foreigners, and assures patients of English-speaking doctors, who also make house calls. In an emergency, dial **155** for an ambulance.

Information See "Tourist Information," earlier in this chapter.

Laundry and Dry Cleaning **Laundry Kings,** 16 Dejvická, is the only American-style coin-operated self-service laundry in Prague. Washes cost 100 Kč to 120 Kč ($3.35 to $4) per load, depending on how much drying power you need. An attendant can do your wash for 30 Kč ($1) additional, but the service takes at least 24 hours. Irons are available free for patrons' use. From Hradčanská metro station, take the "Praha Dejvice" exit and turn left. Laundry Kings is open seven days a week 8am to 10pm.

Rapid Service, Francouzská 15, offers both dry cleaning and

American-style shirt laundering. There are two other Rapid Service locations, at Dejvická 30 and Ječna 29.

Affordable Luxuries (tel. 691-1147) will pick up your wash and dry cleaning and return it to your hotel within 48 hours. They charge 160 Kč ($5.35) per 4 kilogram load (8.8 lb.). Dry cleaning is 44 Kč ($1.50) per shirt, and 69 Kč ($2.30) per trouser.

Libraries The **American Library,** Hybernská 7A, Praha 1, is located near náměstí Republiky. The new facility, formally the American Center for Culture and Commerce, is also the home of the U.S. Information Center. It holds about 8,000 volumes as well as about 140 different magazines and newspapers. Hours are Monday to Thursday from 11am to 5pm, Friday from 11am to 3pm.

The small **English Library** in the National Library, Mariánské náměstí, Praha 1, near Staroměstske náměstí, contains a reading room filled with books and magazines of English origin. The library is open Monday, Wednesday, and Friday from 9am to 3pm; Tuesday and Thursday from 1 to 7pm.

Lost Property If you lose something in Prague, it's probably gone for good, but optimists might try visiting the city's **Lost Property Office,** Bolzanova 5 (tel. 236-8887).

Luggage Storage and Lockers The **Ruzyně Airport Luggage Storage Office** (tel. 36-78-14) never closes, and charges 50 Kč ($1.70) per item, per day. Left-luggage offices are also available at the main train stations, **Hlavní Nádraží** and **Nádraží Holešovice.** Both charge 10 Kč (35¢) per bag per day, and both are technically open 24 hours, but if your train is departing late at night, check to make sure someone will be around. Luggage lockers are available in all of Prague's train stations, but they are not secure and should be avoided.

Finally, you can often leave luggage at a fancy, well-located hotel even if not a guest. At an average cost of 50 Kč ($1.70) per item, your bags can stay at the Paříz, even if you can't.

Mail Post offices are plentiful and are normally open Monday through Friday from 9am to 5pm and on Saturday from 9am to noon. The **Main Post Office,** Jindřišská 14, Praha 1 (tel. 26-41-93), just a few steps from Václavské náměstí, is open 24 hours. You can receive mail in Prague, marked "Poste Restante," and addressed to you, care of this post office. If you carry an American Express Card or Amex traveler's checks, you would be wiser to receive mail care of **American Express,** Václavské nám. (Wenceslas Square) 56, Praha 1 (tel. 22-94-87; fax 26-15-04). They're open Monday through Friday from 9am to 7pm and Saturday from 9am to 3pm.

Newspapers and Magazines Two high-quality English-language newspapers are published in Prague. *Prognosis,* a biweekly published every other Friday, is the more artsy of the two—a kind of *Village Voice,* with in-depth stories about Czech and Slovak societies. The weekly *Prague Post,* published each Wednesday, is straighter and newsier. Both suffer from rather skimpy listings of sightseeing and entertainment happenings. Between them, however, these papers offer the most comprehensive and up-to-date visitor information available in English. It's best to buy both.

Kultura v Praze, a monthly listings booklet, is an excellent Czech-language publication with information on theaters, galleries, concerts, clubs, films, and events around town. It costs less than 15 Kč (50¢), and is not difficult for non-Czechs to understand.

Newsstands are located inside most every metro station, and good-sized, international magazine shops are located in major hotels and on most busy shopping streets.

Photocopies **Copy General,** nám. Gorkého 26, Praha 1 (tel. 26-80-04 or 26-81-02), offers both black-and-white and color copying and employs an English-speaking staff. They're open 24 hours.

Photographic Needs Photo processing in Prague is more expensive than similar services in the U.S. **Fotografia Praha,** Václavské nám. 50 (tel. 26-33-04), with 10 branches in Prague, is one of the best sources for most photographic needs.

Police In an emergency, dial **158.** For other matters, contact the **Central Police Station,** Konviktská 14 (Staré Město), Praha 1 (tel. 212-1111).

Religious Services For a former Communist country that had an official atheist policy, Prague has many places of worship. Most are open to the public, and services in a grand, Gothic church can be a unique experience. For a special treat, think about spending a morning in **St. Vitus Cathedral,** at Prague Castle. Roman Catholic services are held Monday through Friday at 5:45am, Saturday at 7am, and Sunday at 7am, 9:15am, 11am, and 3pm (the latter is a full choral service). **St. Nicholas Church,** Malostranské náměstí, Praha 1, also holds regular Catholic ceremonies. Services are scheduled Monday through Saturday at 7:30am, and Sunday at 8am and 11am. Evening Catholic masses are held at **Church of Our Lady of Týn,** Staroměstské náměstí, Praha 1. Services are scheduled Monday through Friday at 5:30pm, Saturday at 9pm, and Sunday at 11:30am and 9pm.

St. Nicholas Church, Staroměstské náměstí, Praha 1, is the city's main Czechoslovak Hussite (Protestant) church. Services are held Wednesdays at 5pm and Sundays at 12:30pm.

Orthodox Jewish services at Prague's **Old New Synagogue,** Červená 2 (tel. 231-0681), are held Saturday mornings; phone for exact times.

Restrooms My first pick for restrooms are the lobby-level lavatories in Prague's better-known hotels. Most restaurants and pubs also have restrooms you can use if you ask politely.

Safety Whenever you're traveling in an unfamiliar city or country, stay alert. Be aware of your immediate surroundings. Wear a moneybelt and don't sling your camera or purse over your shoulder; wear the strap diagonally across your body. This will minimize the possibility of becoming a victim of crime. Every society has its criminals. It's your responsibility to be aware and alert especially in the most heavily touristed areas.

Tax A 23% value added tax (VAT) was instituted on Jan. 1, 1993. It applies to most restaurant, hotel, and shop items, and is included in the menu, rate card, or ticket price, rather than being tacked on at the register.

Taxis Prague's plethora of cabs can be hailed in the street or at waiting areas near Staroměstské náměstí, Václavské náměstí, and other squares. An illuminated roof light means they're available. If you will need a taxi from your hotel early in the morning, it is advisable to make a reservation the night before. Try **C&H Osobní Taxi** (tel. 231-8044 or 231-8113). *Warning:* Before taking a taxi, see "Getting Around," above.

Telephone There are two kinds of **pay phones** in normal use. The first accepts coins, while the other operates exclusively with a Phonecard, available from post offices and some hotels for 100 Kč ($3.35). The minimum cost of a local call is 1 Kč (3¢). You can deposit several coins at a time, but telephones don't make change, so unless you are calling long distance, use 1 Kč coins exclusively. Phonecard telephones automatically deduct the price of your call from the card. Cards are especially handy if you want to call abroad, as you don't have to continuously chuck in the change.

Prague's **area code** is **02.** All the telephone numbers in this guidebook assume this prefix unless otherwise noted.

To call Prague direct from the United States, dial 011 (international code), 42 (the Czech Republic country code), 2 (Prague's area code, without the "0" prefix, used only in the Czech Republic and Slovakia), and the six-, seven-, or eight-digit local telephone number.

Long-distance phone charges are higher in the Czech Republic than they are in the United States. In addition, hotels usually add their own surcharge, sometimes as hefty as 100% to 200%, which you may be unaware of until you are presented with the bill.

Even if you are not calling person-to-person, collect calls are charged at that high rate, making them pricey too. Charging a long-distance call to your telephone calling card is often the most economical way to phone home.

A fast, convenient way to call the U.S. from Europe is via **USA Direct.** This service bypasses the foreign operator and automatically links you to an AT&T operator in America. The access number in the Czech Republic is 0042-000-101. The same service is also offered via MCI; dial 0042-000-112.

Television There are three Czech television broadcasters. To save money on programming, two go off the air after midnight, while the third broadcasts CNN International (in English) until daybreak. Like so much else in the country, things are changing in TV land. In 1994 a wireless cable system is set to begin operations, with a capacity of 16 channels, including Eurosport, MTV, the Children's

Channel, and a movie channel. Many hotels already receive international programming via satellite.

Time Prague time is the same as the rest of Central Europe, one hour ahead of Britain's Greenwich mean time, and six hours ahead of U.S. eastern time. Clocks here spring forward and fall backward for daylight saving time, but the semiannual ritual follows a slightly different schedule than in the U.S.

Tipping Rules for tipping are not as strict in Prague as they are in the U.S., but when you are presented with good service, a 10% to 15% tip is appreciated.

Tour guides should be tipped, along with any guides at a church or historic site. Washroom and cloakroom attendants usually demand a couple of crowns, and porters in airports and rail stations usually receive 10 Kč to 20 Kč (35¢ to 65¢) per bag.

Taxi drivers should get about 10%, unless they've already ripped you off, in which case they should get nothing more.

Check restaurant menus to see if service is included before leaving an additional tip. Note that tipping is rare in both pubs and theaters.

Transit Information The **American Hospitality Center,** Melantrichova 8, Praha 1 (tel. 02/2422-9961), is your best bet for coherent English-language information on city transportation.

Water No one argues that Prague's water is particularly tasty, but there's lots of debate as to whether water from the tap is safe to drink. Czech bottled water (still and carbonated) is popular, and is sold in stores and restaurants.

3. NETWORKS & RESOURCES

FOR STUDENTS **Charles University** is Prague's most prestigious postsecondary school. Although many of its associated colleges are spread throughout the city, the areas just north and east of Charles Bridge contain most of the university's main buildings. Like many urban schools, this university does not really have a campus, but the pubs and public squares of the neighborhood serve as student hangouts. Since Charles University is largely a commuter school, central Prague lacks the verve and bustle of a college community.

Central European University, chartered in 1991 with a $25 million endowment from Hungarian-American billionaire George Soros, was founded to teach democratic and free-market principles in the former East Bloc. The Prague campus has lured prominent professors from prestigious universities like Oxford, Cambridge,

Stanford, and New York University. To find out about its English-language programs, contact Táboritská 23, POB 114, Praha 3 (tel. 2/27-47-58; fax 2/27-49-13).

In Prague, even non-European youth under age 26 can purchase **Interail train passes** at ČKM Travel, Žitná 9. Passes good for unlimited travel for one month cost 10,000 Kč ($333.35), and are valid on trains in both Eastern and Western Europe.

If you want to make some music or do some magic for money, you can do so legally anywhere in the city. If you want to sell something, beware that city authorities have recently been requiring permits to hawk on Charles Bridge.

FOR GAY MEN & LESBIANS During the bad old days of the Communist regime, homosexuality was met with official silence and popular ignorance. Happily, however, that same government also managed to instill in Czechs a genuine live and let live attitude. In 1991 Czech television broadcast a five-part series about gays called "We Live Among You, But. . . ." It was the first time that this generation of Czechs had seen an honest look at gays in society. Soon after, the film adaptation of Thomas Mann's novella *Death in Venice* was aired during prime time.

Since November 1989, many gays have "come out," and the most prevalent Czech attitude seems to be indifference. Gay sex is legal in the Czech Republic, and parliament is considering a partnership law allowing same-sex "marriages."

The Czech Republic's **Association of Organizations of Homosexual Citizens,** abbreviated SOHO, was founded in 1991 as an umbrella organization uniting several smaller gay organizations. The organization's leaders have even met with President Václav Havel to discuss gay rights issues.

Several bars and nightclubs in Prague cater exclusively to the gay community and are listed under the appropriate heading in Chapter 9, "Prague Nights." The best information on happenings for gay visitors can be found in the weekly entertainment guide **ProGram,** which has one page for gays every other week.

FOR WOMEN Prague is safer than many other cities, but none-theless women must be advised to take special precautions. Use your common sense. Try not to walk alone at night, especially on small, deserted streets. Always carry some emergency money, and don't hesitate to spend it on a taxi if you feel the least bit uneasy.

Every once in a while, women-only events occur in Prague, and are advertised or written about in one of the city's two English-language newspapers. Check the listings for the most up-to-date happenings.

PRAGUE ACCOMMODATIONS

Prague's hotels are nothing to write home about. You've heard all about how cheap Prague is, but for reasons of supply and demand, those utterances don't pertain to hotels. Some experts believe that the situation is finally changing; as competition stiffens, quality is rising and prices falling. Let's hope it's true.

There are several ways you can save money on hotels in Prague. Keep prices down by traveling off-season and off the beaten track. Politely negotiate the price of the room, especially if you sense there are plenty of empty ones from which to choose—you might find yourself paying 25% less than you expected. Negotiate a trade-off; a lower price for a smaller room, one without a television, or one on the top floor. Ask if they will offer a better rate if you stay several nights. If you are a student or an older traveler, ask for a special discount. Be pleasant, not pushy. Make it clear you are shopping around and, if the proprietor is not easily persuaded, try elsewhere or hope for better luck next time.

One of the least expensive ways to keep a roof over your head is by taking advantage of hostels. There are several places offering multishare accommodations listed below.

ROOMS IN PRIVATE APARTMENTS Rooms in private apartments are a traveler's best defense against Prague's sky-high hotel rates. While heavy demand has encouraged most of the city's hotel owners to overprice their rooms, there's a glut of private apartment dwellers itching to trade accommodations for Kč. Although few of these apartments are located right in the city center, most are within walking distance of a subway, tram, or bus stop. If you arrive in Prague by train, chances are you'll be approached by grandmothers offering their spare bedrooms. Several agencies carry listings and make reservations for tourists wishing to stay in private apartments. The best are listed below.

ACCOMMODATIONS AGENCIES Dozens of companies operating room-finding services have opened in the past couple of years;

you'll see their outlets throughout Prague's Staré Město. In addition to the agencies recommended below, you may want to try contacting **Tipatour,** Malé náměstí 2 (tel. 26-55-15); **Top Tour,** Rybná 3 (tel. 269-6526 or 232-1077); or **Accommodation Information Service,** Kaprova 12 (tel. 232-3006).

AVE LTD., Hlavní Nádraží and Nádraží Holešovice. Tel. 236-2560 or 80-75-05.

Arranging beds in hostels, as well as rooms in hotels and apartments, AVE Ltd. has an office in each of Prague's two train stations. Hours vary, but the offices usually stay open for late trains.

ČEDOK, Na příkopě 18. Tel. 212-7512.

The state-run-travel-monopoly-turned-private-travel-agency also arranges housing in private apartments and hotels for a small service charge. A second Čedok office is located at Václavské náměstí 24.

ČKM AGENCY, Žitná 12, Praha 1. Tel. 26-85-07 or 29-99-41.

Geared toward budget travelers, ČKM maintains listings and reservation agreements with many of Prague's least expensive hotels and hostels. A second ČKM Agency is located at Jindřišská 28 (tel. 26-85-07).

PRAGUE SUITES, Melantrichova 8, Praha 1. Tel. 2422-9961 or 2423-0467. Fax 2422-9363. Reservations can be made from the United States and Canada by calling toll free 800/426-8826.

Accommodations in private Czech homes can be arranged 24 hours a day, every day. Rates begin at $15 per person in accommodations outside center city, and $99 for two people in center city. If you make reservations in advance, the company will provide a meet-and-greet service at the train station or airport, and a staff member will escort you to your suite. The outfit can also arrange a room in a regular hotel.

Prices listed below are for summer 1994, and include Prague's 23% value-added tax (VAT). Expect discounts before and after the tourist season.

---

1. NEAR STAROMĚSTSKÉ NÁMĚSTÍ (OLD TOWN SQUARE)

EXPENSIVE

HOTEL INTER-CONTINENTAL PRAHA, nám. Curieových 5, Praha 1. Tel. 2/2488-1111. Fax 2/481-1216. 365

rms, 27 suites. A/C TV TEL MINIBAR **Metro:** Line A to Staroměstská.

$ Rates (including buffet breakfast): 7,011 Kč ($233.70) single;
8,301–10,332 Kč ($276.70–$344.40) double; from 16,605 Kč
($553.50) suite. Children under 10 stay free in parents' room. AE,
DC, MC, V.

Opened in 1974, the Inter-Continental was once the most important
hotel in Prague and the only place in town for Western-style
hospitality. It's hard to blame the building's ugly exterior on the
Communist regime; 1970s architecture was unsightly the world over.
Until 1993, the hotel's inside never reached world-class standards
either. As of this writing, the hotel was still in the process of
updating—a serious, multimillion dollar mending provoked by the
competition. Gone is the dark, Dickensian lobby and drab guest
quarters. They have been replaced by new check-in facilities, a
state-of-the-art health club, and fully remodeled rooms. None of the
guest rooms are particularly large, though they are well dressed in top
business style, with medium-quality wood-and-cloth furniture, good
closets, computer ports, and marble baths containing hairdryers,
magnifying mirrors, and massage shower heads. The hotel's L-shaped
suites are slightly larger than standard guest rooms, and come with
king-size beds, bidets, and fax machines.

Dining/Entertainment: Zlatá Praha, the top-floor continental
restaurant with wraparound windows, offers terrific views of Prague's
spires and rooftops. Main dishes include roasted quail with bacon
and spinach, and roast duck with cabbage. The restaurant is open
daily from noon to 3pm, and again from 7pm to midnight. The
Cechovní síň Brasserie on the lobby level serves three buffet meals
daily. A separate Café is also open all day for light snacks and drinks.
During the summer there is a snack bar on the patio in front of the
hotel.

Services: 24-hour room service, concierge, laundry, massage,
hairdresser, business center, money exchange.

Facilities: Fitness center, Jacuzzi, sauna, gift shop, newsstand,
flower shop.

UNGELT, Štupartská 1, Praha 1. Tel. 2/2481-1330. Fax
2/231-9505. 10 suites. TV TEL **Metro:** Line A to Staroměstská or
line B to náměstí Republiky.

$ Rates: 5,735 Kč ($191.15) one-bedroom suite; 7,165 Kč
($238.85) two-bedroom suite. AE, V.

You can't find a more centrally located hotel in all Prague. Nestled in
a small backstreet, just east of Staroměstské náměstí, the three-story
Ungelt is a hidden gem, with the potential to be one of the most
attractive finds in Europe. The building itself oozes with old-world
charm, and contains 10 one- and two-bedroom suites, which can
sleep two and four persons, respectively. Unfortunately, the hotel

suffers from poor service and worse interior design. Each unit contains a living room, a full kitchen, and hand-held shower in the bath. Bedrooms, which are meagerly dressed with Communist-era beds and couches, are mercifully matched with antique dressers, Bohemian glass chandeliers, and other nice objects. Wall art is practically unknown. The Ungelt's three best rooms have magnificent, hand-painted wood ceilings. It's hard not to wish for the rest of the place to shape up, and honor the building's intrinsic beauty.

There's a bar with terrace seating in summer, and the hotel offers laundry and ironing services year-round.

2. NEAR NÁMĚSTÍ REPUBLIKY & FLORENC

EXPENSIVE

ATRIUM HOTEL, Pobřežní 1, Praha 8. Tel. 2/2484-1111.
Fax 2/232-3791. 788 rms. 20 suites. A/C TEL TV MINIBAR
Metro: Line B to Florenc.
$ Rates: 4,340 Kč ($144.65) single; 4,840–5,800 Kč ($161.35–$193.35) double; from 6,760 Kč ($225.35) suite. AE, CB, DISC, MC, V.

A classic example of modern functionalist architecture, the glass-and-steel cube-shaped Atrium is as imposing as it is huge. True to its name, the entire hotel is built around an enormous glass-topped atrium, dominated by glass elevators and an oversized steel chandelier. The hotel's atrium lobby, impressive even by U.S. standards, would be one of Prague's premier places to lounge if it weren't for a couple of disrupting factors. First, the hotel's location, just outside of center city, is not ideal. Guests must taxi, or take public transportation to reach Prague's main sights. Second, the atrium doesn't encourage relaxation. There is no piano bar or café, and it's hard to take comfort in the few fake leather sofas that are offered. Except for the sound of a hidden waterfall, nothing particularly pleasant reverberates off the hard, carpetless floors.

Guest rooms are quite a bit more intimate than common areas. Most are identical to one another, painted in muted earth tones, and outfitted with queen-size beds, a dressing table, two chairs, and a small TV. While rooms are not large and far from fancy, they are comfortable—good enough for U.S. President Bill Clinton, who stayed here in January 1994.

Dining/Entertainment: The lobby-level Atrium Restaurant, serving breakfast, lunch, and dinner, is the largest of the hotel's six

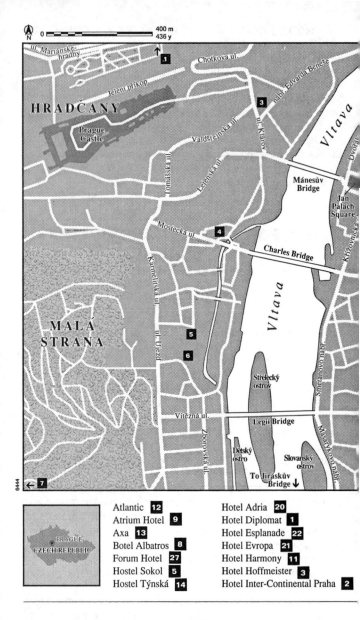

Atlantic **12**	Hotel Adria **20**
Atrium Hotel **9**	Hotel Diplomat **1**
Axa **13**	Hotel Esplanade **22**
Botel Albatros **8**	Hotel Evropa **21**
Forum Hotel **27**	Hotel Harmony **11**
Hostel Sokol **5**	Hotel Hoffmeister **3**
Hostel Týnská **14**	Hotel Inter-Continental Praha **2**

eateries. Chez Louis, on the second floor, serves French food in a relatively upscale dining room. It's open daily for lunch and dinner. Other on-site eateries include a Moravian-style tavern, a traditional Czech beer hall, a French-style café, and an English club room. There's also a lobby bar and a subterranean nightclub offering variety shows and musical entertainment.

Services: 24-hour room service, massage, laundry.

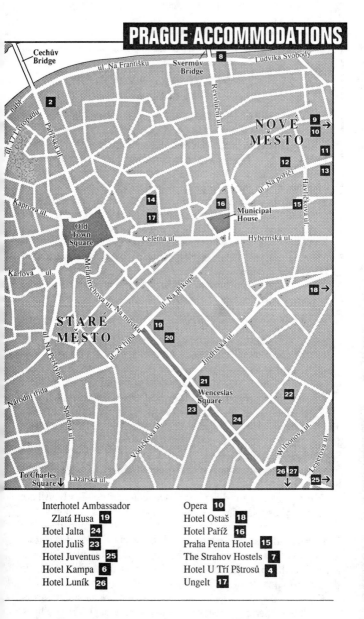

PRAGUE ACCOMMODATIONS

Cechův Bridge

ul. Na Františku

Svermův Bridge

Ludvíka Svobody

8

2

ul. Tři Zlatopadu

Pařížská ul.

Revoluční ul.

NOVÉ MĚSTO

9 →
10 →

11

12

ul. Na poříčí

13

Havlíčkova ul.

Kaprova ul.

14

17

16

Municipal House

15

Old Town Square

Celetná ul.

Hybernská ul.

Karlova ul.

Melantrichova ul. - Na můstku

ul. Na příkopě

18 →

STARÉ MĚSTO

Na Perštýně

ul. 28. října

19

20

Jindřišská ul.

Národní třída

21

Wenceslas Square

22

Spálená ul.

23

Vodičkova ul.

24

Wilsonova ul.

Legerova ul.

To Charles Square ↓

Lazárská ul.

26 27

↓

25 →

Interhotel Ambassador Zlatá Husa **19**
Hotel Jalta **24**
Hotel Juliš **23**
Hotel Juventus **25**
Hotel Kampa **6**
Hotel Luník **26**

Opera **10**
Hotel Ostaš **18**
Hotel Paříž **16**
Praha Penta Hotel **15**
The Strahov Hostels **7**
Hotel U Tří Pštrosů **4**
Ungelt **17**

Facilities: Indoor swimming pool, small gym, tennis courts, sauna, putting greens, beauty salon, gift shop, casino.

HOTEL PAŘÍŽ, U Obecního domu 1, Praha 1. Tel. 2/232-2051 or 236-0820. Fax 2/236-7448. 96 rms, 4 suites. TV TEL **Metro:** Line B to náměstí Republiky.
$ Rates (including breakfast): 4,800–6,600 Kč ($160–$220) sin-

---

🄵 FROMMER'S SMART TRAVELER: HOTELS

1. A hotel room is a perishable commodity; if it's not sold, the revenue is lost forever. Always ask if a hotel has a lower rate, and make it clear that you're shopping around.
2. For the best rates, seek out business-oriented hotels on weekends and in the summer and tourist-oriented apartments during the off-season.
3. Ask about summer discounts, corporate rates, and special packages. Most hotel reservations offices don't tell you about promotional rates unless you ask.
4. Always inquire about telephone charges before you dial. In Prague hotels, long-distance calls are often billed with a significant mark-up.
5. Rent a private apartment, rather than a hotel room. It's always both larger and cheaper.

---

gle; 5,400–7,500 Kč ($180–$250) double; from 10,200 Kč ($340) suite. AE, CB, DC, MC, V.

★ The Paříž is the best hotel in Prague. The building itself, located adjacent to the magnificent Municipal House (Obecní dům), is a neo-Gothic historical landmark, packed with eye-catching art nouveau elements. Acquired by the Brandejs family in 1923, the grand hotel operated as a deluxe property, until it was seized by the Communists in 1948. Returned to the family in September 1992, the Paříž underwent a $1.3 million renovation, and reopened to raves, though it still doesn't compare to grand-luxe hotels in other cities.

Every guest room is different, and amenities vary slightly. All are handsomely decorated, have tall ceilings, and are outfitted with contemporary mahogany furnishings, flowerprint wallpaper, firm beds, soft couches, and wood and brass fittings. Baths feature gooseneck sinks and hand-held showers. The higher-priced rooms, located on the top (fifth) floor, have minibars, safes, and hairdryers in the bathrooms.

Guests and gawkers will want to tour the hotel's public areas, which feature perfectly restored art nouveau wrought-iron railings, and unique deco lighting. *Note:* Be sure to request a room in the back, as front-facing accommodations face two loud and rowdy bars across the street.

Dining/Entertainment: The restaurant Sarah Bernhardt serves meals from 11:30am until midnight, and offers live piano music nightly from 6:30 until 10:30pm. Open longer hours is the Café de Paris, serving from 6:30am to 1am, with free concerts every Thursday beginning at 9pm. The lounge sells refreshments from 11am until 1am.

Services: 24-hour room service, concierge, laundry and dry cleaning, shoeshine, money exchange.

PRAHA PENTA HOTEL, V Celnici 7, Praha 1. Tel. 2/7481-0396 or 2481-0396. Fax 2/231-3133. 309 rms, 14 suites. A/C TEL TV MINIBAR **Metro:** Line B to náměstí Republiky.

$ Rates (including breakfast): 5,819–6,546 Kč ($193.95–$218.20) single; 6,546–7,272 Kč ($218.20–$242.40) double; from 12,730 Kč ($424.30) suite. Additional person 1,274 Kč ($42.45). Children under 16 stay free in parents' room. Weekend packages available. AE, CB, DC, MC, V.

The Praha Penta, a marble monolith completed in 1993, is a top European-style business hotel with well-designed standardized rooms and responsive German management. A conventioners' delight, the hotel's 300-plus guest rooms are almost all identically dressed, and feature good closets and lighting. The lower-priced "standard" rooms are a wee bit on the small side, but thoughtfully outfitted with blond-wood built-in desks and original prints. The higher-priced "king" rooms offer a bit more space for the same Austrian-made furnishings. Corner rooms (ending in numbers 18 and 19) are larger still, but don't offer the quiet of those in the rear. Rooms on the eighth and ninth floors have windows embedded in slanted ceilings, and for reasons of novelty are most recommendable. Suites on the top floor are exceptionally spacious, and have walk-in closets and sizable bathrooms. Baths in all rooms are equipped with hairdryers, telephones, and a small toiletry package. Specially designed wheelchair-accessible rooms are also available.

Dining/Entertainment: Breakfast and lunch are served in the Pavilion, a high-quality buffet-style eatery. The Gazebo, next door, is smaller and brighter, offering fish and meat main dishes ranging from 350 Kč to 450 Kč ($11.65 to $15). The bar is open until 2am.

Services: Room service, concierge, laundry, massage.

Facilities: Indoor swimming pool, fitness center, business center, gift shop.

Note: The Praha Penta, like other Pentas, was recently purchased by Ramada International. Its name might be changed.

MODERATE

ATLANTIC, Na poříčí 9, Praha 1. Tel. 2/2481-1084. Fax 2/2481-2378. 60 rms, 1 suite. TEL TV **Metro:** Line B to náměstí Republiky.

$ Rates: 2,180–2,420 Kč ($72.70–$80.70) single; 2,760 Kč ($92) double; 3,800 Kč ($126.70) suite. Additional person 680 Kč ($22.70). AE, MC, V.

Originally built in 1845, and named The English Court, the hotel catered to society's elite until it fell into disrepair around 1900. Rebuilt in 1935, the five-story Atlantic never reclaimed its past prestige. Instead, the hotel has become one of the best in its moderate class, notable for a fine location and ample-sized though simply furnished guest rooms. It would be a mistake to expect too much from this place, which completed its last makeover just months before the Communist regime fell in November 1989. But the functional rooms are well located, just minutes from náměstí Republiky. There is a pleasant wood-paneled restaurant and lounge, located just behind the lobby, and the hotel offers laundry, dry cleaning, theater booking, and other concierge services.

AXA, Na poříčí 40, Praha 1. Tel. 2/232-7234. Fax 2/232-2172. 127 rms (100 with bath), 5 suites. TEL **Metro:** Line B to náměstí Republiky or Florenc.

$ Rates (including continental breakfast): 1,500 Kč ($50) single with bath; 1,000 Kč ($33.35) double without bath, 2,500 Kč ($83.35) double with bath; 1,800 Kč ($60) triple without bath, 3,100 Kč ($103.35) triple with bath; from 2,000 Kč ($66.70) suite. Free for children under 6. MC, V.

Built in 1932, and completely overhauled in 1992, Axa has all the hallmarks of a typical Prague hotel. It is rather drab on the outside, and sterile within. The lobby and rooms are rather plain; white and functional, and almost devoid of decoration. The small front desk provides all the hotel's services, including check-in, concierge, money exchange, and even a newsstand. Guest rooms are similarly efficient. Frills are few, and so are towels. Beds are "Eastern European Specials"—thin mattresses on pullout-sofalike beds. In addition to a simple bathroom that lacks counter space for toiletries, most guest rooms contain a narrow closet, a table, two chairs, and TV. In most any other city, Axa would be overpriced. So why do I recommend this hotel and so many others like it? Because there's just no other choice.

On the positive side, Axa occupies a good location, close to náměstí Republiky; there's a six-lane indoor lap pool; and the rooms without private toilets are one of the best hotel deals in Prague.

HOTEL HARMONY, Na poříčí 31, Praha 1. Tel. 2/232-0016 or 232-0720. Fax 2/231-0009. 54 rms, 6 suites. TEL **Metro:** Line B to náměstí Republiky or Florenc.

$ Rates (including breakfast): 2,408 Kč ($80.25) single; 3,341 Kč ($111.35) double; from 3,809 Kč ($126.95) suite. There is a 12% discount for guests staying for more than one night. AE, MC, V.

Completely overhauled in 1992, the Harmony is easily the nicest hotel in its class. Contemporary design and brand-new furnishings translates into a sparkling white hotel, inside and out. Double rooms make up the bulk of the hotel's seven floors, each of which really contain two single beds that are pushed together as one. Standard-issue hotel furnishings mean a blond-wood desk and chair, a single small print on an oversized white wall, and miniature table lamps that look like toys. You probably wouldn't have chosen the Smurf-blue carpeting for your own home, and it doesn't look that great here either. Suites are substantially larger and a bit nicer. Many have huge windows, and all come with televisions, minibars, stand-alone closets, larger beds, and good-sized baths. Don't expect frilly bath accessories, however. You'll get enough towels to dry the two of you, and a small bar of soap.

There are two restaurants on the ground floor, and the reception desk becomes the concierge when you need concert tickets or tour reservations.

INEXPENSIVE

OPERA, Těšnov 13, Praha 1. Tel. 2/**231-5609** or 231-5735. Fax 2/231-1477. 58 rms (12 with bath). **Metro:** Line B to Florenc.

$ Rates (including breakfast): 1,050 Kč ($35) single without bath, 1,270 Kč ($42.35) single with bath; 1,360 Kč ($45.35) double without bath, 1,800 Kč ($60) double with bath; 1,690 Kč ($56.35) triple without bath, 2,140 Kč ($71.35) triple with bath. Prices decrease by 10% Oct–Apr. AE, MC, V.

Like so many hotels in Prague, one approaches the stately Opera with great hopes. And like so many hotels in Prague, one is disappointed to discover that the interior lacks even a shred of the facade's charm. Popular with German tour groups, the hotel provides the most basic accommodations and services. Budget-style pine furnishings are set off by grotesque orange curtains. Guest rooms without private baths are outfitted with sinks, and all rooms have small original etchings on the walls.

The Opera is recommendable for being inexpensive and relatively clean compared to others in the neighborhood. The hotel offers laundry and dry-cleaning service, and contains a restaurant and snack bar on the ground floor.

3. VÁCLAVSKÉ NÁMĚSTÍ (WENCESLAS SQUARE)

EXPENSIVE

HOTEL ADRIA, Václavské náměstí 26, Praha 1. Tel. 2/ **2421-1025.** Fax 2/22-13-97. 58 rms, 7 suites. TV TEL MINIBAR **Metro:** Line A or B to Můstek.

$ Rates (including breakfast): 3,030 Kč ($101) single; 3,740 Kč ($124.65) double; from 6,050 Kč ($201.65) suite. AE, DC, MC, V.

Many of Prague's newly privatized hotels have skimped on guest rooms, preferring to spend the bulk of their renovation money on lobbies and exteriors. Adria is no exception. The sliding glass front door on the hotel's 19th-century yellow-and-white storybook exterior opens into a thoroughly contemporary brass-and-glass lobby. Guests file past a stylish espresso bar to the reception desk, and reach their rooms by elevator.

Although this recommendable hotel could theoretically be located in any European capital, several particularly Czech idiosyncracies remind you of your locale. Wall art is scarce, there's always loud music playing in the lobby, service is a bit sluggish, and there are some comical design flaws—like exposed pipes beneath hung ceilings.

Guest rooms are small and modern and far from fancy. Twins contain two single-size beds in a particularly narrow room. Odd-numbered rooms—most of which are doubles—are the same price, but larger. Like other guest rooms, these are dressed with cheap Euro-style built-in furnishings. Bathrooms are clean and neat, and have wall-mounted hairdryers.

Dining/Entertainment: Breakfast is served in the contemporary Neptune Café. The Triton Club restaurant serves Bohemian meals in a unique quartz rock-encrusted cave.

Services: Room service, laundry.

Facilities: Hair salon, sauna, fitness center.

HOTEL JALTA, Václavské náměstí 45, Praha 1. Tel. 2/ 2422-9133. Fax 2/2421-3866. 87 rms, 10 suites. TEL TV MINIBAR **Metro:** Line A or B to Můstek.

$ Rates (including breakfast): 4,500–5,700 Kč ($150–$190) single; 5,400–6,600 Kč ($180–$220) double; from 8,400 Kč ($280) suite. AE, DC, MC, V.

A top-to-bottom gutting and rebuilding has transformed the ancient marble Jalta into a very comfortable, but characterless hotel. Co-owned by Czech and Japanese interests, Jalta has contemporary features like card-lock doors, taro bathrobes, in-room minibars, built-in hairdryers, large mirrors, and respectable furnishings that make this hotel one of the coziest places to stay on Václavské náměstí.

What the guest rooms lack in ornamentation they make up for with high ceilings and a Christmas-like red and green color scheme. Not all rooms in this seven-story hotel are created equal, however. Accommodations facing Václavské náměstí are brightest, and have small balconies overlooking the street. And although they usually don't volunteer this information, note that five of the hotel's double rooms are significantly larger than the others, but rent for the same price. Beware of single rooms, which are furnished with a single-size bed.

Dining/Entertainment: In addition to a ground-floor restaurant with excellent sidewalk seating, the hotel contains a casino, bar, and nightclub.

Services: Room service, laundry.

INTERHOTEL AMBASSADOR ZLATÁ HUSA, Václavské náměstí 5–7, Praha 1. **Tel. 2/2419-3121.** Fax 2/236-3172. 155 rms, 17 suites. TV TEL **Metro:** Line A or B to Můstek.

$ Rates (including breakfast): 3,870–5,400 Kč ($129–$180) single; 5,070–6,600 Kč ($169–$220) double; from 7,200 Kč ($240) suite. Children under 6 stay free in parents' room. AE, CB, DC, MC, V.

One of the grandes dames of Václavské náměstí, the art nouveau Ambassador was opened in 1900, when the square was the toast of the town. The square has tarnished a bit since its heyday; prostitutes and neon proliferate, but a Václavské náměstí address is still notable. The lobby, which seems too small and sedate for such an imposing hotel, welcomes guests with wood paneling, Oriental runners, and 1970s-style leatherette chairs. Above are six floors of medium-size rooms that, although recently renovated, really feel antique. Ceilings are high, and furnishings tend toward faux Louis XVI and marble-topped desks. The single-size beds that furnish most twins leave much to be desired. Bathrooms are marble and some have whirlpools, others just have a stand-up shower. It all sounds pretty nice, but it could be nicer if the building's extra-wide hallways were filled with art and flowers and antiques. Instead, most of the hotel contains cheap fixtures, and little else to entertain the eye.

Dining/Entertainment: Full of nooks and crannies, the sprawling hotel contains many hidden surprises, including a dozen restaurants and bars, a nightclub, and a casino. The Francouzská Restaurant, serving French cuisine, is one of Prague's most beautiful dining rooms. Surrounded by stained-glass windows, patrons eat from gold-embossed dishes and sit on velvet-covered chairs beneath exquisite ceramic ceilings. Staroprazska Rychta, the hotel's tribute to Prague beer halls, is located in the hotel's cellar. Follow the accordion music. Buffet breakfasts are served in Coffeehouse Pasaze, and lunches are available from a grill restaurant and a snack bar. Znojemská Vinárna, and the smaller Vinárna Kecskemet, are two wine bars that specialize in vintages from Moravia. In summer, the best place to sit is at the sidewalk café, which offers some of the best people-watching in the city.

Services: 24-hour room service, concierge, laundry service, currency exchange.

Facilities: Gift shop.

MODERATE

HOTEL EVROPA, Václavské náměstí 25, Praha 1. Tel. 2/2422-8117 or 2422-8118. Fax 2/2422-4544. 104 rms (50 with bath), 3 suites. **Metro:** Line A or B to Můstek.

$ Rates: 1,130 Kč ($37.70) single without bath, 1,780 Kč ($59.35) single with bath; 1,860 Kč ($62) double without bath, 2,360 Kč ($78.70) double with bath; 2,340 Kč ($78) triple without bath, 2,940 Kč ($98) triple with bath; 3,040 Kč ($101.35) quad without bath, 3,520 Kč ($117.35) quad with bath; from 3,260 Kč ($108.70) suite. AE, MC, V.

 Erected in 1889, and rebuilt in the art nouveau style during 1903–5, the Evropa remains one of the most magnificent turn-of-the-century structures in Prague. The fantastic, statue-topped facade is a festival for the eyes, wrapped with hand-sculpted wrought-iron railings, and fronted by a stylish row of cantilevered globe lamps. Seats on the outdoor terrace of the hotel's ground-floor café are some of the city's most coveted—for style and people-watching, not food or service.

The public areas on the hotel's first and second floors are equally impressive, painted yellow and gold, and furnished with busy Louis XVI items. Now the bad news: Rooms are adequate at best, and shabby at worst. There is a great variety of accommodations here. The best rooms are the front-facing doubles, a half-dozen of which have balconies overlooking Václavské náměstí. These are relatively large and have high ceilings. Furnishings are limited to the essentials, however; beds and a table, and belle art is practically unknown. Bathrooms are equally uninspired, have few towels, and contain hand-held showers and aging tubs. The worst rooms are windowless, bathless, charmless boxes tucked way in the back of the hotel.

There's no trick to getting a good room here; luck is the only mitigator. Reservations are accepted by fax. Even if you choose not to check-in here, the hotel is definitely worth checking out.

Dining/Entertainment: The hotel's Cafe Evropa is one of the prettiest in Prague. Food is minimal, and service is sluggish, but the café is a pleasant throwback to the turn of the century, and a pleasant place to while away a morning or afternoon. There's live piano music—and a 20 Kč (70¢) entrance fee—after 3pm. See Chapter 5, "Prague Dining."

The Evropa Restaurant, located at the very back of the hotel's ground floor, is an intimate, romantic room for lunch and dinner, served daily from 11am to 3pm and from 6 until 11:30pm, respectively.

HOTEL JULIŠ, Václavské náměstí 22, 11000 Praha 1. Tel. 2/2421-7092. Fax 2/2421-8545. 54 rms, 4 apartments. **Metro:** Line A or B to Můstek.

$ Rates (including breakfast): May–Sept, 2,290 Kč ($76.35) single; 2,990 Kč ($99.65) double; 3,800 Kč ($126.70) triple. Oct–Apr, 1,790 Kč ($59.65) single; 2,290 Kč ($76.35) double; 2,880 Kč ($96) triple. AE, MC, V.

Except as a reminder of the bad old days, Juliš has nothing exceptional to boast. Sandwiched between two shorter turn-of-the-century gems, the drab, neon-crested, concrete Juliš is one of Václavské náměstí's chief architectural offenders. Guests haul their own luggage up a flight of stairs to the hotel's gloomy lobby, which is staffed by a single employee. Rooms, accessible by elevator, are slightly more comforting, outfitted with the usual Communist-issue beds, tables, and chairs. Some have balconies overlooking Václavské náměstí. Although the hotel was privatized in 1992, it seems as though little has changed. Keep this place in mind if you just have to stay on Václavské náměstí, and can't find accommodations elsewhere.

4. NEAR THE MAIN TRAIN STATION

EXPENSIVE

HOTEL ESPLANADE, Washingtonova 19, Praha 1. Tel. 2/22-25-52 or 22-60-56. Fax 2/2422-9306. 58 rms, 6 suites. TV TEL **Metro:** Line C to Hlavni nádraží.

$ Rates: 5,000 Kč ($166.70) single; 6,500 Kč ($216.70) double; from 7,500 Kč ($250) suite. AE, MC, V.

Physically, the Esplanade has all the makings of a top luxury hotel. Palatial on the outside, and elegant within, the building is graced with a plethora of exquisite embellishments that include rich woods and Oriental rugs throughout. The mansion was constructed in 1927 for an Italian insurance company that maintained offices there. Two years later, the building and all its contents were purchased by hoteliers who preserved the unusual Italian decor. A Bacchus-inspired bas-relief over the hotel's front entrance is complemented by interior decorations that include Murano glass chandeliers and an abundance of quality art.

As with most older hotels, each guest room is different. Most are decorated in a tasteful Louis XVI style, and contain minibars, king-size beds, and large baths with amenities that include built-in hairdryers. Suite room 101 is particularly special; it's outrageously old world, with hand-carved tables and bed, museum-quality chairs, glass chandeliers, and busy wall coverings and carpeting that add to the authentic Laura Ashley–stlye clutter. Not all rooms and suites are as recommendable, however; in fact most are rather plain, with functional 1970s-style furniture. If you have the option, the best strategy for staying here is to wait until you can see your room before committing.

The hotel is located steps from the main railway station, and just a few blocks from Václavské náměstí.

Dining/Entertainment: The comfortable lobby-level café/lounge is decorated with castle-sized original oil paintings and marble floors. The adjacent Esplanade Restaurant serves a continental menu—with main dishes averaging 200 Kč ($6.70)—in a stunning dining room that seems as if it was built just for its spectacular multicolored glass chandelier.

Services: Room service from 6am to 4am, concierge, laundry.

5. NEAR NÁMĚSTÍ MÍRU

INEXPENSIVE

HOTEL JUVENTUS, Blanická 10, Praha 2. Tel. 2/25-51-51 or 25-51-52. 20 rms (none with bath). **Metro:** Line A to náměstí Míru.

$ Rates (including breakfast): 900 Kč ($30) single; 1,500 Kč ($50) double. No credit cards.

Just about as basic a place as you can find in central Prague, the Juventus is typical of hotels in the $50-a-day range (per double) in the

---

Ⓕ FROMMER'S COOL FOR KIDS: HOTELS

Hotel Inter-Continental Praha (see p. 59) With plenty of services and restaurants, and a close proximity to many of Prague's primary sights, the Inter-Continental makes it easier to travel with kids in tow.

Forum Hotel (see p. 75) The only Prague hotel with its own bowling alley, the comfortable Forum also gets high marks for its swimming pool, shops, and services.

Private Apartment (see p. 58) Your best bet may be to rent an apartment for your family. In addition to experiencing life like Praguers, you'll have access to a kitchen allowing you to prepare snacks and meals anytime for your children.

rest of Europe. Rooms are sparsely furnished—no telephones, TVs, or even clocks. A couple of small paintings on the walls constitute the decorations. No rooms have private baths, but all have sinks with cold and (sporadically) hot running water. There is a writing desk, and ceilings are high. At this writing, management is considering to add showers to all rooms, an improvement that would likely raise rates. I hope they also renovate the shabby lobby bar, in which patrons must strain to hear one another over the ever--trumpeting TV.

HOTEL LUNÍK, Londýnská 50, Praha 2. Tel. 2/25-27-01.
Fax 2/25-66-17. 35 rms (all with bath). **Metro:** Line A to náměstí Míru.
$ Rates: 1,900 Kč ($63.35) single; 2,200 Kč ($73.35) double. No credit cards.

Behind Luník's faux off-white stucco front, which brandishes beautiful wooden windows, is a hotel so modest you'd think you're in a hostel. A small elevator takes guests up to 31 identical twins, and four single rooms that have matching wooden beds and closets and that's all. No chairs, no desks, no lamps. Nothing. The only redeeming features of the hotel's complete gutting and rebuilding in 1992 are showers that are pleasantly tiled from floor to ceiling and full-length mirrors. Some rooms have telephones.

6. IN MALÁ STRANA

EXPENSIVE

HOTEL HOFFMEISTER, Pod Bruskou 9, (Malá Strana) Praha 1. Tel. 2/53-83-80, 53-79-14, or 561-8155. Fax 2/53-09-59. 42 rms, 4 suites. TEL TV **Metro:** Line A to Malostranská.
$ Rates (including breakfast): 5,289–6,150 Kč ($176.30–$205) single; 5,904–6,765 Kč ($196.80–$225.50) double; 7,995–12,300 Kč ($266.50–$410) suite. AE, MC, V.

May 1993 was probably the worst time to open a hotel in Prague. Visitor arrivals didn't reach expectations, and room rates were at an all-time high. A small, independently owned hostelry had few avenues of promotion, and before it had a chance to earn its reputation, the tourist season had ended. That's exactly what happened to the Hotel Hoffmeister, and tourists who didn't know about its existence were the biggest losers. The brand-spanking new Hoffmeister is one of the most welcome new arrivals in a city where $200 often buys little more than a thin bed in a nondescript room.

Owned by the son of Adolph Hoffmeister, one of the most famous modern Czech artists, the hotel is one of the few in Prague assembled with a knowledgeable and creative eye.

The hotel's pink exterior resembles a Bohemian alpine cottage, though a corner of the three-floor building's first story is cut away and replaced with a glass-brick wall and contemporary statue-cum-column. The interior is just as stylish, colorful, and artsy. Real Western-style beds are clothed with bright prints that actually match the rooms' other high-quality furnishings and window treatments. Details have not been overlooked. Entry is via card lock, there are good closets, well-placed wall sconces and lamp lighting, sparkling showers, hairdryers, and pants presses. Although there are no views, guests can swing open all the oversized windows.

The hotel's best rooms are only slightly more expensive than the basic ones, and are significantly larger. The bi-level Presidential Suite has a circular staircase connecting a bright office with a cozy bedroom. There's a fax machine, and a bathroom with double sinks and large Jacuzzi tub.

Paintings and prints by Hoffmeister the elder adorn most every wall in the hotel, though unfortunately none is original. To view the real thing, guests must visit the small lobby, where Hoffmeister's line drawings of friends like Salvador Dalí, George Bernard Shaw, and John Steinbeck are on display.

Dining/Entertainment: There's a pretty French restaurant and café with an exceptional 400 Kč ($13.35) fixed-price menu. A separate bar/wine cellar was in the planning stages at presstime.

Services: 24-hour room service, concierge, laundry.

HOTEL U TŘÍ PŠTROSŮ ("At the Three Ostriches"), Dražického náměstí 12, Praha 1. Tel. 2/2451-0779. Fax 2/2451-0783. 18 rms, 3 suites. TEL TV **Metro:** Line A to Malostranská.

$ Rates (including breakfast): 3,300 Kč ($110) single; 4,500–5,500 Kč ($150–$183.35) double; from 6,000 Kč ($200) suite. AE, MC, V.

If you believe a hotel's most important features to be central location and old-world charm, then you can stay nowhere but U tří pštrosů. Sitting at the Malá Strana–side foot of Charles Bridge, this squat, five-story gem is right in the heart of the hustle, with street musicians and sidewalk sellers so close you can almost reach out and touch them without getting out of bed. As for charm, the hotel traces its roots back hundreds of years, when it was owned by a supplier of ostrich feathers. Later the building became one of the first coffeehouses in Bohemia. Rebuilt and reconstructed several times over the centuries, the hotel reopened in 1992, having preserved its painted wooden Renaissance ceilings and smattering of antique furnishings. Double rooms are well sized, fitted with green carpets, decent closets, and rolltop writing desks with inlaid woods. Unfortunately, the same cannot be said for the hotel's single rooms, which are small indeed, and contain a single-size bed. Suites are the hotel's most spectacular accommodations. These corner accommodations offer views of Charles Bridge and Prague Castle, seen over the city's red rooftops.

The small inn is run more like a casual bed-and-breakfast than a professional hotel and some details, ranging from poor telephone placement to lack of services, have been overlooked. Still, if you don't mind the noise that being right in the heart of it all engenders, U tří pštrosů is one of my top hotel picks in Prague.

Dining/Entertainment: The hotel's ground-floor restaurant serves Bohemian specialties in sparkling new vaulted dining rooms that are supposed to look centuries old. It's open to the public daily for lunch from noon to 3pm and for dinner from 6 to 11pm.

MODERATE

HOTEL KAMPA, Všehrdova 16, (Malá Strana) Praha 1. Tel. 2/2451-0409. Fax 2/2451-0377. 85 rms (all with bath). TEL **Metro:** Line A to Malostranská.
$ Rates: 1,800 Kč ($60) single; 2,900 Kč ($96.65) double; 4,000 Kč ($133.35) triple. AE, MC, V.

Located on one of the cutest, quietest, and best-located streets in Prague, Hotel Kampa occupies what was once an armory, built at the beginning of the 17th century. Although renovated in 1992, the rehab was directed by a very modest decorator. Rooms are incredibly simple, and probably will not be acceptable to first-class travelers. Singles are furnished with just a single-size bed and a stand-alone wardrobe. There is no decoration on most walls, and bathrooms are compact. Doubles are larger and marginally nicer. Like singles, they are without TVs, but are outfitted with small clock radios. Try to reserve a double furnished with an extra bed, as these are the largest rooms. There is a restaurant on the premises serving lunch and dinner, but the smartest guests dine elsewhere.

7. HOTELS IN OTHER AREAS

EXPENSIVE

FORUM HOTEL, Kongresová 1, Praha 4. Tel. 2/419-0111. Fax 2/6121-1673. 560 rms, 10 suites. A/C TV TEL MINIBAR **Metro:** Line C to Vyšehrad.
$ Rates (including breakfast): 5,555 Kč ($185.20) single; 6,360 Kč

($212) double; from 10,000 Kč ($333.35) suite. Additional person 1,210 Kč ($40.35). AE, DC, MC, V.

The Forum is something of a Czech anomaly. Located in "Prague Manhattan," a recently sprouted cluster of buildings about seven miles from the center city, the 25-story hotel is a self-contained minicity, complete with restaurants, pubs, shops, a fitness center, and even a bowling alley. Both insulated and American, staying here is as close to staying home as you can get.

Completed in 1988, the hotel is one of the city's best managed, run by a division of the Inter-Continental Hotels Corporation. There are plenty of staffers, a dedicated concierge, and 24-hour room service. Rooms are not quite up to international standard, but they are luxurious for Prague, containing "real" Western-style beds, good lighting, and thoughtful decoration. All have satellite television and nice bathrooms with built-in hairdryers.

Although the city center is not walkable from the hotel, Vyšehrad metro station is just steps away.

Dining/Entertainment: Harmonie Restaurant, serving continental lunches and dinners daily, is the hotel's top eatery. The Czech Restaurant is open for all-day dining, and Café Praha serves pastry, ice cream, and gourmet coffee. There is a typical Czech beer pub, a large lobby bar, and a nightclub, where dance discs spin until about 1am.

Services: 24-hour room service, concierge, business center, laundry.

Facilities: Indoor swimming pool, fitness center, squash court, bowling alley, shops, beauty salon.

HOTEL DIPLOMAT, Evropská 15, Praha 6. Tel. 2/2439-4111. Fax 2/331-4114. 363 rms, 5 studios, 12 suites. A/C TEL TV MINIBAR **Metro:** Line A to Dejvická.

$ Rates (including breakfast): 2,600 Kč ($86.65) single; 2,970 Kč ($99) double; 4,050 Kč ($135) studio; from 4,400 Kč ($146.65) suite. Children under 6 stay free in parents' room. AE, CB, DC, MC, V.

S Hotel Diplomat is one of the most popular in Prague. Constructed in 1990 to an uninspired cubist design, the hotel was built with prefabricated guest rooms that were imported wholesale, making each almost identical to the next. Rooms are small. They have built-in beds and bureaus, alcoves instead of closets, and a shortage of towels that reflects poorly on their generosity of spirit. That said, at about $100 per night, including breakfast, the first-class Diplomat represents one of the best buys in Prague. Its location, just outside the city center, is not ideal, but a metro station just across the street makes getting around a breeze. Operated by an Austrian management team, the nine-story hotel gets praise for efficiency. There's a dedicated concierge, and a full-service business center. Studios are larger than standard rooms, but both earn marks for having clock radios and hairdryers. Suites come with pants presses, minibars, balconies, and larger baths outfitted with hairdryers and bidets.

Dining/Entertainment: Breakfasts are served in the hotel's Brasserie restaurant, which is also open for lunch. The CD-Club is a casual restaurant open for all-day dining. Loreta, the hotel's flagship eatery, serves continental dinners daily. The top-floor Skyline Bar offers live entertainment and dancing nightly.

Facilities: Sauna, whirlpool, exercise room, beauty salon, business center, gift shop, car rental.

Services: 24-hour room service, concierge, laundry and dry cleaning, massage.

MODERATE

BOTEL ALBATROS, nábřeží Ludvika Svobody, Praha 1. Tel. 2/2481-0541 or 231-3600. Fax 2/2481-1214. 80 rms, 4 suites. TEL **Tram:** Lines 5, 14, 26, or 53.

$ Rates: 2,019 Kč ($67.30) single; 2,546 Kč ($84.85) double; 4,037 Kč ($134.55) triple; from 4,509 Kč ($150.30) suite. AE, MC, V.

Located at the end of Revoluční on the River Vltava, the permanently moored blue-and-white Albatros is a converted hotel boat, or "botel." It's no *Queen Mary*. Rooms are predictably cramped; each is just large enough to accommodate two single beds and the tiny table that separates them. At the near end of the berth is a diminutive closet and a miniature bathroom, both entirely devoid of counter space. There is a radio in each room, but no TV. Suites, located toward the back of the boat, are bright exceptions to these otherwise restricted accommodations. Particularly bright, each enjoys wraparound windows and room enough to swing a cat. Although there is a small restaurant on the boat, guests will have more fun on the lively bar barge docked just behind the Albatros.

HOTEL OSTAŠ, Orebitská 8, Praha 3. Tel. 2/627-9386. Fax 2/627-9418. 30 rms, 2 suites. TEL **Tram:** Lines 133, 168, or 207.

$ Rates (including breakfast): 1,360 Kč ($45.35) single; 2,480 Kč ($82.65) double; 2,910 Kč ($97) triple; from 4,200 Kč ($140) suite. No credit cards.

Known primarily to German tour groups, the extremely basic Ostaš is nothing to write home about, and just barely good enough to find inclusion here. Rooms are ascetically styled, with little more than beds and bureaus. And although the hotel was completely remodeled in 1992, furnishings and lighting are strictly functional, only suites have televisions, and guests cannot obtain an outside line directly from their bedside phones. Rack rates here are stiff even by Prague standards. If you decide to stay here, hard bargaining is in order.

8. HOSTELS

There are several dormitory-style accommodations in Prague. Unfortunately, most are far from the center, necessitating both a metro and bus ride to reach them. Still, they're cheap, and you'll meet many other travelers.

HOSTEL SOKOL, Hellichova 1, Praha 1. Tel. 2/53-45-51, ext. 397. 100 beds. Open: June–Sept.
$ Rates: 190 Kč ($6.35) per person. No credit cards.

There's a lot lacking at this hostel; beds are packed 10 to 12 per room, they enforce a 12:30am curfew, and cleanliness is suspect. But Sokol earns mention here for its absolutely fantastic location, smack in the heart of Malá Strana, just a short walk from Charles Bridge. The hostel is closed daily from 10am to 3pm.

HOSTEL TÝNSKÁ, Týnská 17, Praha 1. Tel. 2/231-2509. 80 beds. Open: June–Sept.
$ Rates (including breakfast): 199 Kč ($6.65) per person. No credit cards.

There's not much to recommend about this hostel, except its superlative location, just 150 feet from Staroměstské náměstí.

About 40 bunk beds are crammed together in a single subterranean gymnasium, bisected by a long partition that separates men and women. Baths are far from spotless, but showers are hot, there is a currency exchange and a luggage-deposit box, and the hostel is open 24 hours.

THE STRAHOV HOSTELS, Spartakiádní, Praha 6. 1,500 beds. Open: June–Sept.
$ Rates: 220–270 Kč ($7.35–$9) per person. No credit cards.

Located directly across the street from giant Strahov Stadium, the Strahov Hostels were built to house athletes for Eastern European Olympic-style games that were held annually before the fall of Communism. Today, these dozen concrete high-rises are students' homes throughout the school year, and budget tourist hotels during summer. Most rooms are doubles, none have private baths, and all are open 24 hours.

At least three different companies have contracted with the city to operate these summer hostels. Accommodations in each are identical, but services and prices vary slightly. ESTEC Hostel (tel. 2/52-73-44) is the best known, probably because they run the buildings located closest to the road, and are the first ones tourists see. Petros (tel. 2/35-44-43) and Sakbuild (tel. 2/35-44-42 or 52-06-55) hostels are immediately adjacent to one another, and should be compared for price before committing.

To reach the Strahov Hostels from the city center, take metro line A to Dejvická, then bus 143, 149, or 217 to Strahov Stadium; a 20-minute trip in all.

PRAGUE DINING

It's said that conversations in western Europe always return to love; in Prague, however, they always revert to food. Foreigners swap restaurant tips like trading cards—"My favorite Chinese place for your best local pub"—and when it comes to cuisine, no expatriate is opinionless. News about restaurant openings travels fast, and menu and chef changes are familiar topics of conversation. Seldom will any single eatery gain high marks for an entire menu. "Choose carefully" is tacked on to every restaurant recommendation, along with an implied disclaimer that it was good last time, but next time, who knows? I've been to an untold number of restaurants where the preparations were excellent, but the ingredients were—to western European standards—substandard: meals made with fruit that should have been juiced, and chicken that should have been ground into fast-food "nuggets." It's hard not to pity the proud chefs, who time and again, have to do the best they can with low-quality ingredients. Prague's chefs do their best with game. When available, order goose, duck, or venison, and you'll rarely be disappointed.

If you're willing to part with the equivalent of $100 or more for a meal for two, disregard all of the above. A few of the city's top kitchens are as good as those with similar prices in New York or London. But, even at Prague's smartest eateries (some of which are listed below), service is sorely lacking. Poorly trained waitstaffs, having yet to master the art of intrusiveless service, are almost universal. Waiters are either interfering at inappropriate moments or (more commonly) are as absent as a cop when you need one.

See also "Food and Drink" in Chapter 1 for information on Prague dining.

TAX & TIPPING The Czech government instituted a 23% value-added tax (VAT) on restaurant meals in 1993. At most restaurants, menu prices include VAT. When they don't, it must say so on the menu. In addition to tax, it's common for some restaurants to levy a small cover charge, usually about 10 Kč (35¢).

RESERVATIONS Just a couple of years ago, a table at any number of popular restaurants could only be had with bookings made at least a week in advance. The restaurant boom of 1993 has eased competition among diners, now making it possible for tourists to find a good meal almost on a moment's notice. Still, reservations are mandatory for top eateries, and should be made as far in advance as possible. Lunchtime tables are easier to come by, so if you're only in town for a couple of days, and just have to eat at The Blue Duck, an afternoon meal might be your best bet. *Note:* Telephone numbers in Prague have anywhere from four to eight digits; cellular lines have more. To reach any of the restaurants below from within the city, dial all the numbers provided with a particular listing. Some restaurants with no telephone at presstime may have a phone by the time you visit Prague.

DINING HOURS & PRICES Most Prague restaurants are open daily for lunch from noon to 3pm, and again for dinner from 6 to 11pm. Of course, hours vary, and some restaurants stay open all day. Hours can change, too, as can prices.

WARNINGS It's bad for the travel industry, bad for business, and a shame for the entire country, but tourists in Prague have to be on their guard when dining at Czech restaurants. Although they are not nearly as dishonest as taxi drivers, many restaurateurs (and waiters) make a habit of cheating their patrons. Appetizers and other unordered foods are often offered to trusting diners who only later discover that the small deviled egg or bowl of nuts cost as much as an entire meal. Sometimes when you order a main dish and ask to substitute boiled potatoes for french fries, the menu price inexplicably doubles. Here is the single rule you must **always** follow to avoid being ripped off: Know the price of everything before putting it in your mouth.

Credit cards are new to Czechs, and unscrupulous restaurateurs can easily add an extra zero or change a "1" to a "2." Avoid being ripped off by writing out in letters—anywhere on the charge slip—the total amount of your bill.

1. NEAR VÁCLAVSKÉ NÁMĚSTÍ (WENCESLAS SQUARE)

MODERATE

GANY'S, Národní třída 20, Praha 1. Tel. 29-76-65.
Cuisine: CZECH/INTERNATIONAL. **Reservations:** Not necessary. **Metro:** Line A or B to Můstek.

$ Prices: Appetizers 30–90 Kč ($1–$3); main courses 70–150 Kč ($2.35–$5). AE, DC, MC, V.
Open: Daily 8am–11pm.

You will almost certainly walk past Gany's on your wanderings around Prague; it's situated on a major thoroughfare, equidistant from Václavské náměstí and the National Theater. But, unless you're looking for it, you could easily pass by this gem without knowing it. Don't be discouraged by the disheveled entrance that leads up two flights of dingy stairs to the restaurant. Persevere past the seedy-looking Riviera Disco, to a bona fide institution that is, both literally and figuratively, one of Prague's brightest restaurants. Grand, gracious Gany's is a successful amalgam of new and old. Its fabulous, understated, art nouveau interior, complete with original globe chandeliers, has been perfectly restored, and enlivened with trendy, period-style oil paintings. Gany's is both a restaurant and a café, two distinct and distinctive rooms separated by a contemporary, fountained foyer. The café side, which faces Národní, is bigger and sunnier, and popular with an artistic crowd. What the smaller dining room lacks in views, it makes up for in food, which is good, inexpensive, and plentiful. The restaurant's curious combination of cuisines means a choice of starters that includes smoked salmon, battered and fried asparagus, and ham au gratin with vegetables, and main dishes that encompass everything from trout with horseradish to beans with garlic sauce. In between is an arm's length list of chicken, beef, veal, and pork dishes, each drowned in a complementary, if not extraordinary, sauce. The hen with orange is a visually unusual, but flavorful poultry stir-fry, and one of my top recommendations.

RESTAURANT ADRIA, Národní třída 40, Praha 1. Tel. 2522-8065.
Cuisine: INTERNATIONAL. **Reservations:** Not necessary.
Metro: Line A or B to Můstek.
$ Prices: Appetizers 35–165 Kč ($1.20–$5.50); main courses 55–180 Kč ($1.85–$6); fixed-price menu 90 Kč ($3). AE, MC, V.
Open: Daily 11:30am–11:30pm.

From the street, Restaurant Adria looks awesome. Its grand second-floor terrace, dominated by a colossal statue of wrestling titans, and buzzing with diners, commands attention as it dominates Národní. Unfortunately, the views from the terrace itself are not as magnificent; the buildings across the street are not the prettiest backdrops. Still, in summer, there is hardly a better place in the city to lounge. The food and service at Adria are good, but not exceptional. The same can be said for the bright interior dining room, which features wraparound windows, an open kitchen, and an exposed full bar.

The restaurant's considerable menu is a veritable tour of Czech and eastern European cookery. Many foods, both hot and cold, can be chosen by sight from a glass case in the dining room. Tried and true appetizers include chilled smoked trout filets and surprisingly greaseless fried mushrooms. The plethora of pasta, topped with a variety of seafood, meat, and cheese sauces will win no awards in Italy, but are respectable by Prague standards. The restaurant does its best work with fish, which is grilled and sold by weight, and traditional Czech dishes, including roast pork with dumplings and cabbage. If you're in the mood for the limited offerings of the fixed-price menu, it represents a very good value. Set meals include soup of the day, a choice of goulash with dumplings, roasted pork with cabbage, venison, or deep-fried chicken breast, and dessert.

INEXPENSIVE

COUNTRY LIFE, Jungmannova 1, Praha 1.
Cuisine: VEGETARIAN. **Reservations:** Not accepted. **Metro:** Line B to Národní třída.

$ Prices: Appetizers 10–20 Kč (35¢–70¢); main courses 20–50 Kč (70¢–$1.70). No credit cards.

Open: Mon–Thurs 9am–6:30pm, Fri 9am–3pm.

Among dried beans, fresh breads, and shelves of Bible books, this Seventh-Day Adventist–run health food store-cum-restaurant offers a strictly meatless menu served cafeteria style in pleasant, woody surroundings.

Appetizers like bread with tofu spread, tomato, cucumber, and shredded cabbage are followed by main courses that include spicy goulash, vegetable salads, a zesty wheat bread pizza topped with red pepper, garlic, and onions, and vegetable burgers served on a multigrain buns with garlic-yogurt dressing. Everything is available to go. After procuring your food from the counter, carry your plate to the small upstairs dining loft.

A second Country Life, offering a similar menu with only

🅕 FROMMER'S SMART TRAVELER: RESTAURANTS

1. Avoid imported foods. They are always much more expensive and less fresh than locally produced items.
2. Drinks can add greatly to the cost of any meal.
3. Look for fixed price menus, two-for-one specials, and coupons in the local English-language newspapers.
4. Don't eat anything without first determining the price. Some restaurants gouge customers by charging exorbitant amounts for nuts or other seemingly free premeal snacks.

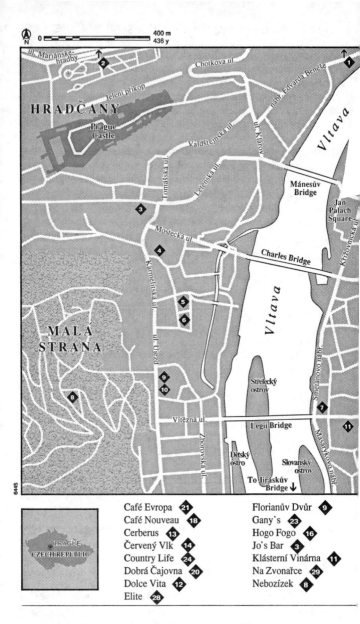

Café Evropa	**21**	Florianův Dvůr	**9**
Café Nouveau	**18**	Gany's	**23**
Cerberus	**13**	Hogo Fogo	**16**
Červený Vlk	**14**	Jo's Bar	**3**
Country Life	**24**	Klásterní Vinárna	**11**
Dobrá Čajovna	**20**	Na Zvonařce	**29**
Dolce Vita	**12**	Nebozízek	**8**
Elite	**28**		

stand-up dining, is located on Melantrichova 15, Praha 1 (no phone). It's open Monday to Thursday from 8:30am to 7pm, Friday from 8:30am to 2:30pm, and Sunday from noon to 6pm.

OBCHOD ČERSTVÝCH UZENIN, Václavské náměstí 36.

Cuisine: CZECH DELICATESSEN. **Reservations:** Not accepted. **Metro:** Line A or B to Můstek.

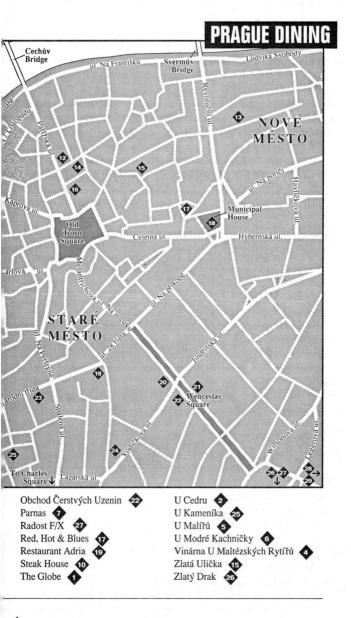

Obchod Čerstvých Uzenin **22**	U Cedru **2**
Parnas **7**	U Kameníka **25**
Radost F/X **27**	U Malířů **5**
Red, Hot & Blues **17**	U Modré Kachničky **6**
Restaurant Adria **19**	Vinárna U Maltézských Rytířů **4**
Steak House **10**	Zlatá Ulička **15**
The Globe **1**	Zlatý Drak **26**

$ Prices: Meats, 25–50 Kč (85¢–$1.70). No credit cards.
    Open: Mon–Fri 7:30am–7pm, Sat 8am–6pm, Sun 10am–4:30pm.

Located on the ground floor of the Melantrich Building, from which Václav Havel addressed the throngs below during the 1989 revolution, this delicatessen is not to be missed. Vegetarians hurry past the meaty aromas that waft over the short line of patrons that often forms out the door. The front of the shop is a takeout deli, offering dozens of kinds of cooked and smoked meats, sausages, and salamis. In back is a small restaurant where cooked meats and beer are served without side dishes or airs, just a dollop of mustard and a slice of dense bread. You have to eat standing up, but the selection is extensive, you can't get it any fresher, and prices are pure Czech. There are almost no tourists here.

2. NEAR NÁMĚSTÍ REPUBLIKY

MODERATE

CAFÉ NOUVEAU, in the Municipal House (Obecní dům), náměstí Republiky 5, Praha 1. Tel. 231-8084.
Cuisine: CONTINENTAL. **Reservations:** Not necessary.
Metro: Line B to náměstí Republiky.
$ Prices: Appetizers 40–60 Kč ($1.35–$2); main courses 140–160 Kč ($4.70–$5.35). AE, MC, V.
Open: Daily noon–midnight (food served only after 5pm).

 No one should miss dining in Prague's flamboyantly styled Obecní dům (Municipal House), the building in which Czechoslovakia was signed into independence in 1918. A long restoration, completed in mid-1993, unveiled Prague's most dazzling art nouveau facade. Lushly encrusted inside and out with ornaments symbolizing the bourgeois values of turn-of-the-century Prague, the building now holds several capitalist-inspired businesses, including this restaurant, owned by a pair of young American entrepreneurs. The ambience of the elegant, grand dining room is very relaxed, but the noise level can be positively deafening—especially when a jazz band is playing, which happens most every night.

Café Nouveau's food is decent, but far from spectacular. Pasta and chicken dishes are the highlights of a rather short menu that's both well priced and adeptly served. Their large selection of salads is a particularly pleasant surprise in this meat and potatoes country. Choose from a Greek salad with cucumbers, tomatoes, black olives, and feta cheese; a salad of marinated vegetables; Caesar salad; or chicken with fresh vegetables and ginger dressing. Soups, sandwiches, and meat- and vegetable-stuffed croissants are also available, but like other foods, are only served after the chefs arrive at 5pm. Until that time only drinks and pastries are served.

CERBERUS, Soukenická 19, Praha 1. Tel. 231-0985.
Cuisine: CZECH/CONTINENTAL. **Reservations:** Not necessary. **Metro:** Line B to náměstí Republiky.
$ Prices: Appetizers 70–150 Kč ($2.35–$5); main courses 90–340 Kč ($3–$11.35). AE, MC, V.

Open: Daily noon–midnight.

It's hard to imagine exactly what the interior designer had in mind when he put together this restaurant's hodgepodge of styles. A long and narrow booth-lined dining room spotlessly sparkles with crimson and cardinal colors like an upscale International House of Pancakes. More tables and chairs are located at the end of the dining hall, in a bright, leafy, gastrodome that's topped by a glass skylight. And although the restaurant is named for the three-headed dog of Greek mythology, Cerberus is devoid of Athenian accents in either the dining rooms or the kitchen.

The menu, which is printed on a faux-medieval paper scroll, is just as eclectic as the decor. In quality, however, the Cerberus's food far surpasses the ambience. Both appetizers and main courses include a liberal variety of meat, fish, pasta. Recommendable starters include rosemary-marinated chicken breasts served with a peppery tomato sauce, and chilled shrimp—sweet small ones from the North Sea—served traditionally, with lemon, on a bed of iceberg lettuce. Pasta, one of the restaurant's best values, is all homemade, and tossed with bacon and mushrooms, basil-tomato sauce, or garlic, green peas, and butter. Main dishes are all à la carte, and run the gamut from poached salmon to stewed rabbit to duck with tomatoes, thyme, and cognac. Several excellent vegetarian meals are also served, including cauliflower soufflé, and potato/vegetable au gratin.

RED, HOT & BLUES, Jakubská 12, Praha 1. Tel. 231-4639.

Cuisine: AMERICAN/CREOLE/CAJUN. **Reservations:** Not necessary. **Metro:** Line B to náměstí Republiky.

$ Prices: Appetizers 55–200 Kč ($1.85–$6.70); main courses 65–200 Kč ($2.20–$6.70). AE, MC, V.

Open: Mon–Sat 11am–11pm, Sun 9am–9:30pm.

There are just two rooms in this trendy American-owned eatery: a small front bar, and a slightly larger back dining room where live jazz is played nightly. During warmer months, a ceilingless atrium opens for eating and drinking, and the musician sometimes move outside, too.

Popular with American twentysomethings, who seem happy to be eating something other than roasted meat, the restaurant attracts few connoisseurs with its food. It's the Créole/Cajun thing that gets them into trouble, along with inedible Czech ketchup, and an inexperienced waitstaff. On the bright side, I can recommend the restaurant's (avocadoless) nachos, and the toasted vegetable and chicken sandwiches; served on French bread, both are excellent. Red, Hot, & Blues shines brightest on Sundays, when they serve the only good à la carte brunch in town, and on special chef nights, when some of the city's most gifted cooks perform. Call ahead to find out who's cooking.

ZLATÁ ULIČKA ["Golden Lane"], Masná 9, Praha 1. Tel. 232-0884.

Cuisine: CZECH/SERBIAN. **Reservations:** Not accepted. **Metro:** Line B to náměstí Republiky.

$ Prices: Appetizers 35–70 Kč ($1.20–$2.35); main courses 70–140 Kč ($2.35–$4.70). No credit cards.

Open: Daily 10am–midnight.

Hidden in the backstreets of Staré Město near Kastel sv. Jakuba (St. James' Church), and named after the Hradčany street of colorful 16th-century cottages (see "Walking Tour 2: Prague Castle," in Chapter 7), pint-sized Zlatá Ulička is one of central Prague's most unique finds. Designed by an architect from Sarajevo, the restaurant's interior has been transformed into a surreal Renaissance-era court-yard, surrounded by faux yellow and blue cottage facades complete with shingle roofs. Stereo speakers sing from birdcages, a ladder climbs to nowhere, and several gold plaques, inscribed with wistful Serbian-language poems are embedded in the restaurant's floor. One translates in part ". . . maybe tomorrow the ships will come."

On the menu, many dishes served here seem similar to those available at any number of Czech restaurants around town. On the plate, however, diners discover the food's Serbian qualities—savory spices that are almost completely absent in Bohemia. Whole trout is pan-fried in olive oil with garlic and parsley. Giant homemade hamburgers are enlivened with a medley of piquant spices, while the very traditional Serbian shish kabob alternates marinated veal and vegetables. Other items worth mentioning include the grilled mush-rooms appetizer and pan-fried squid.

3. NEAR STAROMĚSTSKÉ NÁMĚSTÍ [OLD TOWN SQUARE]

MODERATE

ČERVENÝ VLK ["Red Wolf"], Dušní 10, Praha 1. Tel. 232-9437 or 232-4756.

Cuisine: CZECH. **Reservations:** Not necessary. **Metro:** Line A to Staroměstská.

$ Prices: Appetizers 15–25 Kč (50¢–85¢); main courses 85–100 Kč ($2.85–$3.35). AE, MC, V.

Open: Daily noon–midnight.

On a hidden corner, two blocks down Široká, just east of Pařížská, Červený Vlk serves tasty, well-priced Czech special-ties in an area of Prague where it's sometimes difficult to find either. Avoid the pricey basement club and head straight for the bright, high-ceilinged dining room, which is tastefully furnished with minimalist art.

The lone English-speaking waitress is tiring of translating the entire menu for each American patron, but if you don't read Czech, she will be required to do so. Several sittings have proved the cheese-topped roasted pork to be best on the menu. Other main dishes include grilled beef, Bohemian goulash, and chicken with mushrooms. Portions are filling, even without potato croquets, but you shouldn't miss these savory sides.

One warning: Although it only opened in 1993, Červený Vlk is one of those old-style Czech restaurants that attempt to cheat customers by offering high-priced appetizers that seem innocent enough when they are delivered to your table unexpectedly. Don't eat anything here without knowing the price first.

INEXPENSIVE

HOGO FOGO, Salvátorská 4, Praha 1. Tel. 231-7023.
   Cuisine: CZECH. **Reservations:** Not accepted. **Metro:** Line A to Staroměstská.
   $ Prices: Appetizers 25–35 Kč (85¢–$1.20); main courses 30–65 Kč ($1–$2.15). AE, MC, V.
   Open: Mon–Fri noon–midnight, Sat–Sun noon–2am.
It's hard to determine exactly what attracts Hogo Fogo's loyal following of young Americans and Czechs. The bare basement dining room is unremarkable, service is sluggish, and most of the food is just tolerable. There are some menu standouts, however, such as lentil soup and fried cheese. The rock music is good, and everything is incredibly cheap, especially for a restaurant just two blocks from Staroměstské náměstí. Half liters of beer are just 25 Kč (85¢), and diners are encouraged to sit all day if they wish.

4. NEAR THE NATIONAL THEATER

EXPENSIVE

PARNAS, Smetanovo nábřeží 2, Praha 1. Tel. 2422-7614
   or 2422-9248.
   Cuisine: INTERNATIONAL. **Reservations:** Recommended.
   Metro: Line B to Národní třída.
   $ Prices: Appetizers 95–195 Kč ($3.20–$6.50); main courses 295–495 Kč ($9.85–$16.50); fixed-price menu 775–875 Kč ($25.85–$29.20). AE, DC, MC, V.

Open: Lunch daily noon–3pm; dinner daily 6–11pm.

⭐ One of the few Czech restaurants that would still be considered superior outside eastern Europe, Parnas can always be counted on for excellent and creative dishes served with flair. Located on the embankment facing the Vltava, the restaurant occupies a historical building adjacent to the National Theater, where the composer Smetana once lived. The elegance of Parnas's green-marble pillars and inlaid wood paneling is augmented by a piano-based trio that's almost always entertaining. And although they need to ignore the ceaseless automobile traffic outside, the luckiest diners have window seats, with great views of distant Prague Castle.

Little on the menu is either traditional or plain. Appetizers include cold North Sea shrimp with fresh kiwi, venison pâté with blue cheese, and a piping hot onion, leek, and mushroom tart. Spinach tagliatelle—a house specialty—is tossed with salmon and cream, garlic and herbs, or tomato and olives. Because they ship well, salmon with dill (poached to order and served either hot or cold) and prawns in a hot garlic sauce are the best of almost a dozen seafood main dishes. Even Bohemian standards are accorded special treatment here. Roast duck is stuffed with untraditionally fresh vegetables, and braised rabbit is marinated in a sauce few babushka's know. The chef only slacks when it comes to meatless main courses; the vegetables au gratin and cottage cheese dishes seem like they're from a different restaurant entirely.

Hearty eaters should choose the fixed-price menu, which includes any appetizer, main course, dessert, and coffee or tea.

MODERATE

KLÁSTERNÍ VINÁRNA, Národní třída 8, Praha 1. Tel. 29-05-96.

Cuisine: CZECH. **Reservations:** Not necessary. **Metro:** Line B to Národní třída.

$ Prices: Appetizers 60–100 Kč ($2–$3.35); main courses 50–200 Kč ($1.65–$6.70). AE, MC.

Open: Lunch daily 11:30am–3:30pm; dinner daily 5:30–11pm.

The perfect pre- or posttheater restaurant, Klásterní Vinárna is located in a former 17th-century Ursuline convent, just steps from the National Theater. The main dining room is both large and romantic, an effect achieved by wooden partitions, antique wall coverings, well-spaced tables, and an attentive yet unobtrusive waitstaff. A second dining area, in a smaller anteroom containing a short wooden bar, is more crowded and less desirable.

A traditional Czech kitchen prepares all the standards admirably, including appetizers like Prague ham (served with the traditional horseradish) and caviar (served with butter and toast). Main dishes, like baked chicken breast with peaches, roast pork with ham and melted cheese, and large beefsteaks are equally as genuine and consistent. Even trout and salmon are smothered Bohemian style, with butter sauce or another caloric but savory gravy. The restaurant's mixed vegetables swimming in curry gravy is an excellent, but misguided, attempt at meatlessness.

U KAMENÍKA, V Jirchářích 2, Praha 1. Tel. 29-46-74.
   Cuisine: CZECH. **Reservations:** Recommended. **Metro:** Line B to Národní třída.
$ Prices: Appetizers 50–250 Kč ($1.70–$8.35); main courses 150–500 Kč ($5–$16.70). AE, MC, V.
   Open: Daily 11:30am–11pm.

Family-run, U Kameníka serves patrons the same good-quality food that the family enjoys at home. Little fuss is made over the decor either. Small prints are the only adornments, and red-clothed rectangular tables, each with six chairs, line either side of the dining room. Somehow, it's a lot nicer than it sounds.

Don't expect many fish or vegetarian selections from the meaty menu; they're not the chef's specialties. Roast duck, pork, and beef are trademark dishes here, and most are served with cabbage or boiled vegetables. Recommendable starters include a thick Bohemian-style onion soup and a half-dozen less tempting hot and cold ham rolls made with vegetables and butter. U Kameníka is truly authentic, and an excellent restaurant choice for those unlucky enough not to be invited to dine in a Czech home.

---

5. IN MALÁ STRANA

EXPENSIVE

FLORIANŮV DVŮR ["Florian's Court"], Újezd 16 (Malá Strana), Praha 1. Tel. 53-05-02.
   Cuisine: CONTINENTAL. **Reservations:** Not necessary.
   Metro: Line A to Malostranská, then tram 12 or 22 to Újezd.
$ Prices: 175–695 Kč ($5.85–$23.20); main courses 255–715 Kč ($8.50–$23.85). AE, MC, V.
   Open: Lunch daily 11am–3pm; dinner daily 6pm–midnight.

Almost everything about Florianův Dvůr seems Western—the food, the decor, even the prices. Highlighted by a carved alabaster fireplace and liberal use of backlit stained glass, the restaurant's upscale dining room is as equally suited to business lunches as it is to romantic dinners.

The restaurant's menu changes four times a year—according to seasons in western Europe. In summer, cold appetizers might include stuffed pastries filled with sole and salmon. Fall might mean goose-liver pâté, and winters are warmed with pesto-coated cheese ravioli or garlicky grilled mushrooms. Snail consommé and saffron chowder are typical of the restaurant's creative soups that are always on offer. Fish is the main fare here anytime of year. Good selections of trout, salmon, shrimp, and other fresh and frozen seafoods are always on hand. Duck breast drizzled with a tangy sauce of red pepper and cassis, and lamb cutlets with garlic and rosemary are typical of the imaginative turf offerings. The kitchen is equally competent preparing desserts like chocolate mousse with orange cream and Grand Marnier parfait with pears that are often as complicated as they are creative.

U MALÍŘŮ, Maltézské náměstí 11. Tel. 2451-0269.

Cuisine: FRENCH. **Reservations:** Recommended. **Metro:** Line A to Malostranská.

$ Prices: Appetizers 900–1,100 Kč ($30–$36.70); main courses 1,000–1,200 Kč ($33.35–$40); fixed-price menu 2,600 Kč ($86.70). AE, DC, MC, V.

Open: Lunch daily 11:30am–2:30pm; dinner daily 6–11pm.

The most expensive restaurant in Prague serves quality food at western-European prices. The fixed-price dinner includes eight sample dishes that are representative of the entire menu. After a starter like herb-marinated salmon, the palate is cleansed with green-apple sherbet. Main dishes include braised sole filets with mushrooms and filet of beef rolled in bacon with truffle sauce. An assortment of French cheese is available, along with a tempting selection of desserts prepared by dedicated pastry chefs.

The restaurant itself is intimate and beautiful, consisting of three small, elegant dining rooms plastered with frescoes.

MODERATE

STEAK HOUSE, Újezd 16, Praha 1. Tel. 53-05-02.

Cuisine: AMERICAN. **Reservations:** Not necessary. **Metro:** Line A to Malostranská, then tram 12 or 22 to Újezd.

$ Prices: Appetizers 50–90 Kč ($1.70–$3); main courses 160–190 Kč ($5.35–$6.35). No credit cards.

Open: Daily 11am–11pm.

It almost seems redundant to open a steak house in Prague. But Steak House rises to the occasion, offering some of the best tenderloin, porterhouse, and rib-eye in town.

The entire cloth-tabled restaurant is hardly more than two intimate, wood-paneled dining rooms, each sitting only 16 guests. A diminutive barroom, with honky-tonk piano, rounds out the restaurant, which features tasteful "wild west" oils on most of the walls.

Appetizers include beef soup, asparagus and cheese ham rolls, and a light meal-sized pork steak sandwich smothered in tangy Brazilian sauce. Main courses include Hawaiian chicken (with sweet-and-sour sauce); tenderloin tips with green pepper, onion, and apple; pork ribs; and a good variety of relatively gristleless steaks. There's a small self-service salad bar, and all main dishes come with cottage fries with bacon and onion, or rice and beans.

U MODRÉ KACHNIČKY ["The Blue Duck"], Nebovidská 6, Praha 1. Tel. 0601/20-38-22 (cellular).
  Cuisine: CZECH. **Reservations:** Recommended. **Metro:** Line A to Malostranská.
$ Prices: Appetizers 45–120 Kč ($1.50–$4); main courses 65–210 Kč ($2.20–$7). AE, MC, V.
  Open: Daily noon–4:30pm, and 6:30–11:30pm.

I hesitate to write about my favorite restaurant in Prague because it's not very large, and getting a table here is already difficult enough. It's hard to complain about a restaurant that has everything: charm, intimacy, style, good service, and fine food. Each of the three small dining rooms has vaulted ceilings covered with contemporary frescoes, antique furnishings, Oriental carpets, and a profusion of upholstery patterns and colors compete for the attentions of diners.

From pheasant soup to stag sausage, wild game is the house specialty; if it's hunted, it's probably on the menu. Cold starters include Russian malossol caviar, smoked salmon, goose liver with apples and red wine, and asparagus baked with ham and cheese. They are all excellent. Boar goulash is an interesting twist on the original, duck is smoked before it's served with the traditional cabbage, and rabbit is cooked with cream sauce and cranberries. Deer, beef, pork, and chicken are also available, as is the "hunter's needle," a skewered medley of the kitchen's most interesting meats. Carp, a popular Czech fish, is baked with anchovies, and the single vegetarian main dish, risotto, is made to order with mushrooms and cheese. Last, but not least, several Czech dining companions swore that the traditional Czech crêpes (filled with fruit, nuts, and chocolate) were top of the line.

VINÁRNA U MALTÉZSKÝCH RYTÍŘŮ ["Wine Tavern of the Knights of Malta"], Prokopská 10, Praha 1. Tel. 53-63-57.
  Cuisine: CZECH. **Reservations:** Recommended. **Metro:** Line A to Malostranská.
$ Prices: Appetizers 50–65 Kč ($1.70–$2.20); main courses 105–310 Kč ($3.50–$10.35). AE, MC.
  Open: Daily 11am–11pm.

For price, service, and a big, warm welcome, Nada and Vitězslav Černík's little restaurant is one of the best in Malá Strana. It's not fancy, and there are just four tables in the dignified ground-floor dining room and another 10 or so in the cavernlike cellar below.

A short menu usually indicates intelligent preparations and fresh food, and the somewhat meager list here is no exception. Chateaubriand, filet mignon, pork filet, and a shish kabob are four of the five available main courses. The fifth is vegetable au gratin, Prague's all-purpose vegetarian dish. It's likely that Nada will recommend something special, like the wonderful chicken with pineapple and walnuts that she originally created for *Prague Post* editor-in-chief Alan Levy. If you phone in advance and tell her I sent you, Nada will promise to save you a piece of her homemade apple strudel for dessert; a scrumptious, yet not too sweet, nutty fruit pie that's often served warm.

INEXPENSIVE

JO'S BAR, Malostranské náměstí 7, Praha 1.
   Cuisine: MEXICAN. **Reservations:** Not accepted. **Metro:** Line A to Malostranská.
$ Prices: Main courses 90–150 Kč ($3–$5). No credit cards.
   Open: Daily 11am–1am.

One of Prague's chief hangouts for American visitors in their 20s, Jo's is packed most evenings and weekends with expats craving something other than pork and potatoes. It's not the restaurant's mediocre Mexican cooking that most patrons long for, however, it's beer and camaraderie with other English speakers. Jo's is not a great place. In fact, it's kind of a dive. But in a country where breakfast is practically an unknown meal, this place saves the day with passable breakfast burritos and the other egg dishes. For good tacos, guacamole, and salsa, wait until you return home.

6. NEAR NÁMĚSTÍ MÍRU

MODERATE

ELITE, Korunni 1, náměstí Míru, Praha 2. Tel. 25-88-44.
   Cuisine: CZECH/ITALIAN. **Reservations:** Accepted. **Metro:** Line A to náměstí Míru.
$ Prices: Appetizers 30–50 Kč ($1–$1.70); main courses 90–165 Kč ($3–$5.50). No credit cards.
   Open: Daily 11am–10pm.
There are two different Elites in the same restaurant. The first is

downstairs; a large antiseptic dining room that's too bright, too loud, and too impersonal. The second is upstairs on the balcony, where shadows are long and conversations are intimate. The menu is the same in both places, and curiously combines Czech and Italian dishes. All the local "hits" are here, including chicken, cabbage, duck, cabbage, beef, and cabbage (and more cabbage). If you don't expect Roman standards, the Italian offerings are surprisingly enjoyable, pizzas notwithstanding. Of a half-dozen pasta dishes, tagliatelle with salmon cream sauce rates best. Like other pasta dishes here it's loaded with big chunks of meat, and filling enough to constitute an entire meal.

NA ZVONAŘCE ["At the Bell"], Šafaříkova 1, Praha 2.

Tel. 691-1311 or 25-45-34.

Cuisine: CZECH. **Reservations:** Not necessary. **Metro:** Line C to I. P. Pavlova.

$ Prices: Appetizers 12–69 Kč (40¢–$2.30); main courses 25–76 Kč (85¢–$2.55). V.

Open: Mon–Fri 11am–11pm, Sat–Sun noon–11pm.

Once a pub for bellmakers, then a dingy Communist-era restaurant, Na Zvonařce has blossomed into one of the best all-around Czech restaurants in Prague. There's a book-size menu (in English), relatively good service, a terrific shaded outdoor patio, and top-of-the-line food. And this real find is reasonably priced. Meals are strictly tried-and-true Czech favorites: roasted duck with dumplings and cabbage, pork tongue with potatoes . . . you get the idea. When it's available, however, Na Zvonařce makes one of the best grilled whole trouts in town. Beef in cream sauce with wheat dumplings also gets high marks, along with great Plzeň Urquell beer.

RADOST F/X, Bělehradská 120, Praha 2. Tel. 25-12-10.

Cuisine: VEGETARIAN. **Reservations:** Not accepted. **Metro:** Line C to I. P. Pavlova.

$ Prices: Appetizers 25–40 Kč (85¢–$1.35); main courses 45–70 Kč ($1.50–$2.35). MC, V.

Open: Daily noon–6am.

One of the only real vegetarian restaurants in Prague, Radost is recommendable for good soup, like garlicky spinach and oniony lentil, and hearty sandwiches, like tofu with stir-fried vegetables. There are some disappointments, including an anchovyless Greek salad and lackluster pizzas. But for the most part, Radost is worthy of praise.

The restaurant looks more like a café than a serious dining establishment, and is located above a popular American-style dance club of the same name (see Chapter 9, "Prague Nights"). Consequently, Radost's clientele is almost exclusively young and non-Czech, and the dining room is usually a happening place to be.

Radost is also one of the few restaurants in the city that's open all night. Their fine Bloody Marys compliment 5am breakfasts.

ZLATÝ DRAK ["Golden Dragon"], Anglická 6, Praha 2. Tel. 235-4593.

Cuisine: CHINESE. **Reservations:** Not necessary. **Metro:** Line C to I. P. Pavlova.

$ Prices: Appetizers 60–120 Kč ($2–$4); main courses 130–170 Kč ($4.35–$5.70). V.

Open: Lunch Mon–Sat 11:30am–3pm; dinner daily 6–11:30pm.

If you've just hopped off a plane from Hong Kong, you'll be disappointed. But in a city where just a handful of years ago choices were limited to meats roasted or grilled, Zlatý Drak is a godsend. A single mirror-wrapped dining room is decorated with the obligatory Chinese lanterns and dominated by a large bar.

Moo shu pork, chicken and cashew nuts, beef and bamboo shoots . . . all the major Mandarin dishes are represented, as are some from other parts of China. None are particularly spicy, however, and most taste as if missing a mysterious something. It's hard to pinpoint, but I'm convinced there's an important Chinese ingredient that's unobtainable here. MSG, perhaps?

7. DINING IN OTHER AREAS

MODERATE

NEBOZÍZEK, Petřínské sady 411, Praha 1. Tel. 53-79-05.

Cuisine: CONTINENTAL. **Reservations:** Recommended. **Tram:** 12 or 22 to Újezd, then funicular up Petřín Hill.

$ Prices: Appetizers 35–165 Kč ($1.20–$5.50); main courses 55–180 Kč ($1.85–$6). AE, MC, V.

Open: Lunch daily 11am–6pm; dinner daily 7–11pm.

Getting to Nebozízek is half the fun. No, make that three quarters. Located in the middle of Petřín Hill, overlooking the entire city of Prague, the restaurant is accessible by funicular, a kind of cable car on a track (see "Getting Around" in Chapter 3). Unlike the food, which is mediocre at best, the view is truly unmatched. In fact, dining above the storybook rooftops is so enchanting that dinner reservations are sometimes required days in advance. In summer, the most coveted seats are on a trellised patio. In winter, it's the window seats, of which there are precious few.

Some dining tips: House-prepared appetizers, like roast beef and lobster tail salad, should be passed over in favor of the more trustworthy caviar. Similarly, main dishes, which are heavy on steak

---

ⓕ FROMMER'S COOL FOR KIDS: RESTAURANTS

Restaurant Adria *(see p. 82)* One of the largest menus in Prague makes it very likely your child will find something acceptable to eat.

Red, Hot & Blues *(see p. 87)* Nachos, toasted sandwiches, and an American-oriented staff make this restaurant a good choice for U.S. kids and their families.

Zlatý Drak *(see p. 96)* When your child (or you) tire of Czech fare, this Chinese savior steps in with decent food that's fun to eat.

---

and pork, should be chosen carefully, with an eye toward simple preparations like pepper steak and roast pork. *Note:* The garlic soup is exceptional.

U CEDRU, Národní obrany 27, Praha 6. Tel. 312-2974.
   Cuisine: LEBANESE. **Reservations:** Not necessary. **Metro:** Line A to Dejvická.
$ Prices: Appetizers 30–40 Kč ($1–$1.35); main courses 120–160 Kč ($4–$5.35). AE, MC, V.
   Open: Daily 11am–11pm.
At first glance, the profusion of Czechs eating here suggests that even they tire of pork and cabbage. Upon closer inspection, however, we find that only foreigners are ordering the babaghanouj, tabbouleh, and other Middle Eastern fare. Locals stick to shish kabobs and chicken cutlets, and dabble in rice. Unfortunately, most of the restaurant's chickpea- and eggplant-based dishes aren't nearly as tasty as they are in Jerusalem or New York. There's plenty of irony in the fact that U Cedru's best dishes are those that are similar to the ones you can find in restaurants all over Prague. Still, if you're craving a good gastronomic change, U Cedru is definitely worth a visit.

8. CAFES & TEAROOMS

CAFE EVROPA, Václavské náměstí 25, Praha 1. Tel. 2422-8117.

Cuisine: CAFE. **Metro:** Line A or B to Můstek.

$ Prices: Cappuccino 30 Kč ($1); pastries 30–100 Kč ($1–$3.35). AE, MC, V.

Open: Daily 7am–midnight.

Spin through the etched-glass revolving door into the otherworldliness of Prague's finest art nouveau café. Built in 1906, the café is bedecked with period chandeliers and hand-carved woods, all made even more elegant by musicians, who entertain every afternoon. Drinks are relatively expensive—30 Kč ($1) for coffee—and service is terrible. But compared to western European standards it's cheap, and few diners are in a mood to hurry. There's a 20 Kč (70¢) cover charge after 3pm.

DOBRÁ ČAJOVNA, Václavské náměstí 14, Praha 1.

Cuisine: TEA. **Metro:** Line A or B to Můstek.

$ Prices: Small pot 30 Kč ($1). No credit cards.

Open: Mon–Sat 10am–9pm, Sun 3–9pm.

 Inside the café's intimate, pillow-covered cavern, it's difficult to discern whether you're in Prague or Pakistan. Hidden at the end of a narrow passage, across Václavské náměstí from the Ambassador Hotel, Dobrá Čajovna is truly one of the city's greatest hidden finds. It's not for everyone, mind you. Most patrons sit on the floor, and the teahouse has a decidedly New Age bent. Order at the front counter, which doubles as a health-and-spiritual gift shop, then take a seat in the tea den.

DOLCE VITA, Široká 15, Praha 1. Tel. 232-9192.

Cuisine: CAFÉ. **Metro:** Line A to Staroměstská.

$ Prices: Cappuccino 30 Kč ($1); pastries 30–100 Kč ($1–$3.35). No credit cards.

Open: Daily 8am–11pm.

A half block off Pařížská, in Prague's old Jewish Quarter, is the city's finest Italian café. An excellent espresso machine operated by knowledgeable people is the café's primary draw. But comfortable seating, a good-looking see-and-be-seen crowd, and light pastries and ice creams are the icings on this cake.

THE GLOBE, Janovského 14, Praha 7.

Cuisine: CAFE. **Metro:** Line C to Vltavská.

$ Prices: Sandwiches and desserts 60–100 Kč ($2–$3.35). No credit cards.

Open: Daily 10am–midnight.

Prague's only bookstore/coffeehouse is not only the best place in the city for used paperback literature and nonfiction, it's one of the best places for young American expats to meet. The smart looking barroom serves espresso-based drinks, sandwiches, salads, and desserts, and stocks a full bar.

RESTAURANTS BY CUISINE

American

Red, Hot & Blues *(p. 87)*
Steak House *(p. 92)*

Café/Tearoom

Cafe Evropa *(p. 97)*
Dobrá Čajovna *(p. 98)*
Dolce Vita *(p. 98)*
The Globe *(p. 98)*

Chinese

Zlatý Drak ("Golden Dragon") *(p. 96)*

Continental

Café Nouveau *(p. 86)*
Florianův Dvůr ("Florian's Court") *(p. 91)*
Nebozízek *(p. 96)*

Czech

Cerberus *(p. 86)*
Červený Vlk ("Red Wolf") *(p. 88)*
Elite *(p. 94)*
Gany's *(p. 81)*
Klásterní Vinárna *(p. 90)*
Na Zvonařce ("At the Bell") *(p. 95)*
Obchod Čerstvých Uzenin *(p. 84)*
U Kameníka *(p. 91)*
U Modré Kachničky ("The Blue Duck") *(p. 93)*
Vinárna U Maltézských Rytířů ("Knights of Malta") *(p. 93)*
Zlatá Ulička ("Golden Lane") *(p. 88)*

French

U Malířů *(p. 92)*

International

Hogo Fogo *(p. 89)*
Parnas *(p. 89)*
Restaurant Adria *(p. 82)*

Lebanese

U Cedru *(p. 97)*

Mexican

Jo's Bar *(p. 94)*

Vegetarian

Country Life *(p. 83)*
Radost F/X *(p. 95)*

WHAT TO SEE & DO IN PRAGUE

This city may be deficient regarding accommodations, health foods, and working telephones, but when it comes to sightseeing, Prague is world-class. Because of its exquisite beauty and lengthy history, the Czech capital offers much more for visitors than most cities twice its size. There are few other places in the world where losing one's way can be a pleasure, and taking a bad photo is a near impossibility. Speaking of photography, don't buy film manufactured for use in full sunlight—the best times to capture Prague is early morning and evening, when buildings and monuments that are only gorgeous by day become absolutely stunning.

SUGGESTED ITINERARIES

IF YOU HAVE ONE DAY

The best sights in Prague are outdoors. Walk around, see Staroměstské náměstí (Old Town Square), Charles Bridge, and Václavské náměstí (Wenceslas Square), and lose yourself in the tiny winding cobblestone alleys of Staré Město (Old Town) and Malá Strana. See Chapter 7, ''Strolling Around Prague,'' for walking tours through these areas.

IF YOU HAVE TWO DAYS

Day 1: Spend day 1 as above.
Day 2: On your second day visit Prague Castle in the morning, and spend the afternoon around Staroměstské náměstí (Old Town

Square), visiting Týn Church, Old Town Hall, the Old New Synagogue, and the Old Jewish Cemetery.

IF YOU HAVE THREE DAYS

Days 1 and 2: Spend days 1 and 2 as above.
Day 3: On your third day expand sightseeing to include the Strahov Monastery and Loreto Palace. Visit the Municipal House (Obecní dům), and explore Nové Město (New Town).

IF YOU HAVE FOUR DAYS OR MORE

Days 1 to 3: Spend days 1 to 3 as above.
Beyond Day 3: View the National Gallery museums and the Bertramka (Mozart Museum). Also, visit some of the city's cafés and pubs. Take one of the organized walking or bicycling tours described later in this chapter or travel to one of the towns that surround Prague on your own (see Chapter 10).

1. THE TOP ATTRACTIONS

PRAGUE CASTLE [Pražský hrad], Hradčany. Tel. 2101.
The huge hilltop complex that's known collectively as Prague Castle encompasses dozens of houses, towers, churches, courtyards, and fountains. (It is described in detail in "Walking Tour 2" in Chapter 7.) A visit to the castle could easily take an entire day or more, depending on how thorough you explore it. Happily, the castle's top sights can be seen in the space of a morning or afternoon.

St. Vitus Cathedral is not just the dominant part of the castle, it's also historically the most important. Originally constructed in A.D. 926 as the court church of the Přemyslid princes, the church has long been the center of Prague's religious and political life. It was named after St. Vitus, a wealthy 4th-century Sicilian martyr who became Bohemia's most important patron saint. Of the massive Gothic cathedral's 21 chapels, the Chapel of St. Wenceslas stands out as one of the few indoor sights in Prague that every visitor really must see. Decorated with paintings from the 14th to 16th centuries, and encrusted with hundreds of pieces of jasper and amethyst, the chapel sits on top of the site of the famous saint's grave.

The **Royal Palace,** located in the third courtyard of the castle, was the residence of Bohemian kings and princes for over 700 years beginning in the 9th century. Massive, vaulted Vladislav Hall, the interior's centerpiece, was used for coronations and special occasions. The adjacent Diet was where the king met with his advisers and

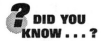

where the supreme court was held. In the 20th century, Czechoslovakia's presidents were inaugurated here.

St. George's Convent, adjacent to the Royal Palace, is the oldest Romanesque structure in Prague, dating from the 10th century. It was also the first convent in Bohemia. No longer serving a religious function, the building now houses a Czech art museum (see "More Attractions," below).

Golden Lane (Zlatá ulička), a picturesque street of 16th-century houses built into the castle fortifications, is one of the most charm-filled roads in Prague. Once home to castle sharpshooters, the houses now contain small shops, galleries, and refreshment bars.

Prague Castle Picture Gallery displays European and Bohemian masterpieces, but few are from the original Imperial collection, which was virtually destroyed during the Thirty Years' War. Of the works that have survived from the days of Emperors Rudolf II and Ferdinand III, the most celebrated is Hans von Aachen's *Portrait of a Girl* (1605–10), depicting the artist's daughter.

Like seemingly everything else in Prague, the castle is currently undergoing major changes. In order to make the building more accessible to the public, plans are underway to remodel and rebuild; enhancements that would be paid for by revenues from restaurants, coffeehouses, and even a hotel that are proposed for the castle site. You might visit the **Prague Castle Information Center,** Vikářská 37, behind St. Vitus Cathedral. The office offers a good selection of guidebooks, maps, and other related information.

IMPRESSIONS

Prague is one of the finest and most picturesque cities on the continent, much more interesting than Berlin or any other German capital. The extraordinary historical treasures of Prague make the whole city worth the closest observation. It would be a foolish enterprise to write a history of the world without previously visiting this ancient capital.
—CHARLES SEALSFIELD, 19TH CENTURY

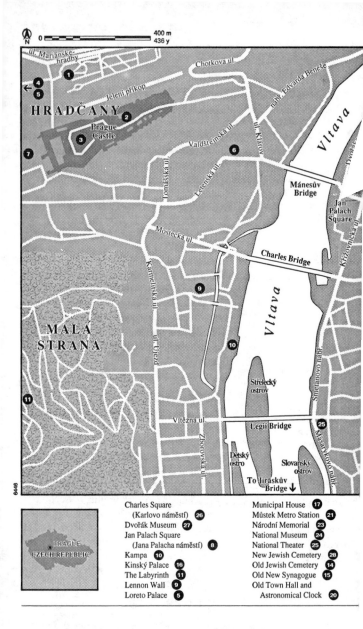

Charles Square (Karlovo náměstí) **26**	Municipal House **17**
Dvořák Museum **27**	Můstek Metro Station **21**
Jan Palach Square (Jana Palacha náměstí) **8**	Národní Memorial **23**
	National Museum **24**
Kampa **10**	National Theater **25**
Kinský Palace **16**	New Jewish Cemetery **28**
The Labyrinth **11**	Old Jewish Cemetery **14**
Lennon Wall **9**	Old New Synagogue **15**
Loreto Palace **5**	Old Town Hall and Astronomical Clock **20**

Admission: Castle 90 Kč ($3); St. Vitus Cathedral and Golden Lane free.

Open: Tues–Sun 9am–5pm. **Metro:** Line A to Malostranská or Hradčanská.

OLD NEW SYNAGOGUE [Staronová synagóga], Červená 2. Tel. 231-0681.

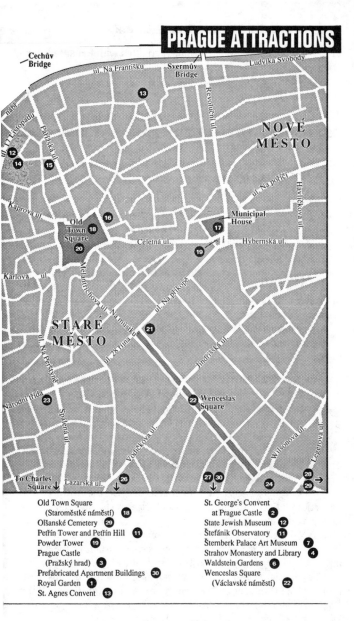

PRAGUE ATTRACTIONS

Originally called the New Synagogue, to distinguish it from an even older one that no longer exists, the Old New Synagogue, built around 1270, is the oldest Jewish house of worship in Europe. The building has been prayed in continuously for over 700 years, interrupted only between 1941 and 1945 because of the Nazi occupation. The synagogue is also one of the largest Gothic buildings in Prague, built with vaulted ceilings and fitted with Renaissance-era columns.

Admission: 30 Kč ($1) adults, 20 Kč (70¢) students.
Open: Sun–Fri 9:30am–5:30pm. **Metro:** Line A to Staroměstská.

OLD JEWISH CEMETERY [Starý židovský hřbitov], U Starého hřbitova.

One of Europe's oldest Jewish burial grounds, located just one block from the Old New Synagogue, was begun in 1439. Because the local government of the time didn't allow Jews to bury their dead elsewhere, graves were dug deep enough to hold 12 bodies vertically, with each tombstone placed in front of the last. The result is one of the world's most crowded cemeteries; a one-block area filled with over 20,000 graves. Among the most famous persons buried here are the celebrated Rabbi Loew (died 1609), who made the legendary Golem (a clay "monster" to protect Prague's Jews), and banker Markus Mordechai Maisel (died 1601), the then richest man in Prague and protector of the city's Jewish community during the reign of Rudolf II.

Admission: 30 Kč ($1) adults, 15 Kč (50¢) children.
Open: Sun–Thurs 9am–5:30pm, Fri 9am–3pm. **Metro:** Line A to Staroměstská.

STRAHOV MONASTERY AND LIBRARY [Strahovský klášter], Strahovské nádvoří. Tel. 53-25-56.

The second-oldest monastery in Prague, Strahov was founded high above Malá Strana in 1143 by Vladislav II. It is still home to Premonstratensian monks, a scholarly order closely related to the Jesuits. Unfortunately, the monks' dormitories and refectory are off-limits to tourists. What draws visitors here are the monastery's ornate libraries, which hold almost 1 million volumes. Over the centuries, the monks have assembled one of the world's best collections of philosophical and theological texts, including many illuminated manuscripts and first editions. The Philosophical Library's 46-foot-high ceilings are decorated with carved wood and frescoes. Ancient wooden printing presses, downstairs in the Museum of Czech Literature, are also worth visiting.

The monastery also contains several altars and the remains of St. Norbert, a 10th-century German-born saint who founded the Premonstratensian order. His bones were brought here in 1627, when he became one of Bohemia's 10 patron saints.

Admission: 20 Kč (70¢) adults, 10 Kč (35¢) students.
Open: Tues–Sun 9am–12:15pm and 1–5pm. **Tram:** 22 from Malostranská metro station.

OLD TOWN HALL [Staroměstské radnice] AND ASTRO-NOMICAL CLOCK [orloj], Staromestské námĕstí. Tel. 28-38-71.

✪ Crowds congregate hourly in front of Old Town Hall's Astronomical Clock (orloj) to witness the glockenspiel spectacle that occurs daily from 8am to 8pm. Originally constructed in 1410, the clock has long been an important symbol of Prague. According to legend, after the timepiece was remodeled at the end of the 15th century, clock artist Master Hanuš was blinded by the Municipal Council so he could not repeat his fine work elsewhere. In retribution, Hanuš threw himself into the clock mechanism and promptly died. The clock was out of kilter for almost a century.

It's not possible to determine the time of day from this timepiece; you have to look at the clock on the very top of Old Town Hall's tower for that. This astronomical clock, with all its hands and markings, is meant to mark the phases of the moon, the equinoxes, the season and day, and innumerable Christian holidays.

When the clock strikes the hour, viewers are treated to a kind of medieval morality play. Two doors slide open and the statues of the Twelve Apostles glide by, while the 15th-century conception of the "evils" of life—the skeleton of Death, a preening Vanity, a corrupt Turk, and an acquisitive Jew—shake and dance below. At the conclusion of World War II, the horns and beard were removed from the moneybag-holding Jew, who is now politely referred to as "Greed."

It's worth climbing Town Hall Tower for an excellent view over the red rooftops of Staroměstské náměstí and the surrounding area.

Admission: Town Hall Tower 10 Kč (35¢) adults, 5 Kč (15¢) students and children.

Open: May–Oct, Tues–Sun 9am–6pm; Nov–Apr, Tues–Sun 9am–5pm. **Metro:** Line A to Staroměstská.

LORETO PALACE [Loreta], Loretánské náměstí 7, Praha 1. Tel. 536-6228.

Loreto Palace was named after the town of Loreto, Italy, where the dwelling of the Virgin Mary was said to have been brought by angels from Palestine in the 13th century. After the Roman Catholics defeated the Protestant Bohemians in 1620, the Loreto cult was chosen as the device for the re-Catholicization of Bohemia. The Loreto legend holds that a cottage in which the Virgin Mary lived had been miraculously transferred from Nazareth to Loreto, an Italian city near Ancona. The Loreto Palace is thought to be an imitation of this cottage, and more than 50 copies have been constructed throughout the Czech lands.

The Loreto's facade is decorated with 18th-century statues of the four writers of the Gospel—Matthew, Mark, Luke, and John, along with a lone female, St. Anne, the mother of the Virgin Mary. Inside the Church of the Nativity here are fully clothed remains of two Spanish saints, St. Felicissimus and St. Marcia. The wax masks on the skeletons' faces strike me as particularly macabre.

Inside the Chapel of Our Lady of Sorrows is a painting of a bearded woman hanging on a cross. This is St. Starosta, or Vilgefortis, who, after taking a vow of virginity was forced to marry the king of Sicily. It is said that God, taking pity on the woman, gave her facial hair to make her undesirable, after which her pagan father had her crucified. Thus, Starosta went into history as the saint of unhappily married women. The painting was created in the 1700s. St. Apolena (or Appollonia), a 3rd-century deacon, had her teeth knocked out as part of a torture for refusing to renounce Christianity. She is often represented in art by a gold tooth or pincer. As the patron saint of dentists, Apolena is sometimes referred to as the "saint of toothaches." Her portrait is also on display here.

Admission: 30 Kč ($1) adults, 10 Kč (35¢) children.

Open: Tues–Sun 9am–noon and 1–5pm. **Tram:** 22 from Malostranská metro.

2. MORE ATTRACTIONS

NOTABLE ARCHITECTURE

In addition to the listings below, architecture buffs should see "Special-Interest Sightseeing," below, for information on specific buildings in a historical context.

PREFABRICATED APARTMENT BUILDINGS (Paneláky).

Prague is full of beautiful sights, but every tourist interested in the "real" Prague should make a point of seeing the worst of the city as well: prefabricated apartment buildings, or *paneláks*. Built during the Communist era, these behemoths now house half of Prague's 1.2 million residents. Created partly out of socialist beliefs and partly out of economic necessity, paneláks are named after the prefabricated concrete slabs used to build them. Ugly, cheap, and badly designed, the apartment buildings are surrounded by a featureless world, seemingly numb to all that is aesthetic. Exteriors are made of cement mixed with sand, and hallways are lined with linoleum. The same room, balcony, and window design was stamped out over and over. The worst paneláks were built in the 1970s, when buildings grew really huge and dense, each 20 or more stories tall. This was the era of Chodov and Háje, suburbs south of the city center with over 100,000 inhabitants.

In a ritual that has continued for the past 30 years, hot water is cut off to nearly all inhabitants of paneláks for three weeks each summer. Residents must brave icy showers and heat water on the stove to wash dishes and clean clothes while repairs are made to the vast underground plumbing network that carries the water to the buildings. But panelák living was not always viewed as a scourge. Unlike the larger, older apartments, paneláks had modern plumbing and heating, and were once considered the politically correct way to live. They're also amazingly cheap. Rent and utility costs still only amount to about 1,000 Kčs ($33.35) per month.

To see a particularly dense cluster of these buildings, take line C of the metro out to Háje.

MUNICIPAL HOUSE (Obecní dům), náměstí Republiky 5, Praha 1. Tel. 232-5858.

⭐ The art nouveau movement that swept across Europe at the end of the 19th century developed with the Continent's ongoing Industrial Revolution. Innovative building materials— primarily steel and glass—opened endless possibilities for artistic flourishes and embellishments. Architects abandoned traditional stone structures, built in a pseudohistorical style, for ones made for their aesthetics. There are several excellent examples of whimsical art nouveau architecture in Prague (see also "Architecture" in Chapter 1), but none is more flamboyant than Municipal House (Obecní dům), built between 1906 and 1911. The building has been an important Czech cultural symbol ever since Czechoslovakia was signed into independence here in 1918. The building is Prague's outstanding monument to itself and its citizens, lushly encrusted inside and out with paintings and ornaments. The dazzling, recently renovated facade is one of the city's most eye-catching. The building's interior is an extravaganza of painted murals, mosaics, sculptures, stained glass, and iron work. The building's most important room, Smetana Hall, has a roof made of stained-glass windows, and is the home of the Prague Symphony Orchestra. Several restaurants and an American-owned bar and nightclub are also located here (see also Chapter 5, "Prague Dining," and Chapter 9, "Prague Nights").

Metro: Line B to náměstí Republiky.

NATIONAL THEATER (Národní divadlo), Národní 2, Praha 1. Tel. 20-53-64.

⭐ Lavishly constructed in the late-Renaissance style of northern Italy, the gold-crowned National Theater, which overlooks the Vltava River, is one of Prague's most recognizable landmarks. Completed in 1881, the theater was built to nurture the Czech National Revival Movement—a drive to replace the dominant German culture with homegrown Czech works. To finance construction, small collection boxes with signs "For the prosperity of a dignified National Theater" were installed in public places.

Almost immediately upon completion, the building was wrecked by fire and rebuilt, opening in 1883 with the premiere of Bedřich Smetana's opera *Libuše*. The magnificent interior contains an allegorical sculpture about music, and busts of Czech theatrical personalities created by some of the country's best-known artists.

Composer Bedřich Smetana conducted the theater's orchestra here until 1874, when deafness forced him to relinquish his post.

See Chapter 9, "Prague Nights," for information on attending performances at the National Theater.

Metro: Line B to Národní třída.

CEMETERIES

NEW JEWISH CEMETERY [Nový židovský hřbitov], Jana Želivského, Praha 3.

Although it's not as visually captivating, nor as historically important as Prague's Old Jewish Cemetery (see "Top Attractions," above), the overgrown, ivy-enveloped New Jewish Cemetery is a popular attraction because the writer Franz Kafka is buried along one of the cemetery's sides. Stop at the main gate and ask the attendant for directions or a map.

Open: Daily dawn–dusk. **Metro:** Line A to Želivského.

OLŠANSKÉ CEMETERY [Olšanské hřbitov], Vinohradská, Praha 3.

One of Prague's most important cemeteries, Olšanské is the burial ground of some of the city's most prominent former residents, including the first Communist president, Klement Gottwald. Olšanské is located just on the other side of Jana Želivského street from the New Jewish Cemetery.

Open: Daily dawn–dusk. **Metro:** Line A to Flora or Želivského.

UNIVERSITIES

Historically, education has always occupied an important place in Czech life. Professors at Charles University—the city's most prestigious and oldest, dating from the 14th century—have been in the political and cultural vanguard, strongly influencing the everyday life of all citizens. During the last 50 years, the university has expanded into some of the city center's largest riverfront buildings, many of which are located between Karlův most (Charles Bridge) and Čechův most (Čech's Bridge).

Central European University, chartered in 1991 with a $25 million endowment from Hungarian-American billionaire George Soros, was founded to teach democratic and free-market principles in the former East Bloc. The Prague campus has lured prominent professors from prestigious universities like Oxford, Cambridge, Stanford, and New York University. To find out about its English-language programs, contact Táboritská 23, POB 114, Praha 3 (tel. 2/27-47-58; fax 2/27-49-13).

HISTORIC BUILDINGS & MONUMENTS

POWDER TOWER [Prašná brána], náměstí Republiky.

Once part of Staré Město's system of fortifications, Powder Tower was built in 1475 as one of the walled city's major gateways. A medieval reminder in a modern world, the round rampart is not just notable for its architecture, but for its spectacular exterior and pretentious decorations that are also centuries old.

The tower marks the beginning of the Royal Way, the traditional three-quarter-mile-long route along which medieval Bohemian monarchs paraded on their way to being crowned in Prague Castle's St. Vitus Cathedral. Powder Tower got its name late in the 18th century, when the development of Nové Město rendered this protective tower obsolete; it was then used as a gunpowder storehouse. Early in this century, the tower served as the daily meeting place of Max Brod and Franz Kafka.

Metro: Line B to náměstí Republiky.

LENNON WALL, Velkopřevorské náměstí, Praha 1.

One of the city's most photographed tourist attractions is a colorful, graffiti-filled wall, located on a quiet side street in Malá Strana's Kampa neighborhood near Charles Bridge. Named the Lennon Wall, after singer John Lennon, whose huge image is spray-painted in the wall's center, this is a kind of pilgrimage site for young locals and tourists who regularly pay homage with flowers and candles.

Following his death in 1980, Lennon became a hero of pacifism and counter-culture throughout Eastern Europe, and this monument was born. During Communist rule, the wall was regularly whitewashed, only to be repainted by the city's faithful. When the new democratically elected government was installed in 1989, it is said that the French ambassador, whose stately offices are located directly across from the wall, phoned Prague's mayor and asked that the city government refrain from interfering with the monument.

Metro: Line A to Malostranská.

NÁRODNÍ MEMORIAL, Národní 16, Praha 1.

Under the arches midway between Václavské náměstí and the National Theater is a striking memorial to hundreds of protesters who were seriously beaten by riot police at this spot at the very beginning of 1989's otherwise nonviolent Velvet Revolution. This violent confrontation, on November 17, marked the beginning of the end for Czechoslovakia's Communist government.

Metro: Line A or B to Můstek.

MŮSTEK METRO STATION, Václavské náměstí.

It's not the metro station itself, which is hardly 50 years old, that warrants an entry in this section. But descend to Můstek's lower escalators and you will see the illuminated stone remains of what was once a bridge that connected the fortifications of Prague's Old and New Towns. In Czech, *můstek* means "little bridge," but the ancient span is not the only medieval remains modern-day excavators discovered. Metro workers had to be inoculated when they also uncovered viable tuberculosis bacterium, which had lain here dormant, encased in horse excrement, since the Middle Ages.

Na příkopě, the pedestrian street above Můstek metro station, literally translates as "on the moat," a reminder that the street was built on top of a river that separated the walls of Staré Město and Nové Město. It was filled in in 1760. The street follows the line of the old fortifications all the way down to the Gothic Powder Tower at náměstí Republiky.

MARKETS

Only since the fall of Communism has private entrepreneurship been encouraged by the government. You will see people selling tourist-related items throughout the busiest parts of central Prague, including Staroměstské náměstí, Charles Bridge, and along the streets that connect the two.

HAVELSKÁ PRODUCE MARKET, Havelská, Praha 1.
Located on a short street that runs perpendicular to Melantrichova, the main route connecting Staroměstské náměstí with Václavské náměstí, this open-air market features dozens of private vendors selling seasonal home-grown fruit and vegetables as well as other goods, including detergent, flowers, and cheese. Designed primarily for locals, prices here are exceedingly low by western European standards. The market is a great place to stop to shop for picnic supplies. See "Parks & Gardens," below, for information on where to place your blanket.

MUSEUMS & GALLERIES

Prague's private galleries are the best places here to see contemporary art. Many terrific eastern European artists, who have not yet gained acceptance into the renowned French and German art markets, are gravitating to Prague, the unofficial art center of the formerly Communist eastern European republics. There are over a dozen fine art galleries in central Prague, most within walking distance of Staroměstské náměstí. Though their primary interest is sales, most welcome window shoppers. See Chapter 8 for information on the city's top art galleries.

MUSEUM OF THE CITY OF PRAGUE [Muzeum hlavního Města Prahy], Švermovy sady 1554, Praha 8. Tel. 236-2449.
Not just another warehouse of history, where unearthed artifacts unwanted by others are chronologically stashed, this delightfully upbeat museum encompasses Prague's illustrious past with pleasant brevity. Sure, the museum holds the expected displays of medieval

weaponry and shop signs, but the best exhibit in this two-story Renaissance-style building is a miniature model of 18th-century Prague, painstakingly re-created in 1:480 scale. It's fascinating to see Staré Město as it used to be, and the Jewish Quarter before its 19th-century facelift. A reproduction of the original calendar face of the Old Town Hall astrological clock is also on display, as are a number of documents relating to Prague's Nazi occupation and the assassination of Nazi commander Reinhard Heydrich. The museum is located one block north of the Florenc metro station.

Admission: 20 Kč (70¢) adults, 10 Kč (35¢) students, free for children under 6.

Open: Tues–Sun 10am–6pm. **Metro:** Line B or C to Florenc.

NATIONAL MUSEUM [Národní muzeum], Václavské náměstí 68, Praha 1. Tel. 269-4517.

The National Museum, which dominates upper Václavské náměstí, looks so much like an important government building, it even fooled the Communists, who fired upon it during their 1968 invasion. If you look closely you can still see shell marks.

The second-oldest museum in the Czech lands, it was opened in 1893. Built in neo-Renaissance style, the museum houses two floors of exhibits. On the first floor is an exhaustive collection of Czechoslovakian minerals, rocks, and meteorites. Only 12,000 of the museum's collection of over 200,000 rocks and gems are on display, all neatly arranged in old wooden cases.

The second-floor exhibits depict the ancient history of the Czech lands, as well as zoological and paleontological displays. Throughout the "prehistory" exhibit are cases of human bones, preserved in soil just as they were found. Nearby, a huge lifelike model of a woolly mammoth is mounted next to the bones of the real thing, and a half-dozen rooms are packed with more stuffed-and-mounted animals than you could shake a shotgun at.

Admission: 20 Kč (70¢) adults, 10 Kč (35¢) students, free for children under 6, free for everyone on the first Mon of each month.

Open: Wed–Mon 9am–5pm. **Metro:** Line A or C to Muzeum.

KINSKÝ PALACE [Palác Kinských], Staroměstské náměstí, Praha 1. Tel. 235-5135.

Housing graphic works from the National Gallery collection, the rococo-style Kinský Palace's permanent collection boasts works by Georges Braque, André Derain, and other modern masters, including Pablo Picasso, whose 1907 *Self-Portrait* has virtually been adopted as the National Gallery's logo.

Good-quality international exhibitions have included Max Ernst and Rembrandt retrospectives, as well as shows on functional art and crafts.

Admission: 20 Kč (70¢) adults, 10 Kč (35¢) students, free for children under 6, free for everyone on the first Mon of each month.

Open: Wed–Mon 9am–5pm. **Metro:** Line A to Staroměstská.

ST. AGNES CONVENT [Klášter sv. Anežky České], U milosrdných 17, Praha 1. Tel. 231-4251.

A complex of early Gothic buildings and churches that date from the 13th century, the convent, tucked away in a corner of Staré Město, was once home to the Order of the Poor Clares. Established in 1234 by St. Agnes of Bohemia, sister of King Wenceslas I, the convent is now home to the National Gallery's collection of 19th- and 20th-century Czech art. In addition to rooms of contemplative oils, the museum contains many bronze studies that preceded the casting of some of the city's greatest public monuments, including the equestrian statue of St. Wenceslas atop the National Theater. A Children's Workshop, downstairs, offers hands-on art activities for kids, most of which incorporate religious themes. The grounds surrounding the convent are pretty nice, too.

The convent is located at the end of Anežka, off of Haštalské náměstí.

Admission: 20 Kč (70¢).

Open: Tues 9am–7pm, Wed–Sun 10am–6pm. **Metro:** Line A to Staroměstská.

ST. GEORGE'S CONVENT AT PRAGUE CASTLE [Klášter sv. Jiřího na Pražském hradě], Jiské náměstí 33, Praha 1. Tel. 535-2469.

Dedicated to displaying old Czech art, the castle convent is especially packed with Gothic and baroque Bohemian iconography as well as portraits of patron saints. The most famous among their unique collection of Czech Gothic panel paintings are those by the Master of the Hohenfurth Altarpiece and the Master of Theodoricus.

The collections are frequently arranged into special exhibitions usually revolving around a specific place, person, or time in history.

Admission: 90 Kč ($3).

Open: Tues 9am–7pm, Wed–Sun 10am–6pm. **Metro:** Line A to Malostranská or Hradčanská.

ŠTERNBERK PALACE ART MUSEUM [Šternberský palác], Hradčanské náměstí 15, Praha 1. Tel. 352-4413, 53-23-79, or 53-44-57.

The biggest jewel in the National Gallery crown, also known as the European Art Museum, the gallery at Šternberk Palace displays non-Czech European artists exclusively. A veritable menu of European art throughout the ages, the museum features six centuries of everything from oils to sculptures. The permanent collection is divided chronologically into pre-19th-century art, 19th- and 20th-century art, and 20th-century French painting and sculpture. The collection includes a good selection of French cubist paintings by

Braque and Picasso, among others. Temporary exhibitions, such as Italian Renaissance bronzes, are always on show.

Admission: 20 Kč (70¢) adults 10 Kč (35¢) students and children.

Open: Tues 9am–7pm, Wed–Sun 10am–6pm. **Metro:** Line A to Malostranská or Hradčanská.

STATE JEWISH MUSEUM [Židovské muzeum], Jachýmova 3, Praha 1. Tel. 231-0634.

Most of Prague's ancient Judaica was destroyed by the Nazis during World War II. Ironically, it was the same Germans who constructed this "exotic museum of an extinct race." Thousands of the objects that were salvaged—including valued Torah covers, books, and silver—were placed in this museum, located adjacent to the Old Jewish Cemetery.

Admission: 80 Kč ($2.70).

Open: Sun–Thurs 9am–5pm, Fri 9am–2pm. **Metro:** Line A to Staroměstská.

DVOŘÁK MUSEUM [Muzeum A. Dvořáka], Ke Karlovu 20, Praha 2. Tel. 29-82-14.

It's no accident that museum authorities chose this particular site to honor Antonín Dvořák, this country's best-loved composer. Built in 1712, the two-story rococo building, tucked away on a Nové Město side street, was home to Dvořák for 24 years until his death in 1901. When it was built in the 18th century, this part of Prague was frontier land, and Czechs willing to open businesses so far from the center were called "Americans" for their pioneer spirit. This building came to be known as "America."

Established in 1932, the museum exhibits an extensive collection of memorabilia including the composer's piano, spectacles, a cap and gown he wore at Cambridge, photographs, and sculptures of the man, as well as his piano. Several of the rooms are furnished as they were around 1900.

Upstairs, a small and ornate recital hall hosts chamber music performances throughout the summer tourist season. See Chapter 9, "Prague Nights," for information.

Admission: 20 Kč (70¢) adults, 10 Kč (35¢) students and children; concerts 90–350 Kč ($3–$11.70).

Open: Tues–Sun 10am–5pm; concerts usually held at 8pm. **Metro:** Line C to I. P. Pavlova.

BERTRAMKA [W. A. Mozart Museum], Mozartova 169, Praha 5. Tel. 55-14-80.

Mozart loved Prague, and when he visited, the composer often stayed here. Now a museum, the villa contains displays that include his written work and his harpsichord. There's also a lock of Mozart's hair, encased in a cube of glass. Much of the Bertramka villa was destroyed by fire in the 1870s, but Mozart's rooms, where he finished composing the opera *Don Giovanni*, have miraculously remained untouched.

Chamber concerts are often held here. See Chapter 9, "Prague Nights," for information.

Admission: 50 Kč ($1.70) adults, 30 Kč ($1) students.

Open: Daily 9:30am–6pm. **Tram:** 2, 6, 7, 9, 14, or 16 from Anděl metro station.

OUTDOOR SQUARES

JAN PALACH SQUARE [Jana Palacha náměstí], Praha 1.

Officially dedicated in 1990, the square formerly known as Red Army Square is named for a 21-year-old philosophy student who immolated himself on the National Museum steps to protest the 1968 Communist invasion. An estimated 800,000 Praguers attended his funeral march from Staroměstské náměstí to the Olšanské Cemetery, where he is buried (see "Cemeteries," above).

Charles University's philosophy department building is located on this square. On the lower left-hand corner of the building's facade is a memorial to the martyred student: a replica of Palach's death mask.

This small square is located at the Staré Město foot of Mánesův Bridge.

Metro: Line A to Staroměstská.

WENCESLAS SQUARE [Václavské náměstí], Praha 1.

One of the city's most historical squares, Wenceslas Square has thrice been the site of riots and revolutions—in 1848, 1968, and 1989. Once the city's most illustrious landmark center, the square has deteriorated and is packed with pimps, prostitutes, and small-time drug dealers. The giant equestrian statue near the top end of the square is of St. Wenceslas on horseback surrounded by four other saints, including his grandmother, St. Ludmilla, and St. Adalbert, the 10th-century bishop of Prague.

Metro: Line A or B to Můstek.

CHARLES SQUARE [Karlovo náměstí], Praha 2.

The largest square in Prague was built by Charles IV in 1348, and once functioned as Prague's primary cattle market. New Town's Town Hall (Novoměstská radnice), which stands on the eastern side of the square, was the sight of Prague's First Defenestration (see "History" in Chapter 1)—a violent protest in which several Catholic councilors were thrown to their deaths from the building's windows—which initiated the 18-year-long Hussite Wars.

Today, Charles Square is a busy commercial center, crisscrossed by tramlines and surrounded by buildings and shops.

Metro: Line B to Karlovo náměstí.

OLD TOWN SQUARE [Staroměstské náměstí], Praha 1.

The most celebrated square in the city, Old Town Square is surrounded by baroque buildings and packed with colorful craftsmen, cafés, and entertainers. In ancient days, the site was a major crossroad on Central European merchant routes. In its center stands a memorial to Jan Hus, the 15th-century martyr who crusaded against Prague's German-dominated religious and political establishment. Unveiled in 1915, on the 500th anniversary of Hus's execution, the monument's most compelling features are the asymmetry of the composition and the fluidity of the figures.

Metro: Line A to Staroměstská.

PANORAMIC VIEWS

EMIR HOFFMAN TV TOWER, Ondříčkova (Televizní Vysíláč), Praha 3. Tel. 27-61-63.

Towering above Prague, from atop a hill in Žižkov, the Emir Hoffman TV Tower is visible in the distance from most everywhere in the city. Conversely, most every place in the city is visible from the TV tower, which is why it's one of the best high places around.

Most everyone agrees that the white, 600-foot antenna-topped tower (completed in late 1989) is one of the most unsightly in Prague. It's not that nice inside either, but the vistas of central Prague and all its suburbs put the entire city and surroundings into solemn perspective. Unfortunately, landmarks are not well marked from the tower's observation cubicles; bring a map.

Admission: 40 Kč ($1.35).

Open: Daily 9am–10pm. **Metro:** Line A to Jiřího z Poděbrad.

PETŘÍN TOWER (Rozhledna), on Petřín Hill, Praha 1.

A one-fifth scale copy of Paris' Eiffel Tower, Prague's Petřín Tower was constructed for the 1891 Jubilee Exhibition of recycled railway track. The tower functioned as Prague's primary telecommunications tower until 1992, when the Emir Hoffman tower opened (see above). Today the Eiffel replica exists solely as a tourist attraction. Those who make the climb to the top are treated to striking views, particularly at night.

Admission: 20 Kč (70¢) adults, 5 Kč (15¢) students and children.

Open: Daily 11am–11pm. **Tram:** 12 or 22 to Újezd, then funicular to the top.

PARKS & GARDENS

KAMPA, Malá Strana.

My favorite Prague park, located near the foot of Charles Bridge in Malá Strana, was named by Spanish soldiers who set up camp here after the Roman Catholics won the Battle of White Mountain in 1620. The park as it is today wasn't formed until the period of Nazi occupation, when the private gardens of three noble families were joined. It's the perfect place to picnic.

ROYAL GARDEN [Královská zahrodna], in Prague Castle, Praha 1.

Prague Castle's Royal Garden, once the site of the sovereign's vineyards, was founded in 1534. Dotted with lemon trees and surrounded by 16th-, 17th-, and 18th-century buildings, the park is consciously and conservatively laid out with abundant shrubbery and fountains.

Admission: 5 Kč (15¢).

Open: Tues–Sun 9am–5pm. **Metro:** Line A to Malostranská or Hradčanská.

PETŘÍN HILL [Petřínské sady], Praha 1.

Looming over Malá Strana, adjacent to Prague Castle, lush green Petřín is easily recognizable by the miniature replica of the Eiffel Tower that tops it. The huge park is dotted with gardens and orchards that bloom throughout spring and summer. Throughout are myriad monuments, churches, a mirror maze, and an observatory (see "Cool for Kids," below). Hunger Wall, a lengthy, decaying 21-foot-high stone wall that runs up through Petřín to the grounds of Prague Castle, was commissioned by Charles IV in the 1360s as a medieval social project designed to provide jobs for Prague's starving poor.

Tram: 12 or 22 to Újezd.

WALDSTEIN GARDENS [Valdštejnská zahrada], Letenská.

⭐ Part of the excitement of Waldstein (or Wallenstein) Gardens is its location, behind a 30-foot wall on the backstreets of Malá Strana. Inside, elegant, leafy gravel paths, dotted by classical bronze statues and gurgling fountains fan out in every direction. Laid out in the 17th century, the baroque park was the personal garden of General Albrecht Waldstein (or Wallenstein; 1581–1634), commander of the Roman Catholic armies during the Thirty Years' War. These gardens are the backyards of Waldstein's Palace—Prague's largest—which replaced 23 houses, three gardens, and the municipal brick kiln.

Admission: Free.

Open: May–Sept, daily 9am–7pm. **Metro:** Line A to Malostranská.

3. COOL FOR KIDS

THE LABYRINTH [Blvdiště], on Petřín Hill.

The Labyrinth was built for the 1891 Jubilee Exhibition; an expo that highlighted the beauty and accomplishments of Bohemia and Moravia. Inside is a gigantic painting/installation depicting the battle between Praguers and the Swedes on the Charles Bridge in 1648, a commemoration of the fighting that ended the Thirty Years' War. In 1892, the building's other historical exhibits were replaced with mirrors, turning the Labyrinth into the funhouse we know today.

Admission: 10 Kč (35¢) adults, 5 Kč (15¢) children.

Open: Daily 9am–6pm. **Tram:** 12 or 22 to Újezd, then funicular to the top.

PRAGUE PLANETARIUM, in Stromovka Park, Praha 7.

The planetarium shows how the sky would look if you could see beyond the smog. There are four shows daily under the dark dome, including one where highlighted constellations are set to music, and another that displays tonight's sky. The shows are in Czech, but the sky's the same.

To reach the planetarium, take tram 5, 12, or 17 to Výstaviště and walk through the park to your left about 350 yards.

Admission: 40 Kč ($1.35).

Open: Mon–Thurs 8am–noon and 1–6pm, Fri 8am–noon, Sat 9:30am–5pm. Shows at 2, 3, 4, and 5pm. **Tram:** 5, 12, or 17 to Výstaviště.

ŠTEFÁNIK OBSERVATORY, on Petřín Hill.

Built in 1930 expressly for the purpose of public stargazing, the observatory is fascinating for astronomers of all levels. Inside, a great number of magnifiers are displayed museum style, and a 90-year-old telescope for viewing the sun during the day, and stars and planets at night.

Admission: 10 Kč (35¢) adults, 5 Kč (15¢) children.

Open: Tues–Fri 2–7pm and 9–11pm; Sat–Sun 10am–noon, 1–7pm, and 9–11pm. **Metro:** 12 or 22 to Újezd, then funicular to top.

4. SPECIAL-INTEREST SIGHTSEEING

FOR THE ARCHITECTURE LOVER

Prague's long history, combined with the good fortune of having avoided heavy war damage, makes it a wonderful city for architecture lovers. Buildings and monuments from the Middle Ages to the present day are interspersed with one another throughout the city.

Prague's earliest extant architectural forms are Romanesque, and date from 1100 to 1250. Parts of Prague Castle, including the Basilica of St. George, are among the best examples of this style.

The long Gothic period spanned three centuries, from about 1250 to 1530. The best examples are in Staré Město, and include the Convent of St. Agnes, Na Františku; the Old New Synagogue,

Pařížská třída; Old Town Hall and the Astronomical Clock, Staroměstské náměstí; Powder Tower, Celetná ulice; and Charles Bridge.

Renaissance architecture came to Prague around 1500 and lasted until the early 17th century. Although examples still standing from this time are few, they include Golden Lane, Malá Strana Town Hall, and Pinkas Synagogue, Široká ulice, in Staré Město.

Many of Prague's best-known structures are pure baroque and rococo, enduring styles that reigned throughout the 17th and 18th centuries. Buildings on Staroměstské náměstí and Nerudova street date from this period, as does St. Nicholas's Church, Malostranské náměstí, in Malá Strana, and the Loreto, Loretánské náměstí, in Hradčany.

Renaissance styles made a comeback in the late 19th century. Two "neo-Renaissance" buildings in particular—the National Theater, Národní třída, and National Museum, Václavské náměstí—have endured as two of Prague's most identifiable landmarks.

The city's most flamboyant buildings are pure art nouveau. Popular from about 1900 to 1918, this style is characterized by frills that raise form to as important a status as function. Prague's most stunning examples are the Municipal House (Obecní dům), náměstí Republiky, the Hotel Evropa, on Václavské náměstí, and the main railroad station, Wilsonova třída.

The late 20th century has played havoc on Prague's architecture—the city's most unappealing structures are quite recent. Communists were partial to characterless, functional designs. Their buildings shed all decorative details and were built solely according to the function of the structure.

Most of these new buildings are situated in the outer districts of Prague. Central Prague examples include the main railroad station's entrance and departure hall; The Máj (K-mart) department store, Národní třída 26; the Kotva department store, náměstí Republiky; and the Inter-Continental Hotel, náměstí Curieových.

5. ORGANIZED TOURS

BUS TOURS

PRAGUE SIGHTSEEING TOURS, Na poříčí 10, Praha 1. Tel. 232-3693 or 232-3925.

Basic sightseeing tours acquaint visitors with the city. The Grand City Tour of Prague lasts three and a half hours and departs twice daily, 9:30am and 2:30pm. The cost is 540 Kč ($18). A shorter Prague–Getting Acquainted tour lasts only 90 minutes, costs 300 Kč ($10), and departs at 9:30am, 11:30am, 1:30pm, and 3:30pm. All tours depart from náměstí Republiky.

BOAT TOURS

If you overlook the more than occasional piece of garbage or dead fish floating in the very polluted Vltava, the river is an enjoyable place from which to view Prague. Several companies run regular sightseeing excursions in the city center. Below are the best.

EVD SHIPS, Čechův most. Tel. 060/120-0687.

The company's three ships, the *Kamenice,* the *Calypso,* and the *Odyssea* offer a plethora of river trips on a daily basis from June through September. One-hour tours glide by Prague's historical center, and include views of Charles Bridge, the National Theater, and Prague Castle. Two-hour tours follow a similar itinerary, but include lunch and live music. Dinner tours are two and a half hours long, and include meal selections from the ship's self-service cafeterias. Boats depart from Čechův most (Čech's Bridge), which is located adjacent to the Inter-Continental Hotel at the end of Pařížská street.

Prices: One-hour tours 150 Kč ($5) adults, 75 Kč ($2.50) children under 15. Lunch tours 390 Kč ($13) adults, 170 Kč ($5.70) children. Dinner tours 490 Kč ($16.35) adults, 300 Kč ($10) children.

PRAGUE PASSENGER SHIPPING, Rašínovo nábřeží, Praha 2. Tel. 29-83-09. Fax 20-58-93.

From June through September, the *Vyšehrad* steamer plies up and down the Vltava River floating beneath Charles Bridge, and past many of the city's main cultural monuments. Although the boat never travels very far, the company has conjured up more than 10 different itineraries that depart throughout the day from 10:30am to 11pm. The shortest tour lasts one hour, the longest is a three-hour dinner cruise. Note that there is no on-board commentary, so bring your own guide, or a map at the very least.

Phone the company for information and reservations, or visit the office at their Palacký Bridge departure point.

Prices: 120–550 Kč ($4–$18.35).

WALKING TOURS

WITTMANN TOURS, Urguayská 7, Praha 2. Tel. 25-12-35.

Sylvia Wittmann's tour company offers daily walks around Prague's compact Jewish Quarter. A thousand years of history is discussed during the two-and-a-half-hour stroll. Tours depart Monday, Wednesday, and Friday at 10am and depart from Pařížská 28, Praha 1, in front of the Lufthansa office.

Prices: 400 Kč ($13.35) adults, 300 Kč ($10) students; children under 10 are free. **Metro:** Line A to Staroměstská.

A THEATER TOUR

ESTATES THEATER [Stavovské divadlo], Ovocný třída 6, Praha 1. Tel. 22-86-58.

The only theater in the world that's still in its original condition from Mozart's day, offers summer tours to groups making advance reservations. Although the historical building is not usually open to the public during off-hours, regularly scheduled tours were offered in 1993, and are likely to continue in the future. The 20-minute tour, with commentary in several languages, including English, is followed by a 30-minute chamber concert. Tours are usually available Monday to Friday from 2 to 6pm, and Saturday and Sunday from 9am to 1pm. For information and reservations, contact Mr. Gregorini (tel. 22-30-32).

Prices: 50–150 Kč ($1.70–$5) per person. **Metro:** Line A or B to Můstek.

6. SPORTS & RECREATION

SPECTATOR SPORTS

Horse Racing

VELKÁ CHUCHLE, Prague 5.

This third-rate track can be a fun way to spend a weekend day. Races are scheduled most every Saturday and on some Sundays from May through October. There are no Triple Crown contenders here, nor does anyone get rich; minimum bets are a low 10 Kč (35¢). You don't need advanced Czech-language skills to wager. Only win (*vítěz*) and place (*místo*) bets are accepted, as are exactas (*pořadí*)—horses to win and place in a specified order.

To reach the track, take metro line B to Smíchovské nádraží, then any bus with a frolicking horse symbol to the track.

Admission: Free.

Post Times: May–Oct, Sat (and sometimes Sun) 2pm.

Ice Hockey

SPARTA, Za elektrárnou 49, Praha 7.

Although the Czech Republic's biggest star, Jaromir Jagr, has left his home country to earn $1.4 million a year as the All-Star forward for America's Pittsburgh Penguins, the Sparta hockey team still has more than its fair share of talent.

For information on tickets and times, visit the American Hospitality Center, Na Můstku 7, Praha 1 (tel. 2422-9961 or 2423-0467).

Soccer

PRAHA SPARTA, Letná Stadium, Praha 7. Tel. 38-22-41.

Praha Sparta, the top local soccer team, has a fanatical following, and games always draw huge crowds. Brawls between opposing fans regularly erupt in the stands, especially when the arch rival Brno team is in town. Tickets for big matches often sell out long before game time, but seats are usually available right up to the last moment for lesser matches.

For game information, visit the American Hospitality Center, Na Mûstku 7, Praha 1 (tel. 2422-9961 or 2423-0467). For tickets, visit the Sparta box office, located across the street from Letná Stadium.

Tickets: 30–80 Kč ($1–$2.70).

Tennis

Some of tennis' brightest stars are Czech-born—Ivan Lendl and Martina Navrátilová are two. Unfortunately for locals, however, the country's biggest talents emigrate. It is expected that as the Czech Republic strengthens economically, the country's tennis scene will thrive.

The Prague Open is played each August at the Štvanice Island Stadium, located near the Vltava metro station. Tickets can be purchased at the gate and cost 60 Kč to 80 Kč ($2 to $2.65).

RECREATION

Ballooning

PRAG TOURIST BALLOONING, Na Balkáně 812, Praha 3. Tel. 684-5387.

Just a couple of years ago ballooning above Bohemia would have seemed ludicrous. Today, it's still a rather preposterous proposition for most Praguers, but for the post-Communist Czech Republic, it's an adventure whose time has come. Flights depart daily, weather permitting, accommodating up to five passengers. Tours last about an hour and a half, champagne is poured in flight, and insurance is included in the price.

Prices: 4,000 Kč ($133.35) per person.

Boating

Many people rent rowboats and paddleboats on the Vltava. Free from commercial boat traffic, the remarkably romantic river slowly snakes through the middle of town, gleaming brightly beneath the city's spires. It's beautiful, but at some moment you'll note something very strange about the behavior of the boaters. Because of pollution, no one is playing with the water; splashing around with paddles is unknown, and no one is lazily lying with their hand trailing in the water. If you do decide to go for a row, there are several places from which to rent, including the following.

RENT-A-BOAT, Slovanský ostrov (Slavic Island), Praha 1.

Both row- and paddleboats can be rented here from March through September. The docks are located at the bottom of the steps on the small island two blocks south of the National Theater.

Prices: Rowboats 50 Kč ($1.70) per hour; paddleboats 70 Kč ($2.35) per hour.

Open: Mar–Oct only, 10am–sunset, weather permitting.

H&S BOATS, Slovanský ostrov (Slavic Island), Praha 1.

Located on the opposite end of the island from Rent-A-Boat (see above), H&S offers similar watercraft at similar rates.

Prices: Rowboats 50 Kč ($1.70) per hour; paddleboats 80 Kč ($2.70) per hour.

Open: Mar–Sept only, 10am–sunset, weather permitting.

Bowling

FORUM HOTEL LANES, in the Forum Hotel, Kongresová 1, Praha 4. Tel. 419-0111.

Prague's only American-style bowling lanes are open daily from 3 to 11pm. Phone for reservations.

Prices: 100 Kč ($3.35) per hour.

Golf

MOTOL PRAHA, Vozovna, Praha 5. Tel. 236-9602.

It's doubtful if any serious duffers have ever made the trip to Prague exclusively for the purpose of playing golf; nine-hole Motol Praha is the only links within city limits. Foreigners are often charged significantly more than natives, but fees usually include balls, a full set of clubs, and a cart.

Greens Fees: 1,500 Kč ($50).

Health Clubs

Although some 80 or so health clubs have opened in Prague since 1989, not all are on par with Western standards. Don't expect rows of gleaming Nautilus machines. Although equipment is largely new, few clubs offer state-of-the-art machines. One of the best centrally located clubs is listed below.

FITNESS FORUM, in the Forum Hotel, Kongresová 1, Praha 4. Tel. 419-0326.

Located on the 25th floor of one of the city's top hotels, this good facility has 13 machines, free weights, exercise bikes, step machines, a small swimming pool, a sauna, and a solarium. They also offer tanning beds, squash courts, a whirlpool, and massages. Take metro line C to Vyšehrad.

Admission: 300 Kč ($10) for a one-day pass.

Open: Mon–Fri 7am–9pm, Sat–Sun 9am–8pm.

Swimming

Summer doesn't last long in Prague, and when it arrives, many city dwellers are only too happy to cool off in one of the city's many swimming pools. In addition to Fitness Forum, in the Forum Hotel, listed under "Health Clubs," above, the best place for tourists to swim is Džbán Reservoir, in the Šárka nature reserve, Prague 6. A natural lake in the ominous shadow of Communist-era panelák block housing, Džbán is fronted by a grassy "beach" that can, and often does, accommodate hundreds of bathers. Waterfront shops sell beer, snacks, and ice cream, and lockers and showers are available. In addition to two artificial swimming pools, the Šárka nature reserve also encompasses a rowboat-rental concession and a special section for nude swimming and sunbathing. To reach Šárka, take tram 20 or 26 from the Dejvická metro station.

CHAPTER 7

STROLLING AROUND PRAGUE

1. **STARÉ MĚSTO (OLD TOWN) & JOSEFOV**
2. **PRAGUE CASTLE**
3. **CHARLES BRIDGE**

Prague is a wonderful city for walking, with glorious vistas and historical buildings seemingly everywhere. The following walking tours lead you through some of the city's most attractive areas.

WALKING TOUR 1 —— STARÉ MĚSTO (OLD TOWN) & JOSEFOV

Start: Municipal House (Obecní dům), náměstí Republiky.
Finish: Old New Synagogue.
Time: Allow approximately one hour, not including rest stops or museum visits.
Best Times: Sunday through Thursday from 9am to 5pm and Friday from 9am to 2pm, when the museums are open.
Worst Times: Friday afternoons and Saturdays, when Jewish museums and monuments are closed.

Staré Město, founded in 1234, was the first of Prague's original five towns. Its establishment was the result of Prague's growing importance along Central European trade routes. Staré Město's ancient streets, most of which meander haphazardly around Staroměstské náměstí, are lined with many important buildings, churches, shops, and theaters.

Josefov, Prague's noted Jewish ghetto, is located entirely within Staré Město. It was once surrounded by a wall, before it was almost all destroyed to make way for 19th-century structures. Prague is considered one of Europe's great Jewish cities: Jews have been here since the end of the 10th century, and by 1708 there were more Jews here than anywhere else in Europe.

Although this tour is far from exhaustive, it takes you past some of the area's most important buildings and monuments. Begin your tour at the:

1. **Municipal House (Obecní dům),** náměstí Republiky 5, at the metro station. One of Prague's most photographed cultural and historical monuments, Municipal House was built between 1906 and 1911 with money raised by the citizens of Prague.

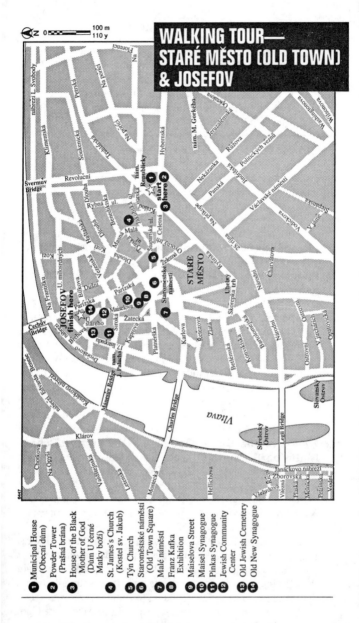

- **1** Municipal House (Obecní dům)
- **2** Powder Tower (Prašná brána)
- **3** House of the Black Mother of God (Dům U černé Matky boží)
- **4** St. James's Church (Kostel sv. Jakub)
- **5** Týn Church
- **6** Staroměstské náměstí (Old Town Square)
- **7** Malé náměstí
- **8** Franz Kafka Exhibition
- **9** Maiselova Street
- **10** Maisel Synagogue
- **11** Pinkas Synagogue
- **12** Jewish Community Center
- **13** Old Jewish Cemetery
- **14** Old New Synagogue

From the beginning, this ornate art nouveau building has held an important place in the national psyche as a Czech cultural symbol—the document granting independence to Czechoslovakia was signed here in 1918. The Prague Symphony performs in Smetana Hall, the building's most important room. It is named for Bedřich Smetana (1824–84), a popular composer and fervent

Czech nationalist. Times are changing. Today, Municipal House also contains Café Nouveau and Brasserie Mozart, two large restaurants owned by North Americans and Swedes, respectively. The building's subterranean beer halls are also foreign run. For more information on Municipal House, see "Architectural Highlights," in Chapter 6.

REFUELING STOP: Café Nouveau, in the Municipal House, náměstí Republiky 5 (tel. 231-8084). The better of two restaurants located in Municipal House, Café Nouveau is recommended not so much for its food, but for its spectacular dining room (see Chapter 5, "Prague Dining").

With your back to the Municipal House, turn right on náměstí Republiky, then right onto Celetná, under the arch of the:

2. Powder Tower (Prašná brána). Once part of Staré Město's system of fortifications, the Powder Tower was built in 1475 as one of the walled city's major gateways. After New Town was incorporated into the City of Prague, the walls that separated Old Town from the new section became obsolete. So did Powder Tower, which was recommissioned as a gunpowder storehouse.

The tower marks the beginning of the Royal Way, the traditional three-quarter-mile route along which medieval Bohemian monarchs paraded on their way to being crowned in Prague Castle's St. Vitus Cathedral.

Continue down Celetná (named after *calt,* a bread that was baked here in the Middle Ages) to the corner of Ovocný to the:

3. House of the Black Mother of God (Dům U černé Matky boží), Celetná 19, important not for its contents, but for its cubist architectural style. Cubism, an angular artistic movement that originated with the paintings of Pablo Picasso and Georges Braque in Paris in 1906, was confined to painting and sculpture in France and most of Europe. As an architectural style, cubism is exclusive to Bohemia.

Constructed in 1921, this house features tall columns, sculpted with rectangular and triangular shapes on either side of an ornate wrought-iron gate. The house is named for the Virgin Mary emblem on the corner of the building's second floor that was salvaged from the last building to stand on this site.

With your back to the House of the Black Mother of God, cross Celetná into Templová, walk two short blocks and turn left onto Jakubská. At the corner, on your right, you'll see:

4. St. James's Church (Kostel sv. Jakub), Prague's second longest, containing 21 altars. Enter the church and look up, just inside the church's front door. The withered object dangling from above is the shriveled arm of a 16th-century thief.

Return to Celetná and continue walking about 300 feet to:

5. Týn Church, one of the largest and prettiest of Prague's many churches. Famous for its twin spires that loom over nearby Staroměstské náměstí, the church was closely connected to the 14th-century Hussite movement of religious reform. After the reformers were crushed by the Roman Catholics, many of the church's Hussite symbols were removed, including statues, insignia, and the tower bells that were once known by Hussite nicknames. Note the tomb of the great Danish astronomer Tycho Brahe (d. 1601), located close to the church's high altar.

Exit the church and continue a few steps down Celetná, which opens up into:

6. Staroměstské náměstí (Old Town Square). Surrounded by baroque buildings, and packed with colorful craftsmen, cafés, and entertainers, Staroměstské náměstí looks just like an old European square is supposed to look. At any hour, it feels more like amusement park than city. If Disney were to re-create the classic European square, it would, no doubt, be very much like this. They would probably even name it "Old Town Square."

In the center of the square is the hulking statue of Jan Hus, a fiery 15th-century preacher who challenged the Roman Catholic hierarchy and was burned at the stake for it. Continue straight through the square, passing Town Hall and the Astronomical Clock (see "The Top Attractions" in Chapter 6 for complete information), into:

7. Malé náměstí. Literally the "lesser square," this small piazza adjacent to Staroměstské náměstí has as much history as its larger companion. Excavations have proven that Malé náměstí was a prime piece of real estate as far back as the 12th century. Archeologists have turned up bits of pottery, evidence of medieval pathways, and human bones that date from the late 1100s, when real estate developers committed the medieval equivalent of paving over a cemetery to build a shopping mall.

From Malé náměstí, turn right, onto U radnice. One block ahead, on the corner, you will see the:

8. Franz Kafka Exhibition, a tribute to the famous writer whose themes at times reflect the life of a Jew in Prague. The small exhibit, on the very site of the building where Kafka was born, re-creates the history of his life and world through words, pictures, and a huge array of Franz Kafka paraphernalia. Unfortunately, it's not as interesting as it sounds. Don't get too enthusiastic about the building itself either; only the gray doorway remains from Kafka's day. The exhibit is open Friday and Saturday from 10am to 6pm. Entrance for all is 10 Kč (35¢).

An unflattering cast-iron bust of Kafka, unveiled in 1965, sits just to the right of the exhibition entrance, at the corner of Maiselova and U radnice. Walk straight, onto:

9. Maiselova Street, one of the two main streets of the old, walled Jewish quarter, founded in 1254. As elsewhere in Europe, Prague's Jews were forced into ghettos following a formal Roman Catholic decision that "the Jews" killed Jesus. By the 16th century, Prague's 10,000 isolated Jews comprised 10% of the city's population.

The ban on Jews living outside the ghetto was lifted in 1848. Eighty percent of the ghetto's Jews moved to other parts of the city, and living conditions on this street, and those that surround it, seriously deteriorated. The authorities responded by razing the entire neighborhood, including numerous old medieval houses and synagogues. The majority of the buildings here now date from the end of the 19th century; several on this street sport stunning art nouveau facades.

About halfway down the street on your right, you'll see:

10. Maisel Synagogue (Maisel Synagóga), a neo-Gothic style temple built on a plot of land donated by Markus Mordechi Maisel, a wealthy inhabitant of Prague's old Jewish town. Though it was later rebuilt, the original synagogue was destroyed by fire in 1689. During the Nazi occupation of Prague the synagogue was used to store furniture seized from the homes of deported Jews. Today, the building holds no religious services; it's home to the Jewish Museum's collection of silver ceremonial objects confiscated from Bohemian synagogues by the Nazis during World War II. The museum is open daily from 9am to 5pm. Admission is 20 Kč (70¢) for adults, 10 Kč (35¢) for students and children.

Continue walking down Maiselova Street and turn left onto Široká. Walk past the former entrance to the Old Jewish Cemetery (Starý židovský hřbitov), through which you can catch a glimpse of its shadowy headstones, to:

11. Pinkas Synagogue (Pinsky Synagóga), Prague's second-oldest Jewish house of worship. After World War II the walls of the Pinkas Synagogue were painted with the names of over 77,000 Czech Jews who perished in Nazi concentration camps. The names were subsequently erased by Czechoslovakia's Communist government; officials claimed the memorial was suffering from "moisture due to flooding." A new fund-raising effort is underway to restore the painted commemoration. Pinkas Synagogue is open daily from 9am until 5pm. Entrance is 20 Kč (70¢) for adults, 10 Kč (35¢) for students and children.

Backtrack up Široká Street and turn left onto Maiselova Street. The pink rococo building on the right-hand side of the street at Maiselova 18 is the:

12. Jewish Community Center, an information and cultural center for locals and tourists. Activities and events of interest to Prague's Jewish community are posted here, and the staff provides visitors with information about Jewish cultural activities and tours.

Continue walking one block along Maiselova and turn left onto U Starého hřbitova to the:

13. Old Jewish Cemetery, Europe's oldest Jewish burial ground dating from 1439. Because the local government of the time didn't allow Jews to bury their dead elsewhere, as many as 12 bodies were placed vertically, with each new tombstone placed in front of the last. Hence, the crowded little cemetery contains more than 20,000 graves.

Like other Jewish cemeteries around the world, many of the tombstones here have small rocks and stones on them—a tradition said to date from the days when Jews were wandering in the desert. Passersby, it is believed, would add rocks to grave sites so as not to lose the deceased to the shifting sands. Along with stones, visitors often also leave small notes of prayer on top of tombstones.

Backtrack along U Starého hřbitova, cross Maiselova, and walk directly into the small alley called Červená. You are now standing between two synagogues. On the right is the High Synagogue (Vysoká synagóga), now an exhibition hall for the Jewish State Museum. On your left is the:

14. Old New Synagogue. Originally called the New Synagogue to distinguish it from an even older one that no longer exists, the Old New Synagogue, built around 1270, is the oldest Jewish temple in Europe. The building has been prayed in continuously for over 700 years, except for 1941 to 1945, during the Nazi occupation in World War II. The synagogue is also one of the largest Gothic buildings in Prague, built with vaulted ceilings and fitted with Renaissance-era columns.

Much of Josefov and Staré Město once was flooded regularly by the Vltava River, until a 19th-century planning effort raised the entire area about 10 feet. The Gothic-era Old New Synagogue, however, has preserved its original floor, which is reached by going *down* a short set of stairs.

Continue to the end of the Červoná alley and turn right, onto Pařížská, or Paris Street, Prague's most elegant thoroughfare, built around the turn of the century. Follow Pařížská back to Staroměstské náměstí.

FINAL REFUELING STOP: Dolce Vita, Široká 15 (tel. 232-9192), a half block off Pařížská, is the city's finest Italian café. Its marble interior contains five tables on the ground floor, and another 10 on a veranda overlooking the action below. The café offers traditional Italian sandwiches, ice cream (gelati), and espresso drinks, served by an Italian-speaking Czech waitstaff. The Dolce Vita is popular with Prague's modeling and well-to-do see-and-be-seen sets, and patrons are encouraged to linger as long as they'd like.

WALKING TOUR 2 — PRAGUE CASTLE

Start: The castle's front entrance, located at Hradčanské náměstí.
Finish: Malostranská metro station.
Time: Allow approximately 2½ hours, not including rest stops.
Best Times: Tuesday through Sunday from 9am to 5pm.
Worst Times: Mondays and late afternoons, when the castle is closed.

The history and development of Prague Castle and the city of Prague are inextricably related; they grew up together and it's impossible to envision one without the other. Popularly known as "the Hrad," Prague Castle dates to the second half of the 9th century when the first Czech royal family, the Přemyslids, moved their seat of government here. Settlements on both sides of the Vltava River developed under the protection of the fortified castle.

Begin your tour from the castle's front entrance, located at Hradčanské náměstí. Walk through the imposing rococo gateway, topped by the colossal *Battling Giants* statue, to the:

1. **First Castle Courtyard (První hradní nádvoří).** An informal changing of the guard ceremony occurs here daily on the hour. It only involves five guards, who do little more than some impressive heel-clicking and rifle-twirling. The guards wore rather drab khaki outfits until 1989, when Václav Havel asked his friend, costume designer Theodor Pištěk (who costumed the actors in the film *Amadeus*) to re-dress them. The guards' smart new blue outfits are reminiscent of those worn during the First Republic.

    Directly ahead is the:
2. **Matthias Gateway (Matyášova brána).** Built in 1614 as a freestanding gate, it was later incorporated into the castle itself. The gateway bears the coats-of-arms of the various lands ruled by Emperor Matthias. Once through the gateway, the stairway on the right leads to the state rooms of the president of the republic. They're not open to the public.

    The gateway leads into the Second Castle Courtyard (Druhé hradní nádvoří). Directly ahead, on the eastern side of the square, is the:
3. **Holy Rood Chapel (kaple sv. Kříže),** constructed in 1763, and redesigned in 1856. The chapel is noted for its high-altar sculpture and ceiling frescoes.

    On the western side of the courtyard is the opulent:
4. **Spanish Hall (Španělský sál),** which was originally constructed in the late 16th century. During restorations in 1993, officials at the castle discovered a series of 18th-century trompe l'oeil murals that lay hidden behind the mirrors that lined the

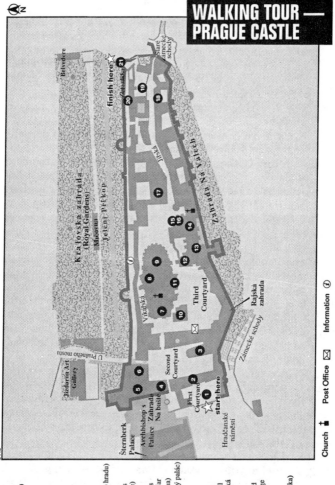

**WALKING TOUR —
PRAGUE CASTLE**

finish here

start here

Church ✝   Post Office ⊠   Information ⓘ

1. First Castle Courtyard (První hradní nádvoří)
2. Matthias Gateway (Matyášova brána)
3. Holy Rood Chapel (kaple sv. Kříže)
4. Spanish Hall (Španělský sál)
5. Rudolf Gallery
6. Picture Gallery of Prague Castle (Obrazárna Pražského hradu)
7. St. Vitus Cathedral
8. Chapel of St. Wenceslas (Svatováclavská kaple)
9. Royal Crypt
10. Memorial to the Victims of the First World War
11. Golden Gate (Zlatá brána)
12. Royal Palace (Královský palác)
13. Vladislav Hall (Vladislavský sál)
14. Ludwig Wing (Ludvíkovo křídlo)
15. Chamber of the Imperial Court Council (Říšská dvorská rada)
16. Old Diet (Sněmovna)
17. St. George's Basilica and Convent of St. George
18. Lobkowicz Palace
19. Burgrave's Palace
20. Golden Lane (Zlatá ulička)
21. Daliborka tower

hall's walls. The paintings were made to look as if the viewer were looking out of a window at detailed city scenery.

Adjoining Spanish Hall is:

5. Rudolf Gallery, an official reception hall that once housed the art collections of Rudolf II. The last remodeling of this space—rococo-style stucco decorations—occurred in 1868.

On the northern side of the square is the:

6. Picture Gallery of Prague Castle (Obrazárna Pražského hradu). Containing both European and Bohemian masterpieces, the gallery holds few works from the original Imperial collection, which was virtually destroyed during the Thirty Years' War. Of the works that have survived from the days of Emperors Rudolf II and Ferdinand III, the most celebrated is Hans von Aachen's *Portrait of a Girl* (1605–10), depicting the artist's daughter.

A covered passageway leads to the Third Castle Courtyard (Třetí hradní nádvoří), dominated by hulking:

7. St. Vitus Cathedral. Begun in 1334, under the watchful eye of Charles IV, Prague's most celebrated Gothic cathedral has undergone three serious reconstructions. The tower galleries date from 1562, the baroque onion roof was constructed in 1770, and the entire western part of the cathedral was begun in 1873.

Before entering the cathedral, notice the facade, decorated with statues of saints. The bronze doors are embellished with reliefs. The central door depicts the construction history of the cathedral. The door on the left features representations from the lives of St. Adalbert (on the right) and St. Wenceslas (on the left).

Inside the cathedral's busy main body are several chapels, coats-of-arms of the city of Prague, a memorial to Bohemian casualties of World War I, and a Renaissance-era organ loft (with an organ dating from 1757).

According to legend, St. Vitus died in Rome but was then transported by angel to a small town in southern Italy. Since his remains were brought here in 1355, Vitus, the patron saint of Prague, has remained the most popular saint in the country. Nearly all of the Czech Republic's churches have altars dedicated to him.

The most celebrated chapel, located on your right, is the:

8. Chapel of St. Wenceslas (Svatováclavská kaple), built atop the saint's actual tomb. The chapel's altar and walls are decorated with a multitude of polished semiprecious stones. Stoneless spaces are filled in with 14th-century mural paintings depicting Christ's sufferings and the life of St. Wenceslas.

Below the church's main body is the:

9. Royal Crypt, which contains the sarcophagi of Kings Václav IV, George of Poděbrady, Rudolf II, and Charles IV and his four wives.

Exit the cathedral from the same door you entered and turn left into the courtyard past the:

10. Memorial to the Victims of the First World War, a marble monolith measuring over 35 feet tall. Just behind the memorial is an equestrian statue of St. George, a Gothic work produced in 1373.

Continue walking around the courtyard. In the southern wall

of St. Vitus Cathedral you will see a ceremonial entrance known as the:

11. **Golden Gate (Zlatá brána).** The closed doorway is decorated with a 14th-century mosaic known as the Last Judgment, depicting a kneeling Charles IV with his wife Elizabeth of Pomerania. The doorway's 1950s-era decorative grille is designed with zodiac figures.

   An archway in the Third Castle Courtyard connects St. Vitus Cathedral with:

12. **The Royal Palace (Královský palác),** which was, until the second half of the 16th century, the official residence of royalty. Inside, to the left, is the Green Chamber (Zelená světnice), where Charles IV presided over minor court sessions. A fresco of the court of Solomon is painted on the ceiling.

   The adjacent room is:

13. **Vladislav Hall (Vladislavský sál),** a ceremonial room that has held coronation banquets, political assemblies, and knightly tournaments. Since 1934, elections of the president of the republic have taken place here. In addition to the historical and political associations, it's worth visiting this hall to view the exquisite 40-foot-tall twisted-rib vaulted ceiling.

   At the end of Vladislav Hall is a door giving access to the:

14. **Ludwig Wing (Ludvikovo křidlo),** built in 1509. Here you'll find two rooms of the Chancellery of Bohemia (Česká kancelář), once the administrative body of the Land of the Crown of Bohemia. When the king was absent, Bohemia's nobles summoned assemblies here. On May 23, 1618, two hated governors, together with their secretary, were thrown out of the eastern window of the rear room. This act, known as the First Defenestration, marked the beginning of the Thirty Years' War.

   A spiral staircase leads to the:

15. **Chamber of the Imperial Court Council (Říšská dvorská rada),** which met here during the reign of Rudolf II. From this room the 27 rebellious squires and burghers who fomented the defenestration were sentenced to death and consequently executed on June 21, 1621, in Staroměstské náměstí. All portraits on the walls of the chamber are of Habsburgs. The eastern part of Vladislav Hall opens onto a terrace from which there is a lovely view of the castle gardens and the city of Prague.

   Also located in the palace is the:

16. **Old Diet (Sněmovna),** where the Provincial Court once assembled. It's interesting to notice the arrangement of the diet's 19th-century furniture, which is all centered around the royal throne. To the sovereign's right is the chair of the archbishop; behind him are benches for the prelates. Along the walls are seats for the federal officials; opposite the throne is a bench for the representatives of the Estates. By the window on the right is a

gallery for the representatives of the royal towns. Portraits of the Habsburgs adorn the walls.

Stairs lead down to St. George's Square (náměstí U Svatého Jiří), a courtyard at the eastern end of St. Vitus Cathedral. The square is dominated by:

17. St. George's Basilica and the Convent of St. George, founded in 973 by Benedictine Nuns. In 1967, the convent's premises were acquired by the National Gallery, which now uses the buildings to warehouse and display their collections of Bohemian art from Gothic to baroque periods. See Chapter 6, "What to See and Do in Prague," for complete information.

Leave the basilica and continue walking through the castle compound on Jiské Street, the exit at the southeastern corner of St. George's Square. About 200 feet ahead on your right is the entrance to the:

18. Lobkowicz Palace, a 16th-century manor that now houses the Permanent History Exhibition of the National Museum, a gallery devoted exclusively to the history of the Czech lands.

Opposite Lobkowicz Palace is:

19. Burgrave's Palace, now the House of Czech Children, a 16th-century building used for cultural programs and exhibitions aimed toward children.

Walk up the steps located to the left of Burgrave's Palace to:

20. Golden Lane (Zlatá ulička), a picturesque street of 16th-century houses built into the castle fortifications. Once home to castle sharpshooters, this charm-filled lane now contains small shops, galleries, and refreshment bars.

Turn right on Golden Lane and walk to the end, where stands:

21. Daliborka tower, part of the castle's late-Gothic fortifications dating from 1496. The tower's name comes from Squire Dalibor of Kozojedy, who in 1498 became the first unlucky soul to be imprisoned here.

Turn right at Daliborka tower, then left, through the passageway and down the old castle steps (Staré zámecké schody) to the Malostranská station on line A of Prague's metro.

WALKING TOUR 3 — CHARLES BRIDGE

Dating from the 14th century, Charles Bridge is the oldest and most celebrated span in the city. As the primary link between Staré Město and the castle, Charles Bridge has always figured prominently in the city's commercial and military history. For most of its 600 years, Charles Bridge has been a pedestrian promenade, just as it is today. The first sculpture, depicting St. John of Nepomuk, was placed on the bridge in 1683. It was such a hit that the church commissioned another 21, which were created between 1698 and 1713. Since then the number has increased to 30. The location of the Charles Bridge statues, the most looked at sculptures in Prague, is shown on the accompanying map. The tour takes at most one hour.

Start your walk from the Staré Město side of the bridge. The first statue on the right is of the:

1. **Madonna,** attending to a kneeling **St. Bernard,** flanked by cherubs. Like most of the statues on the bridge, this is a copy; the originals were removed to protect them from weather-related deterioration.

   Directly across the bridge is a statue of:

2. **St. Ives,** the patron saint of lawyers, depicted promising to help a person who petitioned him. Justice, with a sword on his right, is also portrayed. If you see his outstretched hand holding a glass of beer, you will know that Prague's law students have just completed their finals.

   Cross the bridge again, and continue to do so after you view each statue.

3. **St. Dominic** and **St. Thomas Aquinas** (1708) are shown receiving a rosary from the hands of the Madonna. Below the Madonna is a cloud-enshrouded globe and a dog with a torch in its jaws, the symbol of the Dominican order.

4. **St. Barbara, St. Margaret,** and **St. Elizabeth** were sculpted by two brothers who worked under the watchful eye of their father, Jan Brokoff, who signed the work as a whole. Franz Kafka writes about the finely sculpted hands of St. Barbara, the patron saint of miners, situated in the center of the monument. To art experts, however, the sculpture of St. Elizabeth (on the left) is the artistically most valuable figure in this group.

5. Originally produced for positioning on a bridge in Dresden, Germany, this bronze **crucifix** was purchased by the Prague magistrate and placed on Charles Bridge in 1657. The statue's gilded Hebrew inscription translates as "holy, holy, holy, God," and is believed to have been paid for with money extorted from an unknown Jew who had mocked a wooden crucifix that formerly stood on this site.

6. The **Lamenting of Christ** depicts Jesus lying in the Virgin Mary's lap with St. John in the center and Mary Magdalene on the right. Executions were regularly held on this site during the Middle Ages.

7. Created in 1707, this statue depicts Mary's mother, **St. Anne,** holding baby Jesus, while the child embraces the globe.

8. This statue of **St. Joseph** with Jesus dates from 1854, and was put here to replace another that was destroyed by gunfire six years earlier by anti-Habsburg rioters.

9. These two saints, **Cyril** and **Methodius,** are the Catholic missionaries credited with introducing Christianity to the Slavs.

10. St. Francis Xavier, the 18th-century cofounder of the Jesuit order, is depicted here carrying four pagan princes on his shoulders—an Indian, a Tartar, a Chinese, and a Moor, symbollizing the cultures targeted for proselytizing. This statue is widely regarded as one of the most outstanding Czech baroque sculptural works.

11. St. John the Baptist is depicted here with a cross and a shell, symbols of baptism.

12. St. Christopher, the patron saint of raftsmen, is shown here carrying baby Jesus on his shoulder. The statue stands on the site of the original bridge watch-house, which collapsed into the river along with several soldiers during the Great Flood of 1784.

13. The three saints portrayed here—**St. Norbert, St. Wenceslas,** and **St. Sigismund**—are patron saints of Bohemian provinces.

14. St. Francis Borgia, a Jesuit general, is depicted with two angels holding a painting of the Madonna. Look on the lower part of the sculpture's pedestal, where you'll see the three symbols of the life of the saint: a helmet, a ducal crown, and a cardinal's hat.

15. St. John of Nepomuk was thrown to his death from this bridge, and this, the oldest sculpture on the span, was placed here to commemorate him. The bronze figure, sporting a gold-leaf halo, was completed in 1683. The bridge's sole bronze statue, St. John of Nepomuk is now green with age and worn from years of being touched for good luck.

16. This statue shows **St. Ludmilla** pointing to a Bible from which St. Wenceslas is learning to read. In her left hand, St. Ludmilla is holding the veil with which she was suffocated. The statue's relief depicts the murder of St. Wenceslas.

17. Dedicated in 1707, this statue of **St. Anthony of Padua** depicts the preacher with baby Jesus and a lily. The relief is designed around a motif inspired by the saint's life.

18. St. Francis of Assisi, the first Roman Catholic martyr to be incorporated into Bohemian liturgy, is shown here contemplatively, between two angels.

19. St. Judas Thaddeus is depicted here holding both the Gospel and the club with which he was fatally beaten.

20. St. Vincent Ferrer is depicted here boasting to **St. Procopius** of his many conversions: 8,000 Muslims and 25,000 Jews.

21. A 1974 copy of a 1708 work, the sculpture depicts church teacher **St. Augustine** holding a burning heart and walking on "heretical" books. On the pedestal there is the emblem of the Augustinians.

22. St. Nicholas of Tolentino is depicted handing out bread to the poor. Behind him is a house with a Madonna, a mangle, and

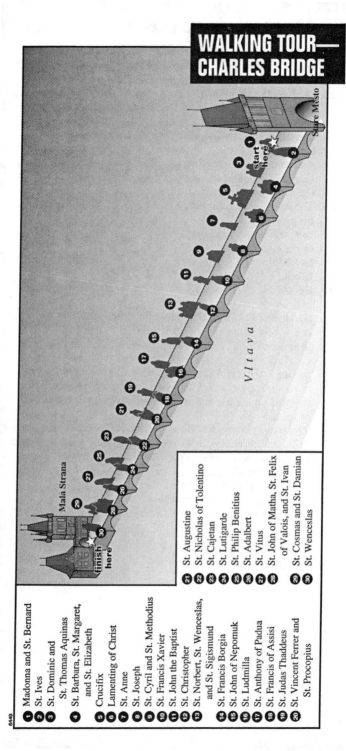

WALKING TOUR—
CHARLES BRIDGE

Stare Mesto

Start here

finish here

Mala Strana

V l t a v a

1. Madonna and St. Bernard
2. St. Ives
3. St. Dominic and St. Thomas Aquinas
4. St. Barbara, St. Margaret, and St. Elizabeth
5. Crucifix
6. Lamenting of Christ
7. St. Anne
8. St. Joseph
9. St. Cyril and St. Methodius
10. St. Francis Xavier
11. St. John the Baptist
12. St. Christopher
13. St. Norbert, St. Wenceslas, and St. Sigismund
14. St. Francis Borgia
15. St. John of Nepomuk
16. St. Ludmilla
17. St. Anthony of Padua
18. St. Francis of Assisi
19. St. Judas Thaddeus
20. St. Vincent Ferrer and St. Procopius
21. St. Augustine
22. St. Nicholas of Tolentino
23. St. Cajetan
24. St. Lutigarde
25. St. Philip Benitius
26. St. Adalbert
27. St. Vitus
28. St. John of Matha, St. Felix of Valois, and St. Ivan
29. St. Cosmas and St. Damian
30. St. Wenceslas

6449

a lantern on its top-floor balcony. Walk quickly. Legend holds that if the lantern goes out while you are passing by the statue, you will die within the year.

23. St. Cajetan stands here in front of a column of cherubs, while holding a sacred heart. Behind the statue of the saint is a triangle symbolizing the Holy Trinity.

24. Created in 1710 by 26-year-old M. B. Braun, this statue of **St. Lutigarde** is widely considered to be the most valuable sculpture on Charles Bridge. The sculpture portrays St. Lutigarde, a blind nun, seeing Christ on the cross, in order that she might kiss his wounds.

25. The only marble statue on the bridge is of **St. Philip Benitius,** the general of the Servite order. He is portrayed with a cross, a twig, and a book. The papal tiara is lying at his feet as a symbol of the saint's refusal of the papal see in 1268.

26. St. Adalbert (1709), the first bishop of Bohemia, is blessing the Czech lands after returning from Rome.

27. St. Vitus, attired as a Roman legionary, is standing on a rock between the lions to which he fell victim.

28. St. John of Matha, St. Felix of Valois, and **St. Ivan,** were commissioned for the Trinitarian order, which rescued Christians from Turkish captivity. In the huge rock is a prison, in front of which there is a dog and a Turk with a cat-o'-nine-tails guarding the imprisoned Christians. With money for their freedom, St. John is standing on the summit of the rock. St. Ivan is seated on the left and St. Felix is loosening the bonds of the prisoners.

29. This statue portrays **St. Cosmas** and **St. Damian,** the patron saints of physicians, who were known for dispensing free medical services to the poor. The saints, which were commissioned by the medical faculty in Prague, are attired in gowns and are holding containers of medicines.

30. This statue of **St. Wenceslas** was sculpted in 1858, on a commission by Prague's Klar Institute for the Blind.

PRAGUE SHOPPING

1. THE SHOPPING SCENE

2. SHOPPING A TO Z

Only since the fall of Communism has Prague been open to international retailers. But it has not taken long for shops to open and quality goods to become available. And while the city still lags far behind western European capitals for fashion and accessories, Prague offers many bargains that are unmatched elsewhere. Craft and specialty shops abound, and good deals on unique and interesting items are often found in street markets and in art studios and galleries.

---

1. THE SHOPPING SCENE

SHOPPING AREAS   Throughout Prague, you'll find artists and crafts people selling their jewelry, prints, handcrafts, and other wares. They're concentrated on Charles Bridge, in Staroměstské náměstí (Old Town Square), and on Na příkopě. "Golden Cross," a shopping district formed by Václavské náměstí (Wenceslas Square), Na příkopě, and Národní třída, is packed with shops selling Bohemian crystal, ceramics, jewelry, and souvenirs.

BEST BUYS   **Garnets** are not only the official Czech national gem, the reddish stones are among the country's top exports. Most are mined near Teplice, about 39 miles northwest of Prague. There are at least five specific kinds of garnets in the world. Bohemian garnets are of the Pyrope type, an amalgam of calcium and magnesium that's almost always deep red. For garnets set in silver, expect to pay anywhere from 200 Kč to 2,000 Kč ($6.70 to $66.70). For stones set in gold, be prepared to pay anywhere from 2,000 Kč to 40,000 Kč ($66.70 to $1,335). *Beware:* Fake garnets are common; purchase your stones from a reputable shop.

   Handmade glass is another Czech specialty. Of the country's estimated 200 artists in glass, only about a half dozen have international reputations. In addition to hand-blown functional pieces, galleries contain much unusual sculpture. The Museum of Applied Arts often exhibits glass. See "Glass/Crystal," below, for a list of Prague's most prominent glass retailers.

   Antikvariáts, shops selling **secondhand books, prints, and**

antiques, are some of the best things about Prague. They're located all over the city, but especially around Staroměstské náměstí, in Nové Město (New Town), and in Hradčany (Castle District). Although few books are in English, the occasional find makes browsing worthwhile. Several Antikvariáts are listed below.

HOURS & TAXES   Prague's centrally located shops rely on tourist business and keep fairly long hours. Most are open Monday through Saturday from about 10am to 6pm. Many open on Sunday as well, though usually for fewer hours.

Prices for goods in shops include the government's 23% value-added tax (VAT). While some European countries encourage tourists to part with their dollars by offering to refund the VAT, the Czech Republic offers no such program.

The limit on duty-free items Americans can bring back into the U.S. is $400, including one liter of alcohol. Beyond the allotted exemption, the next $1,000 worth of goods is taxed at a flat rate of 10%.

2. SHOPPING A TO Z

ANTIQUES

ANTIQUE, Panská 1, Železná 10, Praha 1. Tel. 22-06-79.

Located in a former monastery, secular silence has been replaced by the rhythmic ticking of antique pendulum clocks, table clocks, and wall clocks, all displayed amid period furniture, paintings, and porcelain. **Open:** Mon–Fri 10am–6pm, Sat 10am–2pm.

ANTIQUE SHOP ON VALDŠTEJN SQUARE, Valdštejnské náměstí 7, Praha 1.

Historical junk, some valuable, some not, is displayed in this 18th-century Renaissance house. The shop's English-speaking clerks keep the historical records of some of their holdings. **Open:** Mon–Fri 10am–6pm, Sat–Sun 10am–5pm.

AVENTIS, Jilská 20, Praha 1. Tel. 26-15-07 or 26-76-32.

A collector's heaven of Bohemian glass, art nouveau jewelry, and signed paintings, the shop is run by professional collectors who are knowledgeable about their subject. **Open:** Mon–Sat 10am–noon and 1–6pm.

JIŘÍ VANDAS, Pařížská 8, Praha 1. Tel. 231-3285.

It's amazing how many different kinds of Czechoslovak and Czech coins, medals, and paper currency have been issued over the years. The shop's extensive holdings attest to the country's continuously changing politics and economics. Even if you're just browsing, ask to see the Order of the White Lion with Sword, 1st Class—the highest Czechoslovak state medal, awarded to heads of state. Only 12 have ever been made, and theirs is priced at 390,000 Kč ($13,000). **Open:** Mon–Fri 10am–7pm, Sat 10am–6pm.

LUKAS ANTIQUES, Národní 21, Praha 1. Tel. 22-53-11.

The shop's proprietors boast 25-plus years of experience collaborating with the Czech Association of Antique Dealers. Goods range from paintings of masters of the Renaissance, baroque, and Romantic ages to rare jewelry, old glass, weapons, and porcelain. **Open:** Mon–Sat 10am–1pm and 2–6pm.

MILITARY ANTIQUES, Charvátova 11, Praha 1. Tel. 26-07-88.

Old weapons, uniforms, and army accessories are offered for sale here. The shop also deals in coins and paintings. **Open:** Daily 10am–6pm.

ART GALLERIES

CENTRAL EUROPE GALLERY AND PUBLISHING HOUSE, Husova ulice 19–21, Praha 1. Tel. 236-0700.

The gallery's a kind of clearinghouse where contemporary Czech artists sell and display their works. Its well-planned exhibitions are most always accompanied by catalogs with English-language descriptions and color reproductions.

DÍLO, Galerie Platýz, Národní 37, Praha 1.

A member of Czech Fund of Creative Arts, Dílo displays and sells works by contemporary Czech painters, sculptors, and graphic artists on a rotating basis. The gallery is located in one of the oldest apartment houses in Prague. **Open:** Mon–Fri 10am–6pm, Sat 9am–noon.

GALERIE PEITHNER-LICHENFELS, Michalská 12, Praha 1. Tel. 26-14-24.

Contemporary Czech and Austrian pieces by major artists, including Anderle, Brauer, Čapek, Crepaz, Hoffmeister, Jíra, Kubin, Valter, and Wagner. **Open:** Daily 10am–7pm.

VLASTA WASSERBAUEROVÁ–GALERIE VLASTA, Staroměstské náměstí 5, Praha 1. Tel. 231-8119.

Delicate lace, most produced by the gallery owner herself, is the primary attraction here. Filled with dainty beauty, the shop is located in Old Town Square. **Open:** Mon–Fri 10am–6pm, Sat 10am–1pm.

A+G FLORA, Štěpánská 61, Praha 1. Tel. 22-22-05.

In addition to painting and wall hangings, A+G Flora specializes in original wearable art, including clothes, accessories, and jewelry. **Open:** Mon–Fri 10am–7pm, Sat 9am–1pm.

GALLERY-BOUTIQUE VALENTINO, Hellichova 14, Praha 1. Tel. 53-54-15.

Browse the store's quality selection of ceramics, traditional Czech marionettes, and handmade clothes on your way to the garden café. **Open:** Tues–Sun 10am–6pm.

ATELIER KAVKA, Vězeňská 4, Praha 1. Tel. 232-0847.

In addition to the typical gallery fare of paintings and graphic art, this shop offers unique furniture, lights, and textiles. **Open:** Daily 10am–6pm.

BOOKS

ALBATROS, Národní třída 24 and Havelská 20, Praha 1. Tel. 54-90-06.

Both Czech- and foreign-language books are sold in the two stores, along with posters and cutouts. **Open:** Mon–Fri 9:30am–6pm, Sat 9:30am–noon.

THE GLOBE, Janovského 14, Praha 7.

Prague's only bookstore/coffeehouse opened in 1993. It stocks over 10,000 titles, and is the best place in the city for used paperback literature and nonfiction. The smart looking barroom serves espresso drinks, sandwiches, salads and desserts, and stocks a full bar. To reach The Globe, take the metro to Vltavská or tram 1, 3, 5, 8, 12, 14, 17, 25, or 26. **Open:** Daily 10am–midnight.

COSMETICS

LANTANA, Václavské náměstí 56, Praha 1. Tel. 235-9822.

In addition to cosmetic departments in the department stores (see below), full lines of international brands can be purchased at this stylish Wenceslas Square shop. **Open:** Mon–Fri 9am–7pm, Sat 9am–2pm.

DEPARTMENT STORES

KOTVA, náměstí Republiky 8, Praha 1. Tel. 235-0001 or 235-0010.

Prague's largest department store is trying to spruce up with the times, but it's tough going when you run a service-oriented business with historically unmotivated employees. There are four floors of goods, and a large supermarket in the basement. **Open:** Mon–Wed and Fri 8am–7pm, Thurs 8am–8pm, Sat 8am–4pm.

MÁJ/K-MART, Národní třída 26, Praha 1. Tel. 26-23-41.

One of Prague's oldest and largest department stores, Máj was bought recently by America's K-mart corporation. The Prague K-mart is one of 13 Czech stores now owned by the company. Sparkling display cases and Muzak have replaced drab displays and the din of mumbling shoppers. **Open:** Mon–Wed and Fri 8am–7pm, Thurs 8am–8pm, Sat 8am–4pm.

KRONE, Václavské náměstí 21, Praha 1. Tel. 26-38-42.

The largest store on Wenceslas Square, Krone sells a wide variety of goods from what seems like hundreds of departments. The store's best feature is the basement supermarket, which has a good selection at favorable prices. **Open:** Mon–Fri 8am–7pm, Sat 8:30am–1pm.

EYEGLASSES

OPTICS IN CELETNÁ–VISUS AND MALÍK, Celetná 32, Praha 1. Tel. 22-26-20.

If you look through it, it's sold here. Eyeglasses, sunglasses, telescopes, and even microscopes are available, as are saline solution and other contact-lens supplies. **Open:** Mon–Fri 9am–7pm, Sat–Sun 10am–4pm.

FASHIONS

ANO ANO, Panská 9, Praha 1. Tel. 22-76-96 or 22-05-19.

Name-brand men's and women's fashions are sold in elegant surroundings; designs are by Hugo Boss, Betty Barclay, Sabu, Esquire, and others. **Open:** Mon–Fri 10am–6pm, Sat 10am–1pm.

AQUASCUTUM, náměstí Republiky 8, Praha 1. Tel. 286-1111.

This prominent British retailer was among the first to set up shop in Prague. True to its name, which means "rain protection" in Greek, the shop sells weather-protective coats, raincoats, and suits, as well as wool skirts, shirts, and ties. **Open:** Mon–Wed and Fri 8am–7pm, Thurs 8am–8pm, Sat 8am–4pm.

CRÉATION STUMMER, Jungmannova 18, Praha 1. Tel. 26-36-31 or 26-43-49.

Here you can buy colorful children's fashions, some of which are really unique. **Open:** Mon–Fri 9am–6pm, Sat 9am–noon.

DIOR, Pařížská 7, Praha 1. Tel. 232-7382 or 232-6229.

No clothing is sold here, just novelties, perfumes, cosmetics, and accessories by such famous designers as Christian Dior and Christian Lacroix. **Open:** Mon–Fri 10am–6pm, Sat 10am–2pm.

POINT, Londýnská 81, Praha 2. Tel. 25-74-43.

It may not be politically correct in the United States, but in Prague there's no better way than fur to fight winters. Choose from mink, raccoon, and several types of fox. Leather coats, belts, bags, and gloves are also sold. **Open:** Mon–Fri 10am–6pm, Sat 10am–1pm.

GARNETS

GRANÁT TURNOV, Dlouhá třída 30, Praha 1.

Granát Turnov, the monopoly that controls the Czech Republic's garnet industry, is *the* place to visit if you're serious about shopping for garnets. Expect to pay between 600 Kč ($20) and 900 Kč ($30) for a middle-priced ring or bracelet that incorporates one of these ruby-colored jewels. **Open:** Mon–Fri 9am–5pm.

GIFTS/SOUVENIRS

DeLAURO GIFTS & INTERNATIONAL BOOKSTORE, in Betlémsk Pala, Husova 5, Praha 1. Tel. 2424-8693.

Owned by Peter Magurean, one of Prague's most important social heavyweights, DeLauro is the best place in the city for high-end stationery, gifts, and art books. Classic European keepsakes include carved wooden containers, hand-made paper, and top-of-the-line Czech gifts for the well-heeled that just can't be found anywhere else in Prague. Even if you're not looking for something in particular, stop by and say "hello" to Peter—tell him I sent you. **Open:** Mon–Sat 9am–6pm, Sun 10am–4pm.

EXCLUSIVE, Vodičkova 28, Praha 1. Tel. 2142-2586.

Bohemian glass, porcelain, jewelry, and other specialty items can be packed and shipped directly from this store. **Open:** Mon–Fri 9am–7pm, Sat–Sun 10am–6pm.

FOTOANTIQUE, Pařížská 12, Praha 1.

Original photographs by the most famous Czech photographers are sold alongside old cameras, ferrotypes, and magazines and catalogs from the beginnings of photography. **Open:** Tues–Fri 10am–6pm, Sat 9am–2pm.

KARLOVARSKÝ PORCELÁN, Na příkopě 22, Praha 1. Tel. 22-18-51.

Some of the best pieces from the 21,000 tons of decorative and domestic porcelain that are produced annually in Karlovy Vary are on display in this high-quality shop. **Open:** Mon–Fri 9am–7pm.

MUSIC PRAHA CENTER, Revoluční 14, Praha 1. Tel. 231-1693.

What better gift for the budding musician than an instrument from the land where "every Czech is a musician." Most every kind of eastern European–made stringed instrument is sold. **Open:** Mon–Fri 9am–6pm.

PRIOR MÁJ, Maiselova 16, Praha 1. Tel. 231-8447.

In the heart of the old Jewish ghetto, this small shop sells antique watches and clocks, as well as porcelain, crystal, antique typewriters, and a variety of other collectibles. **Open:** June–July, Mon–Fri 10am–noon and 2–5pm; Aug–May, Mon–Fri 9am–noon and 1–5pm.

TERRA NOVA, Jindřišská 19, Praha 1. Tel. 26-83-82.

The name means "New Land," and that's just what it is for owner

Mrs. Hubacz who reentered her Czech homeland after a 30-year absence. She sells original Czech gifts as well as specialties imported from the United States. **Open:** Mon–Fri 10am–6pm, Sat 10am–1pm.

LOUTKAMI, Nerudova 47, Malá Strana, Praha 1.

This busy shop offers what is probably the widest selection of puppets, old and new, for sale anywhere in Prague. There are many kinds of puppets, including hand, glove, rod, and marionettes. No ventriloquist dummies, however. **Open:** Mon–Sat 9am–6pm.

SPARTA SPORT STORE, Betlémské náměstí, Praha 1.

Shirts, shorts, and other clothing sporting the name "Sparta Praha," the city's most popular soccer team. **Open:** Mon–Fri 10am–6pm, Sat 10am–1pm.

FUN EXPLOSIVE, Národní 20, Praha 1. Tel. 312-1916.

Pop artist Jiří Votruba sells his whimsical designs printed on T-shirts, postcards, posters, and scarves. They're really worth checking out. **Open:** Mon–Fri 9am–6pm, Sat 10am–3pm.

GLASS/CRYSTAL

ČESKÉ SKLO A BIŽUTERIE, Křemencova 10, Praha 1. Tel. 20-35-61.

This specialized shop markets cut-glass chandeliers, as well as Czech porcelain and costume jewelry. **Open:** Mon–Sat 11am–10pm.

GALERIE BÖHM, Anglická 1, Praha 2. Tel. 236-2016.

The first gallery in Prague to focus exclusively on original works of contemporary Czech glass artists, Galerie Böhm is still the most important. Many of the best-known Czech glass artists display their works here. Exhibits change often so there's always something fresh. **Open:** Tues–Fri 2–6pm, Sat–Sun 10am–3pm.

GLASS FOR YOU, Jungmannovo náměstí 5, Praha 1. Tel. 235-5602.

This shop sells hand-cut crystal from the Bohemian Glassworks in Poděbrady as well as pieces from the glassworks in Nový Bor. Prices are high. **Open:** Mon–Fri 9:30am–7pm, Sat 9am–7:30pm, Sun 1–7pm.

MOSER, Na příkopě 12, Praha 1. Tel. 22-18-51 or 22-18-52.

The Jewish Moser family opened Prague's most prestigious crystal shop in 1857, and continued to produce their own works until the Nazis forced them to flee during World War II. Prague's Communist government nationalized the firm, but managed to retain the company's exacting standards. Even if you're not buying, the inimitable old-world shop is definitely worth a browse. **Open:** Mon–Fri 9am–7pm, Sat 9am–1pm.

HATS

MODEL, Mikulandská 2, Praha 1. Tel. 20-50-85.
In addition to the hundreds of handcrafted hats on display, the haberdashery can specially produce a topper according to your specifications in just three days. Both men's and women's hats are sold.

JEWELRY

BIJOUTERIE V JÁMĚ, V jámě 5, Praha 1. Tel. 2142-2089.
Neoclassical Czech costume jewelry, Bohemian crystal, evening bags, and hair clips are just the tip of this store's proverbial iceberg of accessories. **Open:** Mon–Fri 10am–2pm and 2:30–6pm, Sat–Sun 10am–2pm.

DUŠÁK [Watchmaker and Goldsmith], Na příkopě 17, Praha 1. Tel. 22-47-40.
Located on one of Prague's busiest shopping streets, Dušák is regarded as one of Prague's best watch shops. Noted brands, including Omega, Swatch, Raymond Weil, Pierre Balmain, Seiko, and Rado, are sold, and watches of all kinds are repaired. **Open:** Mon–Sat 9am–7pm.

S+S, Michalská 11, Praha 1. Tel. 26-13-08.
Close to Staroměstské náměstí's Astronomical Clock, this costume-jewelry shop sells baubles and bangles from all around the world. It's worth stopping in just to see the store's interesting historical architecture. **Open:** Mon–Fri 10am–7pm, Sat 11am–7pm.

MUSIC

CRAZY MUSIC SHOP, Října 8, Praha 1. Tel. 235-5811.
For a taste of Czech rock and pop, visit this hip shop, which also sells the latest Western releases. **Open:** Mon–Fri 10am–7pm, Sat 11am–7pm.

POPRON, Jungmannova 30, Praha 1. Tel. 22-30-06.
Satisfying most musical tastes, Popron offers everything from classical to contemporary, on formats ranging from vinyl to compact disc. **Open:** Mon–Fri 10am–7pm, Sat 11am–7pm.

SHOES

BUTIQUE ELISABETH, Pařížská 7, Praha 1. Tel. 232-3085.
Located on Prague's most fashionable street, Butique Elisabeth is known for its small but excellent selection of top Italian women's footwear. Ties, umbrellas, and other accessories are also sold. **Open:** Daily 10am–7pm.

SPORTING GOODS

ARMS SHOP, Národní 38, Praha 1. Tel. 22-39-21.

Eastern European sporting and hunting weapons are sold here, along with some unique shooting accessories. **Open:** Mon–Fri 8am–6pm, Sat 9am–noon.

KASTNER AND OHLER, Václavské náměstí 66, Praha 1. Tel. 236-73-61 or 22-89-85.

From track suits to skis, to in-line skates, this large sporting emporium is stocked with a wide variety of sporting essentials. **Open:** Mon–Fri 10am–6pm, Sat 10am–2pm.

PRAGUE NIGHTS

It has been said that "every Czech is a musician," and from the numerous concerts and theater performances that are scheduled in Prague at any one time, this certainly seems the case. Especially during summer, the city is so bustling with activity that on any given night you may have difficulty choosing which of the many performances to attend.

Prague's players are having their problems, though. Once well supported by the Communist state, the city's cultural entertainment companies now must fight for fewer government subsidies—and for their very existence. It seems certain that over the next couple of seasons, there will be a significant shake-up in Prague's serious music scene—one that may force less-popular companies to fold.

Turn to the two English-language newspapers *Prague Post* and *Prognosis* for listings on cultural events and nightlife around the city. *ProGram,* a Czech-language weekly with more comprehensive listings, is easy enough for non-Czechs to decipher, and is available at most metro station newsstands.

1. THE PERFORMING ARTS

Citizens of Prague have a historical love for serious music. In the 19th century, operas were received with enthusiasm, and Prague was a much-loved stop on the symphony tour. Both Mozart and Vivaldi had close relationships with Prague, which was also visited by Beethoven, Chopin, Paganini, and many other composers.

With the exception of the Czech Philharmonic, which remains top of the line by any standard, Prague's music and dance companies have declined since the 1989 revolution. Now that the best talents are allowed to leave the country, many are doing so. Singers and musicians are moving to where the money is, and Prague's operas and orchestras simply can't afford to compete with foreign companies. Don't worry, though. There are still plenty of fine players in Prague, as well as a regular supply of visiting talent.

Ticketpro (tel. 311-8780), Prague's computerized ticket service, sells seats to most events around town. You can purchase tickets by phone using your credit card (VISA, MasterCard, Diners Club, or American Express), or visit one of their many central Prague locations: PIS, Staroměstské náměstí 22; PIS, Na příkopě 20; American Hospitality Center, Na Můstku 7; Lucerna, Štěpánská 61; Melantrich, Václavské náměstí; Reduta, Národní 20; or Laterna Magika, Národní 20. You should know that tickets are sometimes—but not always—cheaper when purchased directly from theater box offices.

MAJOR PERFORMING ARTS COMPANIES

Classical-Music Orchestras and Venues

CZECH PHILHARMONIC ORCHESTRA, in the Rudolfinum, náměstí Jana Palacha, Praha 1.

Despite economic problems that have plagued the organization since the fall of Communism, Prague's most prestigious orchestra is still world-class. In addition to being seriously in debt, the orchestra is dogged by an internal controversy that led to the 1993 departure of the orchestra's conductor emeritus, Václav Neumann, after 45 years of collaboration. Still, when the orchestra is at its worst it is better than many; when in top form, it's among the very best. Catch them if you can.

Tickets: 300–400 Kč ($10–$13.35). **Metro:** Line A to Staroměstská.

PRAGUE SYMPHONY ORCHESTRA, in Smetana Hall, náměstí Republiky 5, Praha 1. Tel. 232-9164.

The city's second orchestra regularly performs in many churches around Prague, as well as outside and in select gardens during summer months. Most of their concerts are given on their home stage, Smetana Hall (Smetanova síň), at the Municipal House (Obecní dům).

Tickets: 200–300 Kč ($6.70–$10).

CONCERTS IN CHURCHES AND MUSEUMS
Many classical concerts take place in churches and museums around the city. Some of the more popular venues are listed below. Contact ticket agencies or ask at your hotel's front desk to see what is playing during your stay.

BERTRAMKA (W. A. MOZART MUSEUM), Mozartova 169, Praha 5. Tel. 54-38-93 or 54-00-12.

Intimate classical concerts featuring the music of Mozart are offered throughout the year. Music schedules vary, and although activities are clustered around warm summer months when the musicians perform in the back garden, events are planned year-round. Phone for the latest.

See Chapter 6, "What to See and Do in Prague," for information on Bertramka.

Admission: 50–200 Kč ($1.70–$6.70). **Tram:** 4, 6, 7, or 9 from Anděl metro.

CHAPEL OF MIRRORS [Klementinum], Karlova, Praha 1.

Almost every evening brings with it a different classical concert that may highlight strings, winds, or the organ. Programs are varied, but often rely on popular works by Handel, Bach, Beethoven, and, of course, Prague's beloved Mozart. Contact any of the above-listed ticket agencies for tickets and program information.

Tickets: 50–150 Kč ($1.70–$5). **Metro:** Line A to Staroměstská.

CHURCH OF ST. NICHOLAS [Kostel sv. Mikuláše], Staroměstské náměstí, Praha 1.

Built in the first half of the 18th century, St. Nicholas is one of the city's finest baroque gems. Chamber concerts and organ recitals are popular here; there are often two or more programs scheduled for the same day. Check *Prague Post* and ticket agencies for specific program information.

Tickets: 50–150 Kč ($1.70–$5). **Metro:** Line A to Staroměstská.

DVOŘÁK MUSEUM [Muzeum A. Dvořáka], Ke Karlovu 20, Praha 2. Tel. 29-82-14.

Inside this small museum, established in 1932 to honor composer Antonín Dvořák, is a beautiful baroque recital room where chamber concerts are held most evenings during the tourist season. Programs tend toward trios and quartets playing the music of Dvořák, Mozart, and other Czech-loved stars.

Theater performances are also occasionally staged here, usually in English. Check the local papers for the latest.

Tickets: 90–350 Kč ($3–$11.70). **Metro:** Line C to I. P. Pavlova.

HOUSE AT THE STONE BELL [Dům U kamenného zvonu], Staroměstské náměstí 13, Praha 1. Tel. 231-0272.

Chamber concerts and other small gigs, including operatic arias and duets, are often performed here by soloists of the National Theater and State Opera.

Tickets: 50–150 Kč ($1.70–$5). **Metro:** Line A to Staroměstská.

Theater

Theater has a long tradition of importance in Czech life. It's influence and position was reconfirmed during the revolutionary events of 1989, when theaters became the opposition's strategy rooms.

Most of the city's theater offerings are in Czech, but there are several active English-language troupes, especially during the touristy summer months. These vary annually, with the arrival and departure of touring troupes, so check the listings in the local English-language newspapers for the latest.

IMAGE BLACK LIGHT THEATRE, at Theatre Image, Pařížská 4, Praha 1. Tel. 232-9191 or 74-39-81.

Black-light theater is popular in Prague, with performances on up to six stages at any one time. The concept is simple: Actors and props coated with luminescent paint cavort under black lights that only illuminate bright objects. The result is pantomime shows packed with light comic entertainment and exceptional Houdini-esque visual tricks. Afterward, the theater transforms into a disco, and guests are invited to dance until 3am.

Tickets: 80–150 Kč ($2.70–$5). **Metro:** Line A to Staroměstská.

NATIONAL MARIONETTE THEATER [Národní divadlo marionet], Žatecká 1, Praha 1. Tel. 232-3429.

Marionette theater is a centuries-old tradition in Bohemia. One of the most popular and accessible Czech cultural treasures, puppet theater is performed in most every town in the country, and many families have collections of traditional marionettes. Charles University is the only major school in the world offering a degree in puppet-theater direction, and the National Marionette Theater was built specifically to nurture the spirit of this art form. Both the marionettes and their costumed operators are part of the action, which usually includes humor and song. Productions run the gamut from whimsical interpretations of Mozart's *Don Giovanni* to serious stagings of ancient Greek literary classics, and performances are usually scheduled nightly.

Tickets: 80–200 Kč ($2.70–$6.70).

Box Office Open: Tues–Sun 10am–8pm. **Metro:** Line A to Staroměstská.

Opera

NATIONAL OPERA, in the National Theater [Národní divadlo), Národní 2, Praha 1. Tel. 20-53-64.

In addition to hosting theatrical and symphonic events, the National Theater is also home to the country's primary opera company. Although not a particularly adventurous company, the National Opera is well regarded, and sometimes attracts internationally acclaimed soloists.

Tickets: 50–500 Kč ($1.70–$16.70). **Metro:** Line B to Národní třída.

STATE OPERA COMPANY [Státní opera], in the State Opera House, Wilsonova 4, Praha 2. Tel. 236-0642 or 26-53-53.

The State Opera Company's existence is the result of an acrimonious 1992 split with the National Opera (see above). The State Opera is slightly more flamboyant than its rival, staging grand productions of time-honored works like *Rigoletto* and *Aïda*. However, the State Opera offers popular, big-money crowd-pleasers almost exclusively.

Tickets: 50–500 Kč ($1.70–$16.70).

Box Office Open: Daily 10am–5pm, and one hour before performances. **Metro:** Line A or C to Muzeum.

Dance

CZECH BALLET THEATER, at the Palace of Culture, Května 65, Praha 4.

A new company of young dancers, the Czech Ballet Theater premiered in 1993 to critical praise. Its inspired performances mix classical and modern works.

Tickets: 200–300 Kč ($6.70–$10). **Metro:** Line C to Vyšehrad.

NATIONAL BALLET, at the National Theater (Národní divadlo), Národní 2, Praha 1. Tel. 20-53-64.

Although most of its top talent has gone west since 1989, the ballet still puts on a good show. Some critics complain that Prague's top troupe has been performing virtually the same dances for many years and that they are in serious need of refocusing. But the difficulty of attracting locals to unfamiliar works has proved insurmountable. *Swan Lake* sells out every time, while more experimental pieces are virtually ignored.

Tickets: 200–500 Kč ($6.70–$16.70). **Metro:** Line B to Národní třída.

PRAGUE FESTIVAL BALLET. Tel. 26-13-50 or 22-87-38.

Only a few years old, this troupe has already undertaken an extensive world tour featuring contemporary programs by eastern European choreographers. When in Prague, the company usually performs at the Palace of Culture in Prague 4, just outside the Vyšehrad metro station.

Tickets: 200–300 Kč ($6.70–$10).

MAJOR CONCERT HALLS & ALL-PURPOSE AUDITORIUMS

In addition to the auditoriums listed below, there are dozens of lesser showrooms in the city regularly staging concerts and theater performances. Check the local English-language newspapers and ticket agencies for up-to-date listings on current events.

ESTATES THEATER (Stavovské divadlo), Ovocný třída 6, Praha 1. Tel. 22-86-58.

In a city full of spectacularly beautiful theaters, the massive, pale green Estates ranks as one of the most awesome. Built in 1782, this is the only theater in the world that's still in its original condition from Mozart's day. The Estates was home to the premiere of Mozart's *Don Giovanni*, which was conducted by the composer himself. The building, an example of the late baroque style, was reopened on the 200th anniversary of Mozart's death in 1991, after nearly nine years of reconstruction.

Simultaneous English translation, transmitted via headphone, is available for most plays staged here.

Tickets: Plays 20–75 Kč (70¢–$2.50); operas 50–300 Kč ($1.70–$10).

Box Office Open: Mon–Fri 10am–6pm, Sat–Sun (performance days only) noon–1pm and 2:30–6pm, and half hour prior to curtain. **Metro:** Line A or B to Můstek.

LABYRINTH THEATER [Divadlo Labyrint], Štefánikova 57, Praha 5. Tel. 548-5459.

One of Prague's best alternative cultural venues, Labyrinth is a bold combination of art gallery, concert hall, legitimate theater, and acting studio. Known as the Realistic Theater in the 1980s, the playhouse presented programs that were well within the bounds of acceptable socialist realism. Labyrinth became nationally famous in 1989, when it became one of the city's main centers of revolutionary activity. Today, the theater's main hall and newer studio, which seat 400 and 100, respectively, are lit most every night for Czech-language farces and satires.

Tickets: 50–300 Kč ($1.70–$10).

Box Office Open: Daily 10am–7pm. **Tram:** 9 to Kinský Gardens (Kinského zahrada).

NATIONAL THEATER [Národní divadlo], Národní 2, Praha 1. Tel. 20-53-64.

One of Prague's most glorious landmarks, the neo-Renaissance-style National Theater, identifiable by its gold crown, hosts grand scale opera, ballet, or drama almost every night of the week.

Programs are usually scheduled at 7pm, with additional performances on Saturdays and Sundays at 2pm. See "More Attractions" in Chapter 6 for complete information on the National Theater.

The **Magic Lantern Theater** (Laterna magika) is a three-building extension of the National Theater.

Tickets: 30–300 Kč ($1–$10).

Box Office Open: Mon–Fri 10am–8pm, Sat–Sun noon–8pm. **Metro:** Line B to Národní třída.

PALACE OF CULTURE [Palác kultury], Května 65, Praha 4. Tel. 417-2711.

Prague's largest showhouse stages anything and everything from classical to rock to opera. Each June, the Palace becomes one of the main venues for the AghaRTA Festival, a contemporary music fair named for the local jazz club that hosts it.

Tickets: 50–300 Kč ($1.70–$10).

Box Office Open: Mon–Fri 10am–6pm, Sat–Sun noon–6pm, and half hour prior to curtain. **Metro:** Line C to Vyšehrad.

RUDOLFINUM, náměstí Jana Palacha, Praha 1.

Named for Prince Rudolf, and home to the Czech Philharmonic (see above), the beautifully restored Rudolfinum has been one of the city's premier concert venues since it opened in the 19th century. The Rudolfinum's aptly named Little Hall mostly presents chamber concerts, while the larger, more celebrated Dvořák Hall is home to the Czech Philharmonic Orchestra; its first all-Dvořák program was played here in 1896. When the Philharmonic vacations, Dvořák Hall hosts visiting performers that sometimes include notables like Polish pianist Emanuel Ax and Leonard Slatkin, conductor of the St. Louis Orchestra.

Tickets: 50–350 Kč ($1.70–$11.70).

Box Office Open: Mon–Fri 10am–5pm, Sat 11am–5pm, and half hour before show time. **Metro:** Line A to Staroměstská.

SMETANA HALL [Smetanova síň], at the Municipal House (Obecní dům), náměstí Republiky 5, Praha 1. Tel. 232-2501 or 231-9164.

Named for Bedřich Smetana (1824–84), a popular composer and fervent Czech nationalist, Smetana Hall is home to the Prague Symphony in summer, and a host of performances by others throughout the year. The hall itself is located within the Municipal House (Obecní dům), one of the most distinctive art nouveau buildings in town (see Chapter 6, "What to See and Do in Prague," for complete information).

Tickets: 100–300 Kč ($3.35–$10).

Box Office Open: Mon–Sat 8am–8pm, Sun noon–5pm. **Metro:** Line B to náměstí Republiky.

STATE OPERA HOUSE [Státní opera], Wilsonova 4, Praha 2. Tel. 236-0642 or 236-4625.

Originally called the New German Theater, then the Smetana Theater, the State Opera was built in the 1880s for the purpose of staging Germanic music and drama. Based on a Viennese design, the Renaissance-style theater was painstakingly rebuilt after suffering serious damage during the bombing of Prague in 1945. Over the years, the auditorium has hosted many great names, including Richard Wagner, Richard Strauss, and Gustav Mahler, whose Seventh Symphony premiered here. In addition to being home to the State Opera, the house stages other music and dance events.

Tickets: 50–500 Kč ($1.70–$16.70).

Box Office Open: Mon–Fri 10am–5pm, Sat 11am–5pm, and half hour before show time. **Metro:** Line A and C to Muzeum.

VINOHRADY THEATER [Divadlo na Vinohradech], náměstí Míru 7, Praha 2. Tel. 25-70-41.

Because it's just outside center city and rarely, if ever, stages English-language productions, the fantastically ornamented art nouveau-style Vinohrady Theater is often overlooked by tourists. It shouldn't be. Built in 1907, the building is one of the city's finest, and the players are some of the country's most gifted. Originally constructed as a legitimate theater, the Vinohrady is still restricted to plays, most every one of which is in the Czech language.

Tickets: 50-350 Kč ($1.70-$11.70).

Box Office Open: Mon-Fri 10am-5pm, and 30 minutes before performances. **Metro:** Line A to náměstí Míru.

2. THE CLUB & MUSIC SCENE

The Prague club and music scene is limited but lively. Each summer, several top international names stop here on tours of Europe, but these events are relatively few and far between. Excellent Czech musicians and bands perform around town almost nightly, and are definitely worth checking out. Rockers to look out for include Ecstasy of St. Theresa, the first Czech band ever to breach the Western music charts; Lucie Bílá, the current darling of the Czech music press and the first Czech to have a video aired on MTV Europe; Support Lesbians, a kind of postpunk quintet; and Vladimír Mišik, a lively folk rocker who opened for the Rolling Stones when they played here in 1990.

ROCK & DANCE CLUBS

BORÁT, Újezd 18, Praha 1. Tel. 53-83-62.

Under Communism, this multilevel house was the best "underground" club. After November 1989, this living room-size place went legit, becoming at once both more mainstream and less interesting. There's a snug dance floor and a snugger stage on which live bands perform three to four nights each week. The music usually kicks in about 9pm.

Admission: 30 Kč ($1).

Open: Tues-Thurs and Sun 6pm-2am, Fri-Sat 6pm-6am. **Tram:** 12 or 22 from Malostranská metro station.

BUNKR, Lodecká 2, Praha 1. Tel. 231-4535.

A long, deep basement that once was a 1950s Civil Guard bunker and nuclear shelter, club Bunkr opened in November 1991, followed a few months later by a like-named street-level café. Despised by its neighbors, the club features loud DJ nights and a plethora of live bands. Owner Richard Nemčok has honest credentials; he was jailed by the socialists and signed Charter 77, before immigrating to the U.S. in 1981. Packed with lots of young twentysomething European tourists, Bunkr is sometimes laughed at by knowledgeable locals. Still it's hard to argue with its success; Havel has been spotted here, and every time I'm here I have a lot of fun. Music usually starts at 9pm.

Admission: 20–70 Kč (70¢–$2.35).

Open: Café, daily 11am–3am; club, daily 6pm–5am. **Metro:** Line B to náměstí Republiky.

LÁVKA, Novotného lávka 1, Praha 1. Tel. 22-82-34.

Because of its location, next to the Staré Město foot of Charles Bridge, Lávka attracts a lot of tourists. This is not such a bad thing, however, because this club is also one of the nicest in town, offering a large bar, good dance floor, and fantastic outdoor seating. Straightforward dance hits attract a good-looking young crowd.

Admission: 40–60 Kčs ($1.35–$2).

Open: Daily 9pm–4am. **Metro:** Line A to Staroměstská.

MALOSTRANSKÁ BESEDA, Malostranské náměstí 21, Praha 1. Tel. 53-86-51 or 53-90-24.

This Beseda, or "meeting place," on Malá Strana's main square is located in a building that was once the area's town hall. Situated on the second floor of the arcaded side of the square, the club consists of little more than two smallish rooms; one holds the bar, the other a stage on which live bands perform most every night. Music usually begins at 8pm. Although this is not the best place to hang out, it's hard to beat when a good band is playing.

Admission: 20–30 Kč (70¢–$1); free after 11pm.

Open: Daily 7pm–1am. **Tram:** 12 or 22 from Malostranská metro station.

RADOST F/X, Bělehradská 120, Praha 2. Tel. 25-12-10 or 25-89-38.

Popular with a very mixed gay and model crowd, Radost is built in the American mold; a subterranean labyrinth of nooks and crannies, and a pulsating dance floor with good sightlines for wallflowers. It's worth going just to stare at the spectacular painting hanging over the back bar.

Radost's vegetarian café of the same name, upstairs, is usually combined with a trip to the club, and listed separately in Chapter 5.

Admission: 40–50 Kč ($1.35–$1.70).

Open: Daily 9pm–5am. **Metro:** Line C to I. P. Pavlova.

REPRE, in the Municipal House (Obecní dům), náměstí Republiky 5, Praha 1. Tel. 231-8084.

Prague's club-of-the-moment is also the best. Hidden in the basement of the Municipal House, the cavernous club consists of two rooms: a couch- and chair-filled bar and a rathskellerlike beer hall, where bands perform and dance discs spin. My friends Leora and

Thatcher swear that the club is permeated by some kind of sex gas—a vapor that destroys inhibitions, and from what I've seen here, I almost believe them.

Admission: 30 Kč ($1) on concert nights; 20 Kč (70¢) other times.

Open: Daily 9pm–5am. **Metro:** Line B to náměstí Republiky.

JAZZ

AGHARTA JAZZ CENTRUM, Krakovská 5, Praha 1. Tel. 22-45-58.

Relatively high prices guarantee this small jazz room a predominantly foreign clientele. Upscale by Czech standards, the AghaRTA jazzery regularly features some of the best music in town, running the gamut from standard acoustic trios to Dixieland, to funk and fusion. Hot Line, the house band led by AghaRTA part-owner and drummer extraordinaire Michael Hejuna, regularly takes its keyboard-and-sax Crusaders-like sound to this stage. Bands usually begin at 9pm.

Admission: 40–50 Kč ($1.35–$1.70).

Open: Daily 8pm–midnight. **Metro:** Line A and C to Muzeum.

CAFE NOUVEAU'S MARTINI BAR, in the Municipal House (Obecní dům), náměstí Republiky 5, Praha 1. Tel. 231-8084.

American-owned Café Nouveau's balcony-level Martini Bar overlooks a large dining room in which a jazz band usually performs. When you're tired of the clamor, retreat to the back room pool table.

Admission: Free.

Open: Daily 6pm–2am. **Metro:** Line B to náměstí Republiky.

REDUTA JAZZ CLUB, Národní 20, Praha 1. Tel. 20-38-25.

Reduta is a smoky subterranean jazz room that looks exactly like a jazz cellar is supposed to look. An adventurous booking policy means different bands playing almost every night of the week. Music usually starts around 9:30pm.

Admission: 80 Kč ($2.70).

Open: Mon–Sat 9pm–2am. **Metro:** Line B to Národní třída.

3. THE BAR SCENE

PUBS/BEER HALLS

U BONAPARTA, Nerudova 29. Tel. 53-97-80.

Don't let the climb uphill to this restaurant deter you; this is one of the better beer bars in the Malá Strana. Smoky and boisterous,

Bonaparta's three rooms are often filled with drinkers who snack on the pub's mediocre sausages.

Open: Daily 10am–midnight. **Metro:** Line A to Malostranská.

U FLEKŮ, Křemencova 11. Tel. 29-32-46.

Originally a brewery dating back to 1459, U Fleků is Prague's most famous beer hall, and the only one that still brews its own beer. It's a huge place with a myriad of timber-lined rooms and a large, loud courtyard where an oompah band performs. The ornately decorated medieval-style wood ceilings and courtyard columns are charming, but not very old. The recipe for U Fleků's special dark beer is the real thing, and very good as well. It's not available anywhere else; they brew only enough to service their own restaurant. Sausages, goulash, and other traditional foods are served, but not recommended.

Admission: Free; 30 Kč ($1) to the garden when the band performs.

Open: Daily 10am–midnight. **Metro:** Line B to Národní třída.

VELRYBA ["The Whale"], Opatovická 24, Praha 1. Tel. 2491-2391.

Velryba was opened in July 1992 as a Czech literary café and quickly caught on with the city's intellectuals and theater types. Sort of down and dirty, the pub has become one of Prague's trendiest cafés; a "real" place that doesn't particularly appreciate foreign tourists. In addition to café drinks, Velryba serves well-priced pasta and Czech dishes.

Open: Daily 11am–2am. **Metro:** Line B to Národní třída.

GAY BARS & CLUBS

The Czech Republic's Association of Organizations of Homosexual Citizens, abbreviated SOHO (tel. 25-78-91), was founded in 1991 as an umbrella organization uniting several smaller gay organizations. *SOHO Magazine,* available at larger newsstands around the city, lists nightspots and events. The weekly entertainment guide *Pro-Gram* also includes listings for gays, though it only amounts to one page every other week.

CLUB AMERICA, Petřínská 5, Smíchov.

Started by an American expatriate and his Czech partner in hopes of revitalizing Prague's gay nightlife, America was gay Prague's postrevolution toast of the town—until newer clubs grabbed the spotlight.

Admission: 30 Kč ($1).

Open: Mon–Thurs 8:30pm–4am, Fri–Sun 8:30pm–5am. **Tram:** 12 or 22 from Malostranská metro station.

CLUB DAVID, Sokolovská 77, Praha 8.

One of the brightest spots of 1993, David's cellar dance floor is packed most every night of the week with both Czechs and visitors.
Admission: 20 Kč (70¢), with a 30 Kč ($1) drink minimum.
Open: Daily 8:30pm–5am. **Metro:** Line B to Křižikova.

MERCURY, Kolínská 11, Vinohrady.

Another hot club-of-the-moment, Mercury is a contemporary disco and restaurant named for the late rocker Freddie Mercury. Compact and ultramodern, the club packs up to 200 revelers on weekends.
Admission: 25 Kč (85¢).
Open: Daily 7:30pm–6am. **Metro:** Line B to Křižikova.

WHISKEY CLUB OLD ENGLAND, Šafaříkova 6, Praha 2.

Opened in July 1993, this small, nook-and-cranny-packed bar contains an intimate dance floor and a telephone at every table through which callers can ring up other diners for a dance. The club caters equally to men and women.
Admission: Free; beer 35 Kč ($1.20).
Open: Daily 24 hours. **Metro:** Line C to I. P. Pavlova.

4. MORE ENTERTAINMENT

READINGS

You've learned that Prague is the Left Bank of the 90s, but where are the bohemian writers and poets? Many come out of the woodwork weekly at the **Beefstew Readings,** held every Sunday from 6 to 9pm at Radost F/X, Bělehradská 120, Praha 2 (tel. 25-12-10 or 25-89-38), a basement nightclub near the I. P. Pavlova metro station. Started in 1992 by a visiting American writer, the readings have become a kind of expatriate institution, attracting up to 100 poets, novelists, and songsters per week. Everyone is welcome and admission is free.

MOVIES

In the Czech Republic, foreign films are generally screened in the original language, with Czech subtitles. Most cinemas in the city center show Hollywood-style movies exclusively. Many others show "smaller" American films, Czech films, and other international features. Most every theater offers just two screenings daily; typically at 5:30 and 8pm. Check the (sometimes unreliable) newspapers and phone the theaters for the latest.

First-run Films

Many of city's major centrally located cinemas are on or near Václavské náměstí (Wenceslas Square). Most screen major American and European releases in their original languages with Czech subtitles. The largest cinemas are listed below.

Alfa, Václavské náměstí 28, Praha 1. Tel. 22-07-24. Metro: Line A or B to Můstek.

Blaník, Václavské náměstí 56, Praha 1. Tel. 235-2162. Metro: Line A or C to Muzeum.

DIF Centrum—Kinokavárna, Václavské náměstí 43, Praha 1. Tel. 26-46-88. Metro: Line A or B to Můstek.

Kotva, náměstí Republiky 8, Praha 1. Tel. 231-3639. Metro: Line B to náměstí Republiky.

Lucerna, Vodičkova 36, Praha 1. Tel. 235-2648. Metro: Line A or B to Můstek.

Paříž, Václavské náměstí 22, Praha 1. Metro: Line A or B to Můstek.

Pasáž, Václavské náměstí 5, Praha 1. Tel. 235-5040. Metro: Line A or B to Můstek.

Sevastopol, Na příkopé 31, Praha 1. Tel. 26-43-28. Metro: Line A or B to Můstek.

Světozor, Vodičkova 39, Praha 1. Tel. 26-36-16. Metro: Line A or B to Můstek.

Alternative & Repertory Movie Houses

Miš Maš, Veletržní 61, Praha 7 (tel. 37-92-78), shows the only late-night movies in Prague. There are usually two shows, at 8 and 10pm, with additional midnight showings added on weekends. The bar stays open throughout the movie, which is usually an offbeat, independent American release.

Dlabačov, Bělohorská 24, Praha 6 (tel. 311-5328), screens alternative films from September to February, before reverting to more mainstream features. Tickets cost 15 Kč to 20 Kč (50¢ to 70¢).

Ponrepo, Národní 40, Praha 1 (tel. 26-05-55 or 26-00-87), one of the city's newest film clubs, opened on January 3, 1993, to commemorate the 50th anniversary of the National Film Archives, where it is located. Films are screened here twice daily. There is also a silent-movie theater, where images are presented with live music every Monday at 7pm. Membership is required, and costs 120 Kč ($4) for adults, 80 Kč ($2.70) for students. Tickets are another 15 Kč (50¢).

CASINOS

There are many casinos in Prague, most offering the same games (always blackjack and roulette). **Casino de France,** in the Hotel Atrium, Pobřežní 1, also offers slot machines and poker. It's open daily from 2pm to 6am (metro: line B or C to Florenc). **Casino Palais Savarin,** Na příkopé 10, occupying a former rococo palace, is the most beautiful gameroom in the city. My friend Nico Lowry won a car here. It's open daily from 6pm to 3am (metro: line A or B to Můstek).

EASY EXCURSIONS FROM PRAGUE

1. KARLŠTEJN (KARLSTEIN) & KUTNÁ HORA
2. KARLOVY VARY (CARLSBAD)
3. MARIÁNSKÉ LÁZNĚ (MARIENBAD)
4. ČESKÉ BUDĚJOVICE
5. ČESKÝ KRUMLOV
6. TEREZÍN

Just as New York is not representative of the entire United States, and London does not embody all England, Prague is quite different from nearby towns. Even if you don't have much time, try to spend a day outside the city to explore the countryside. If you can spare a few days, there are several not-too-distant Bohemian destinations that are really worth a trip.

Most destinations listed below are accessible from Prague by train. It's important that you know from which of Prague's several stations your train is departing; these change, so check with **Čedok,** Na příkopě 18 or Václavské náměstí 24 (tel. 212-7512). Long-haul trains in the Czech Republic are very popular, especially in summer and on Friday and Sunday evenings, so although seats can be purchased up until the moment of departure, prebooking is recommended. If you want a couchette, it's always advisable to make your reservations several days in advance.

Because trains often follow circuitous routes, bus transportation can be a better option. There's a pretty good bus system operating in the Czech Republic. State-run ČSAD buses are relatively inexpensive, surprisingly abundant, and offer terrific coverage of the country. Prague's main bus station is located above the Florenc metro stop (line C). Unfortunately, few employees speak English there, making it a bit tricky for non-Czech speakers to obtain schedule information. If you have some time before you depart Prague, your best bet for bus information and tickets is to visit **ČSAD Travel Agency,** Na příkopě 31 (tel. 236-5332), in Sevastopol Passage or **Bohemia Tour,** Zlatnická 7 (tel. 232-3877). Neither agency charges an additional fee for their services, and both are open Monday through Friday from 9am to 5pm.

Students should always show identification cards and ask for discounts. They are sometimes, but not always, available on buses, trains, and even planes.

ORGANIZED DAY TOURS

Central European Adventures, Staroměstské náměstí 1, Praha 1 (tel. 22-44-53), offers several one-day adventure tours in the Bohemi-

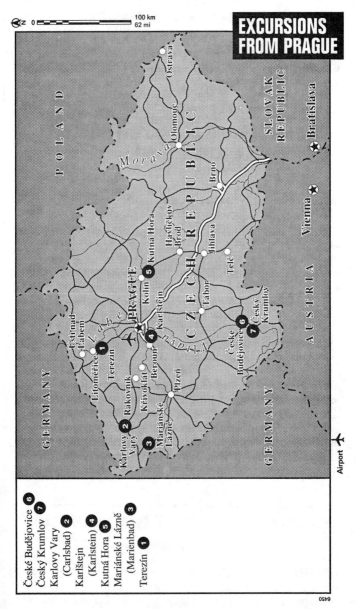

an countryside from May to September. Their bicycle tour around Karlštejn includes bus transportation from Prague and admission to Koneprusy Cave. The tour costs 600 Kč ($20), and departs from the Staroměstské náměstí (Old Town Square) office daily except Monday at 8:40am. A canoe tour of a mild 10-mile stretch of the nearby Berounka River departs every Saturday and Sunday and includes life jackets and lunch. It costs 700 Kč ($23.35) per person. The company also offers guided countryside hikes, that include bus transportation from and to Prague, and light refreshments. Hikes depart on Saturdays only, at 8:40am from the company's Staroměstské náměstí office; phone or stop-in for complete information.

1. KARLŠTEJN (KARLSTEIN) & KUTNÁ HORA

Medieval **Karlštejn castle,** located 17 miles southwest of Prague, was founded in 1348 by Charles IV. It hasn't changed much since. Probably the most popular short trip from Prague, this dramatic castle was once the Royal Treasury. It is more spectacular from the outside than it is from the inside, which is only accessible by guided tour. Tours are offered Tuesday through Sunday from 9am to 7pm, and cost 20 Kč (65¢). Trains depart from Prague's Smíchov Station hourly throughout the day and take about 40 minutes to reach Karlštejn.

Kutná Hora, a medieval town that grew fantastically rich from the silver deposits beneath it, is probably the second most popular day trip from Prague. Small enough to be seen in a single day at a brisk pace, the town's ancient heart is much decayed, but it is also mercifully free of the ugly Communist-era functionalist-style buildings that plague many of the country's small towns. Kutná Hora's main draw is the macabre Bone Church (Kostnice), filled with human bones assembled in bizarre sculptures. It's located a mile up the road in Sedlec; board a local bus on Masarykova street. Kutná Hora is best reached by bus, which departs from the terminal at Prague's Želivského metro station, and takes about 90 minutes.

2. KARLOVY VARY (CARLSBAD)

75 miles W of Prague

GETTING THERE By Train Avoid the train from Prague, which takes over four hours on a circuitous route. If you're arriving from another direction, you'll want to know that Karlovy Vary's main train station is connected to the town center by bus no. 13.

By Bus Frequent express buses make the trip from Prague's Florenc station to Karlovy Vary's Horakova náměstí in about 2½ hours. The trip costs 53 Kč ($1.80) each way. Take a 10-minute walk or local bus no. 4 into Karlovy Vary's town center.

ESSENTIALS Karlovy Vary's **telephone area code** is 017. All phone numbers in this section assume this prefix, unless otherwise noted.

INFORMATION There are two privately run **Info-Centrum** booths in Karlovy Vary: one in the train station and the other in a parking lot at the base of Jana Palacha ulice. Both give away free maps and a brochure of current cultural listings and events called Promenáda. Info-Centrum also books accommodations in private rooms and sells tours.

ORIENTATION Karlovy Vary is shaped like a T with the Teplá River running up the stem and the Ohře River at the top of the T. Most of the major streets here are pedestrian promenades lining both sides of the Teplá River.

Famous for its thermal spas, Karlovy Vary (Carlsbad) attracts over 80,000 people each year, who come here specifically for a spa treatment lasting two weeks or more. Tens of thousands of others come just for a day or two. In addition to the health spas, the area offers rural beauty. There are about 60 miles of walking paths around the hills and woods surrounding Karlovy Vary, and those taking the cure often enjoy lengthy strolls there. The town's many pedestrian promenades, lined with turn-of-the-century art nouveau buildings, are also truly beautiful.

WHAT TO SEE & DO

Spa Cures

Most visitors to Karlovy Vary come for the specific reason of getting a spa treatment, a therapy that lasts one to three weeks. After consulting with a spa physician, guests are given a specific regimen of activities that may include mineral baths, massages, waxings, mud packs, electrotherapy, and pure oxygen inhalation. The common denominator of all the cures is an ample daily dose of hot mineral water, which bubbles up from 12 different springs. After spending the morning at a spa, or sanatorium, guests are usually directed to walk the paths of the town's surrounding forest.

The minimum treatment lasts one week and must be arranged in advance. For information and reservations in the United States, contact **Čedok,** 10 E. 40th St., New York, NY 10016 (tel. 212/689-9720). For information and reservations in Prague contact **Čedok,** Na příkopě 18 or Václavské náměstí 24 (tel. 212-7512). Rates, which traditionally include room, full board, and complete therapy regimen, vary from about $40 to $100 per person per day, depending on season and facilities. Rates are lowest from November through February, and highest from May through September.

Visitors to Karlovy Vary for just a day or two can experience the waters on an "outpatient" basis. The **State Baths III** (tel. 017/256-41) welcomes day-trippers with mineral baths, massages, saunas, and a cold pool. They're open for men on Tuesday, Thursday, and Saturday, and for women on Monday, Wednesday, and Friday from 7:45am to 3pm. **Vojenský lázeňský ustav,** Mlýnské nábřeží 7 (tel. 017/222-06), offers similar services, and costs about 750 Kč ($25) per day.

SHOPPING

Crystal and porcelain are Karlovy Vary's other claims to fame. There are dozens of shops throughout the town selling everything from plates to chandeliers. Ludvík Moser first founded his first glassware shop in 1857, and became one of this country's foremost names in glass. You can visit the **Moser Factory,** kapitána Jaroše 19 (tel. 41-61-11), just west of the town center (take bus no. 1, 10, or 16). It's open Monday through Friday only, from 7:30am to 3:30pm. The **Moser Store,** Stará Louka 40, is right in the heart of town, and open Monday through Friday from 9am to 5pm.

WHERE TO STAY

For quality and price, private rooms are the best places to stay in Karlovy Vary. Arrange your room through **Info-Centrum** (see above) or **Čedok,** Karla IV č. 1 (tel. 017/261-10 or 267-05; fax 017/278-35). The office is open Monday through Friday from 9am to 5pm and on Saturday from 9am to noon. Expect to pay about 300 Kč ($10) for a single and 500 Kč ($16.35) for a double.

Unless they're particularly poorly occupied, the town's major spa hotels only accommodate those who are paying for complete treatments. The following hotels will accept guests for any length of time.

Moderate

GRAND HOTEL PUPP, Mírové náměstí 2, 36091 Karlovy Vary. Tel. 017/209-111. Fax 017/240-32. Telex 156220. 358 rms (all with shower or bath). TV TEL

$ Rates (including breakfast): 2,300 Kč ($76.70) single with shower; 4,000 Kč ($135) double with shower, 6,000 Kč ($200) double with bath. 25% discounts Nov–Apr (except Christmastime). AE, DC, MC, V.

Well known as one of Karlovy Vary's best hotels, Grand Hotel Pupp, built in 1701, is also one of Europe's oldest. While the hotel's public areas are oozing with splendor and charm, the guest rooms are not as

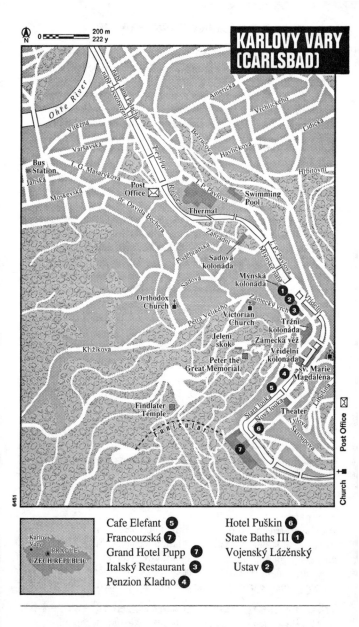

KARLOVY VARY (CARLSBAD)

Cafe Elefant ⑤
Francouzská ⑦
Grand Hotel Pupp ⑦
Italský Restaurant ③
Penzion Kladno ④

Hotel Puškin ⑥
State Baths III ①
Vojenský Lázeňský
  Ustav ②

---

consistent in their enchantment. The best rooms have good views, sturdy wooden furniture, and plenty of intrinsic appeal.

Inexpensive

PENZION KLADNO, Stará Louka č. 2, 36001 Karlovy Vary. Tel. 017/251-95. 22 rms (3 with bath). TEL

$ Rates (including breakfast): 500 Kč ($16.35) single without bath; 600 Kč ($20) double without bath, 900 Kč ($30) double with bath. No credit cards.

Located just 150 feet from a hot spring, this basic hotel, in a beautiful 19th-century building, is very clean, well maintained, and quiet. Many rooms have balconies overlooking a major promenade.

HOTEL PUŠKIN, Tržiště 37, 36001 Karlovy Vary. Tel. 017/226-46 or 221-93. 20 rms (none with bath). **Bus:** 11 from the train or bus station.

$ Rates (including breakfast): 700 Kč ($24.35) single or double. No credit cards.

Named for the great Russian poet we know as Pushkin, this hotel occupies an intricately ornamented 19th-century building. The building shows its age, and rooms are rather basic, but they are comfortable enough, and terrifically located, close to the springs.

WHERE TO DINE

CAFE ELEFANT, Stará Louka 32. Tel. 234-06.
 Cuisine: CAFE.
$ Prices: Cakes 10–30 Kč (35¢–$1).
 Open: Daily 9am–10pm.

Not a restaurant, but a café, Elefant is widely known for its belle époque style that includes pink walls and mirrors. Famous for freshly baked cakes, the café has a large number of outdoor tables overlooking the pedestrian promenade.

FRANCOUZSKÁ, in the Grand Hotel Pupp, Mírové náměstí 2. Tel. 221-21.
 Cuisine: CONTINENTAL. **Reservations:** Recommended.
$ Prices: Appetizers 25–55 Kč (85¢–$1.85); main courses 125–300 Kč ($4.15–$10). 15% service and cover charge. AE, DC, MC, V.
 Open: Daily noon–10pm.

It's no surprise that the Grand Hotel Pupp has the nicest dining room in town, an elegant eatery with tall ceilings, huge mirrors, and glistening chandeliers. A large menu gives way to larger portions of chicken, veal, pork, turkey, and beef in a variety of heavy and heavier sauces. Even the trout with mushrooms is prepared in a butter sauce.

ITALSKÝ RESTAURANT, Zámecký Vrch 14. Tel. 291-97.
 Cuisine: ITALIAN/CZECH. **Reservations:** Accepted.
$ Prices: Appetizers 30–50 Kč ($1–$1.65); main courses 60–100 Kč ($2–$3.35). AE, MC, V.
 Open: Lunch daily 11:30am–3pm; dinner daily 6–10pm.

When you get tired of roasted meats and dumplings, this atypical restaurant saves the day with giant-size portions of soups, salads, pastas, and pizzas. Traditional Bohemian fare is also always available.

3. MARIÁNSKÉ LÁZNĚ [MARIENBAD]

29 miles SW of Karlovy Vary, 100 miles W of Prague

GETTING THERE   By Train   The express train from Prague takes just over three hours, and costs 105 Kč ($3.50) in first class, 70 Kč ($2.35) in second class. Mariánské Lázně train station, Nádražní náměstí 292 (tel. 5321), is located south of the town center; take bus no. 5 into town.

By Bus   The bus from Prague takes about 3½ hours and costs about 60 Kč ($2). The Mariánské Lázně bus station is situated adjacent to the train station on Nádražní náměstí; take bus no. 5 into town.

ESSENTIALS   Mariánské Lázně's **telephone area code** is 0165; all phone numbers in this section assume this prefix, unless otherwise noted.

INFORMATION   City Service, at Hlavní třída 1 (tel. and fax 0165/4218 or 3816), on the town's main street, just across from the Hotel Bohemia, is the best place for information. In addition to dispensing advice, they sell maps and arrange accommodations in hotels and private homes. They're open Monday through Friday from 7am to 7pm, and on Saturday and Sunday from 9am to 6pm.

ORIENTATION   Geographically, there's not much to Mariánské Lázně, which is laid out around Hlavní třída, the main street. Several hotels, restaurants, travel agencies, and stores front this street. Lázeňska Colonnade, a long, covered block beginning at the northern end of Hlavní třída, contains six of the resort's eight major springs.

Smaller, and slightly less touristed then neighboring Karlovy Vary, Mariánské Lázně (Marienbad) is the Czech Republic's second most famous spa town. Nestled among forested hills and packed with romantic and elegant pastel hotels and spa houses, the town's 19th-century heyday meant frequent visits from European royalty. Today, Mariánské Lázně is frequented predominantly by older Germans looking for beauty, comfort, and cures. Note that all spas here are closed on Sunday.

WHAT TO SEE & DO

CITY MUSEUM [Muzeum Hlavního Msta], Goethovo náměstí 11. Tel. 2740.

There's not much to the history of Mariánské Lázně; the town only began in 1805, when the first house was built here. But engaging brevity is what makes this two-story museum recommendable. Chronologically arranged displays include photos and documents of famous visitors including Frédéric Chopin, Thomas Edison, and Mark Twain. Goethe slept here, in the upstairs rooms in 1823, when he was 74 years old. If you ask nicely, the museum guards will play an English-language tape that describes the contents of each of the museum's rooms. You can also request to see the museum's English-language film about the town.

Admission: 15 Kč (50¢).

Open: Tues–Sun 9am–4pm. **Directions:** Walk one block east from Kreuzbrunnen Colonnade.

KREUZBRUNNEN COLONNADE, off Skalníkovy sady.

The eye-catching cast-iron and glass Kreuzbrunnen Colonnade, adorned with ceiling frescoes and Corinthian columns, is the main strip for spagoers. Built in 1889, the colonnade connects a half-dozen major springs. Visitors dip cups in the springs and drink their "liquid health."

For a relaxing mineral bubble bath or massage, make reservations through the State Spa Office, Masarykova 22 (tel. 2170). Treatments cost anywhere from 300 Kč to 900 Kč ($10 to $30) each.

Admission: Free.

Open: Daily 24 hours; water distributed daily 6am–noon and 4–6pm. **Bus:** 3 or 5. **Directions:** From Hlavní třída, walk east on Vrchlického ulice.

WHERE TO STAY

There are many hotels in Mariánské Lázně. If you feel comfortable enough to do so, my best advice is to walk along Hlavní třída, the main street, and take your pick of rooms from over a dozen hotels; most charge from 900 Kč to 1,500 Kč ($30 to $50) for a double.

Moderate

HOTEL PALACE, Hlavní třída 67, 35301 Mariánské Lázně.
Tel. 0165/2222. Fax 0165/4262. 73 rms, 9 suites. TV TEL MINIBAR **Bus:** 5 from the train or bus station.
$ Rates: 1,500 Kč ($50) single; 3,000 Kč ($100) double; from 3,300 Kč ($110) suite. AE, DC, MC, V.

One of the top hotels in town, the 1920s-era Palace is a beautiful art nouveau–style hotel located just 300 feet from the spa colonnade. While rooms are far from international standard, they are extremely comfortable, and contain direct-dial telephones, TVs, and minibars. In addition to a good Bohemian restaurant, the hotel contains a café, wine room, and snack bar.

Inexpensive

HOTEL CORSO, Hlavní třída 61, 35301 Mariánské Lázně.
Tel. 0165/3091 or 3092. Fax 0165/3093. 27 rms (4 with full

bath, 6 with shower but no toilet). TV TEL **Bus:** 5 from the train or bus station.

$ Rates: 400 Kč ($13.10) single without bath; 650 Kč ($22) double without bath, 775 Kč ($25.85) double with shower but no toilet, 1,000 Kč ($33.35) double with full bath. Showers 100 Kč ($3.35) extra. AE, DC, MC, V.

The dignified Corso is not the most beautiful in town, but it's hard to beat its location, on the main street in the very heart of town. Rooms are basic and clean, and some in front have balconies overlooking the street. The US Club restaurant on the ground floor serves Bohemian food along with rock videos.

HOTEL CRISTAL PALACE, Hlavní třída 61, 35344 Mariánské Lázně. Tel. 0165/2056 or 2057. Fax 0165/2058. 94 rms (4 with bath). **Bus:** 5 from the train or bus station.

$ Rates: 500 Kč ($16.65) single without bath; 1,000 Kč ($33) double without bath, 1,500 Kč ($48.35) double with bath; 1,300 Kč ($43.65) triple without bath. AE, DC, MC, V.

Neither "cristal" nor a palace, this decent hotel enjoys an enviable location just a few minutes south of the town center. Rooms are outfitted with 1950s-style furnishings and double doors to screenout hallway noise. The hotel contains a restaurant, café, wine room, and brasserie.

WHERE TO DINE

Moderate

HOTEL PALACE RESTAURANT, Hlavní třída 67. Tel. 2222. Cuisine: CZECH. **Reservations:** Recommended.

$ Prices: Soups 10–40 Kč (35¢–$1.35); main courses 140–320 Kč ($4.60–$10.65). AE, DC, MC, V.

Open: Daily 7am–11pm.

The restaurant's mirror- and glass-packed neoclassical dining room is one of the prettiest in town. Bow-tied waiters serve traditional Bohemian specialties like roast duck, boiled trout, and chateaubriand. Most everything comes with dumplings and sauerkraut. During good weather, the best tables are outside, on a small streetfront porch.

---

4. ČESKÉ BUDĚJOVICE

92 miles S of Prague

GETTING THERE   By Train   Express trains from Prague make the trip to České Budějovice in about three hours, and cost about 100 Kč ($3.35) in first class, 60 Kč ($2) in second class.

ESSENTIALS   České Budějovice's **telephone area code** is 038.

All phone numbers in this section assume this prefix, unless otherwise noted.

ORIENTATION České Budějovice's circular Staré Msto (Old Town) centers around the Czech Republic's largest cobblestone square, called náměstí Přemysla Otakara II.

INFORMATION Although there is no official tourist agency in town, several places in the heart of Staré Msto can sell you a map, make accommodations arrangements, and dispense information.

Southern Bohemia's well-preserved Renaissance town of České Budějovice is steeped in history and small enough to be comfortably seen in a day. At its center is one of the largest squares in Central Europe, containing the ornate Fountain of Sampson, an 18th-century water well that was once the town's principle water supply.

WHAT TO SEE & DO

CERNÁ VĚŽ [Black Tower], U Černé věže. Tel. 386-38.

The most famous symbol of České Budějovice, this 232-foot-tall 16th-century tower was built as a belfry for the adjacent St. Nicholas Church. Visitors regularly ascend the tower's 255 steps for a glimpse of downtown and the surrounding countryside.

Admission: 20 Kč (70¢) adults, 10 Kč (35¢) students.

Open: Mar–June, Tues–Sun 10am–6pm; July–Aug, daily 10am–7pm; Sept–Nov, Tues–Sun 9am–5pm. **Closed:** Dec–Feb.

CHURCH OF ST. NICOLAS (Kostel sv. Mikuláše), U Černé věže. Tel. 98-967.

One of the most important sights in České Budějovice, this 13th-century church was a bastion of Roman Catholicism during the 15th century Hussite rebellion. The church's flamboyant white-and-cream 17th-century baroque interior shouldn't be missed.

Admission: Free.
Open: Daily 8am–6pm.

WHERE TO STAY

For quality and price, private rooms are the best places to stay in České Budějovice. Arrange your room through **Nimbus Travel, Žižkova 3** (tel. 038/570-85).

Moderate

HOTEL ZVON, Žižkovo náměstí, 37042 České Budějovice. Tel. 038/353-61. 45 rms (10 with bath). TV TEL

$ Rates: 550 Kč ($18.30) single without bath, 1,000 Kč ($33.35) single with bath; 900 Kč ($30) double without bath, 1,500 Kč ($50)

double with bath; 1,000 Kč ($33.35) triple without bath, 1,900 Kč ($63.35) triple with bath. Bath or shower 56 Kč ($1.90) extra. No credit cards.

Location is everything to this hotel, directly on náměstí Přemysla Otakara II, the town's main square. And although the rooms themselves are relatively plain and functional, the views from those in front can't be topped. Rooms facing the square aren't only brighter, they're larger and nicer, too. There is no elevator, but if you don't mind the climb, locate on the fourth floor.

WHERE TO DINE

MASNÉ KRÁMY ["Meat Shops"], Krajinská 29. Tel. 326-52.

Cuisine: CZECH.
$ Prices: Appetizers 30–60 Kč ($1–$2); main courses 90–150 Kč ($3–$5). No credit cards.
Open: Daily 10am–11pm.

Located just northwest of náměstí Přemysla Otakara II, labyrinthine Masné Krámy occupies a series of drinking rooms on either side of a long hallway. The food is pure Bohemia, inexpensive and filling, and includes several pork, duck, and trout offerings. Come here for the atmosphere, which is always boisterous and lively.

RYBÁŘSKY SÁL, in the Hotel Gomel, Míru třída 14. Tel. 289-49.

Cuisine: CZECH/INTERNATIONAL.
$ Prices: Appetizers 15–30 Kč (50¢–$1); main courses 60–150 Kč ($2–$5). AE, DC, MC, V.
Open: Mon–Thurs 6am–10pm, Fri–Sat 6am–11pm.

Generally acknowledged as the best food in town, Rybářsky sál is a popular restaurant known for four freshwater fish: carp, trout, perch, and pike. Chicken Kiev and other "turf" dishes are also served. The dining room is modern and minimally decorated with hanging fishnets.

---

5. ČESKÝ KRUMLOV

12 miles SW of České Budějovice

GETTING THERE   By Train   The only way to reach Český Krumlov by train from Prague is via České Budějovice, a slow ride that will deposit you at a station relatively far from the town center.

By Bus   The 3½-hour bus ride from Prague usually involves a transfer in České Budějovice. The bus station in Český Krumlov is a 15-minute walk from the town's main square.

ESSENTIALS   Český Krumlov's **telephone area code** is 0337;

all phone numbers in this section assume this prefix, unless otherwise noted.

ORIENTATION   Surrounded by a circular sweep of the Vltava River, Český Krumlov is very easy to negotiate. The main square, náměstí Svornosti is located at the very center of the Old Town. The bridge that spans the Vltava a few blocks away leads to a rocky hill, above which is a castle known as the Český Krumlov Chateau.

INFORMATION   Služby Turistům (Tourist Service), Zámek 59 (tel. and fax 337/4605), located on the street leading up to the castle entrance, is the best source of information in town. In addition to dispensing information, the company's English-speaking staff books private rooms and tours and sells maps and guidebooks. It's open daily from 9am to 6pm.

Český Krumlov, a living gallery of elegant Renaissance-era buildings housing charming cafés, pubs, restaurants, shops, and galleries, is one of the prettiest towns in all of Bohemia. In 1992 UNESCO named Český Krumlov a World Heritage Site for its historical importance and physical beauty. Bustling since medieval times, centuries of embellishment have left the town exquisitely beautiful.

WHAT TO SEE & DO

ČESKÝ KRUMLOV CHATEAU. Tel. 2075.

Reputedly the largest castle in Bohemia after Prague Castle, Český Krumlov Château was constructed in the 13th century as part of a private estate. Throughout the ages, the castle has passed on to a variety of private owners, including the Rožmberk family, the largest landholders in Bohemia.

Perched high atop a rocky hill, the château is open to tourists from April to October only, exclusively by guided tour. Visits begin in the palace's rococo Chapel of St. George, continue through portrait-packed Renaissance Hall, and end with the Royal Family Apartments, outfitted with ornate furnishings that include Flemish wall tapestries and European paintings.

Tours last one hour and depart frequently. Most are in Czech or German, however. Should you wish an English-language tour, arrange it ahead of time through Prague's **Čedok,** Na příkopě 18 (tel. 212-7512).

Admission: Tour 90 Kč ($3) adults, 45 Kč ($1.50) students.

Open: May–Aug, Tues–Sun 7:45am–noon and 12:45–4pm; Sept, Tues–Sun 8:45am–noon and 12:45–4pm; Apr and Oct, Tues–Sun 8:45am–noon and 12:45–3pm (last entrance 60 minutes before closing). **Closed:** Nov–Mar.

REGIONAL MUSEUM [Muzeum esk Krumlov], Horní ulice 152. Tel. 2049.

Once a Jesuit seminary, the three-story Regional Museum now contains artifacts and displays relating to Český Krumlov's 1,000-year history. The highlight of this mass of folk art, clothing, furniture, and statues is a giant model of the town that offers a bird's-eye view of the buildings. Ask for an English-language pamphlet at the entrance.

Admission: 20 Kč (70¢) adults, 10 Kč (35¢) students.

Open: May–Sept, daily 10am–12:30pm and 1–6pm; Feb–Apr and Oct–Dec, Tues–Fri 9am–noon and 12:30–5pm, Sat–Sun 1–5pm. **Closed:** Jan.

WHERE TO STAY

"Pension" and "Zimmer Frei" signs line Horní and Rooseveltova streets, and offer the best values in town; expect to pay about 200 Kč to 500 Kč ($3.35 to $13.35) per person.

Moderate

HOTEL RŮŽE ("Rose Hotel"), Horní 153, 38101 Český Krumlov. Tel. 0337/2245 or 5481. 70 rms (all with bath). TV TEL
$ Rates: 1,300–3,000 Kč ($36.70–$100) single or double. AE, MC, V.

Once a Jesuit seminary, this stunning Italian Renaissance structure has been turned into a plush hotel. Comfortable in a big-city kind of way, the hotel is packed with amenities, and is the top place to stay in Český Krumlov.

Inexpensive

HOTEL KRUMLOV, náměstí Svornosti 14, 38101 Český Krumlov. Tel. 0337/2040. 30 rms (5 with full bath, 8 with shower only). TV TEL
$ Rates: 300 Kč ($10) single without bath, 450 Kč ($14.35) single with shower only; 300–550 Kč ($10–$18.35) double without bath, 500 Kč ($16.35) double with shower only, 750 Kč ($25) double with bath. AE, DC, V.

Located on the town's main square, a few minutes' walk from Český Krumlov Château, Hotel Krumlov is an aging belle dating from 1309. Like so many others in the republic, there's nothing fancy here, just satisfactory rooms right in the heart of the city. The hotel's restaurant serves typical Bohemian fare daily from 7am to 11pm.

PENSIONE VE VĚŽI ("In the Tower"), Latrán 28, 38101 Český Krumlov. Tel. 0337/5287 or 4972. 4 rms (none with bath).
$ Rates (including breakfast): 350 Kč ($11.70) single; 700 Kč ($23.35) double. No credit cards.

A recommendable private pension located in a renovated medieval tower just five minutes by foot from the castle, Ve Věži is one of the most magnificent places to stay in town. It's not the accommodations themselves that are so grand; none has private baths, and all are sparsely decorated. The ancient ambience is what fills this place; advance reservations are always recommended.

WHERE TO DINE

Moderate

RYBÁŘSKÁ BAŠTA JAKUBA KRČÍNA, Kájovská 54. Tel. 67-183.

Cuisine: CZECH. **Reservations:** Recommended.

$ Prices: Appetizers 30–60 Kč ($1–$2); main courses 120–300 Kč ($4–$10). AE, MC, V.

Open: Daily 7am–11pm.

One of the most celebrated restaurants in town, the restaurant specializes in freshwater fish from surrounding lakes. Trout, perch, pike, and eel are sautéed, grilled, baked, and fried in a variety of herbs and spices. Venison, rabbit, and other game are also available, along with the requisite roasted beefs and porks.

Inexpensive

U MĚSTA VÍDNĚ, Latrán 78.

Cuisine: CZECH.

$ Prices: Main courses 30–75 Kč ($1–$2.50). No credit cards.

Open: Daily 10am–10pm.

This locals' kind of pub is not only a good restaurant, it's one of the best hangouts in town. Traditional meat-and-dumplings style food is augmented by a couple of egg-based vegetarian dishes. Natives swear by the pub's locally brewed Českokrumlovské beer.

6. TEREZÍN

Prague's Jewish population was decimated during World War II, when the occupying Nazi army deported most of Bohemia's Jews to Terezín, a concentration camp located just 30 miles northwest of the city. There were no gas chambers, mass machine-gun executions, or medical testing rooms here. Terezín was a "show" camp, used by the Nazis to demonstrate to the world (via the International Red Cross) that Jews, Gypsies, gays, and political prisoners were not being mistreated. Yet thousands died here, most from disease and starvation. For most inmates, Terezín was little more than a stopping-off point on their way to greater suffering and death at Auschwitz or Buchenwald. Of the 139,654 prisoners sent to Terezín, there were only 17,472 left to be liberated at the war's end.

Today, the Terezín Camp exists as a memorial to the dead and a monument to human depravity. Visitors can tour the camp's dank cells and execution fields, and visit an adjacent museum that exhibits historical and personal artifacts illustrating camp life. Several short documentary films are available for viewing on request, including a Nazi-made propaganda piece.

Terezín Camp (tel. 0416/922-25) is open daily from 8am to 4:30pm. Admission is 50 Kč ($1.65) for adults, 25 Kč (85¢) for children. From Florenc Bus Station (metro line C), take any bus from stand number 17 or 19. The ride takes about an hour and costs 30 Kč ($1) each way. Prague-based **Wittmann Tours** (tel. 231-2895) offers irregularly scheduled group tours to Terezín on most Sundays and Thursdays. Tours depart from the Jewish Community Center, Maiselova 18, near the Old New Synagogue, and cost 450 Kč ($15) for adults and 350 Kč ($11.65) for students.

A. CZECH LANGUAGE

CZECH ALPHABET

There are 32 vowels and consonants in the Czech alphabet, and most of the consonants are pronounced about as they are in English. Accent marks over vowels lengthen the sound of the vowel, as does the *kroužek,* or little circle (" ˙ "), which appears only over "o" and "u."

A, a	*fa*ther	N, n	*n*o
B, b	*b*oy	Ň, ň	Ta*ny*a
C, c	ge*ts*	O, o	*aw*ful
Č, č	*ch*oice	P, p	*p*en
D, d	*d*ay	R, r	slightly trilled *r*
D', d'	*Di*or	Ř, ř	slightly trilled *r* + *sh* as in cru*sh*
E, e	n*e*ver	S, s	*s*eat
F, f	*f*ood	Š, š	cru*sh*
G, g	*g*oal	T, t	*t*oo
H, h	un*h*and	T', t'	no*t y*et
Ch, ch	Lo*ch* Lomond	U, u	r*oo*m
I, i	n*ee*d	V, v	*v*ery
J, j	*y*es	W, w	*v*ague
K, k	*k*ey	Y, y	f*u*nny
L, l	*l*ord	Z, z	*z*ebra
M, m	*m*ama	Ž, ž	a*z*ure, plea*s*ure

CZECH VOCABULARY

Everyday Expressions

ENGLISH	CZECH	PRONOUNCED
Hello	**Dobrý den**	*daw*-bree den
Good morning	**Dobré jitro**	*daw*-breh *yee*-traw
Good evening	**Dobrý večer**	*daw*-bree *veh*-chair
How are you?	**Jak se máte?**	*yahk* seh *mah*-teh
Very well	**Velmi dobře**	*vel*-mee
		daw-brsheh
Thank you	**Děkuji vam**	*dyek*-ooee vahm
You're welcome	**Prosím**	*praw*-seem
Please	**Prosím**	*praw*-seem
Yes	**Ano**	*ah*-no
No	**Ne**	neh
Excuse me	**Promiňte**	*praw*-min-teh

ENGLISH	CZECH	PRONOUNCED
How much does it cost?	**Kolik to stojí?**	*kaw*-leek taw *staw*-ee
I don't understand.	**Nerozumím.**	*neh*-raw-zoo-meem
Just a moment.	**Moment, prosím.**	*maw*-ment, *praw*-seem
Good-bye,	**Na shledanou.**	*nah* skleh-dah-noh-oo

Traveling

Where is the? . . .	**Kde je?** . . .	*gde* **yeh?** . . .
bus station	**autobusové nádraží**	*ahoo*-taw-boos-oh-veh *nah*-drah-shee
train station	**nádraží**	*nah*-drah-shee
airport	**letiště**	*leh*-tyish-tyeh
baggage check	**úschovna zavazadel**	*oo*-skohv-nah *zah*-vahz-ah-del
Where can I find a taxi?	**Kde najdu taxi?**	*gde nai*-doo *tahks*-eh
Where can I find a gas station?	**Kde najdu benzínovou pumpu?**	*gde nai*-doo *ben*-zeen-oh-voh *poomp*-oo
How much is gas?	**Kolik stojí benzín?**	*koh*-leek *stoh*-yee *ben*-zeen
Please fill the tank.	**Naplňte mi nádrž, prosím.**	*nah*-puln-teh mee *nah*-dursh, *praw*-seem
How much is the fare?	**Kolik je jízdné?**	*koh*-leek yeh *yeesd*-neh
I am going to . . .	**Pojedu do** . . .	*poh*-yeh-doo doh . . .
One-way ticket	**Jízdenka**	*yeez*-den-kah
Round-trip ticket	**Zpáteční jízdenka**	*zpah*-tech-nee *jeez*-den-kah
Car-rental office	**Pujčovna aut**	*poo*-eech-awv-nah ah-oot

Accommodations

I'm looking for . . .	**Hledám** . . .	*hleh*-dahm . . .
a hotel	**hotel**	*haw*-tel
a youth hostel	**studentskou ubytovnu**	*stoo*-dent-skoh *oo*-beet-ohv-noo
I am staying . . .	**Zůstanu** . . .	*zoo*-stah-noo . . .

ENGLISH	CZECH	PRONOUNCED
a few days	**několik dnů**	*nyeh*-koh-leek dnoo
two weeks	**dva týdny**	dvah tid-*neh*
a month	**jeden měsíc**	*yeh*-den *myeh*-seets
I have a reservation.	**Mám zamluvený nocleh.**	mahm *zah*-mloo-veh-ni *nawts*-leh.
My name is . . .	**Jmenují se . . .**	*meh*-noo-yee seh . . .
Do you have a room? . . .	**Máte pokoj? . . .**	*mah*-teh *poh*-koy? . . .
for tonight	**na dnešek**	*nah* dneh-sheck
for three nights	**na tři dny**	*nah* trshee dnee
for a week	**na týden**	*nah* tee-den
I would like . . .	**Chci . . .**	khtsee . . .
a single	**jednolůžkový pokoj**	*jed*-noh-loosh-koh-vee *poh*-koy
a double	**dvojlůžkový pokoj**	*dvoy*-loosh-koh-vee *poh*-koy
I want a room . . .	**Chci pokoj . . .**	khtsee *poh*-koy . . .
with a bath	**s koupelnou**	*skoh*-pehl-noh
without a bath	**bez koupelny**	*behz* koh-pehl-nee
with a shower	**se sprchou**	*seh* spur-choh
without a shower	**bez sprchy**	*bez* sprech-*eh*
with a view	**s pohledem**	*spoh*-hlehd-ehm
How much is the room? . . .	**Kolik stojí pokoj? . . .**	*koh*-leek *stoh*-yee *paw*-koy? . . .
with breakfast	**se snídaní**	*seh* snee-dan-nyee
May I see the room?	**Mohu vidět ten pokoj?**	*moh*-hoo *vee*-dyet ten *paw*-koy
The key	**Klíč**	kleech
The bill, please.	**Dejte mi učet, prosím.**	*day*-teh mee oo-cheht, *praw*-seem

Getting Around

I'm looking for . . .	**Hledám . . .**	*hleh*-dahm . . .
a bank	**banku**	*bahnk*-oo
the church	**kostel**	*kaws*-tell
the city center	**centrum**	*tsent*-room
the museum	**muzeum**	*moo*-zeh-oom
a pharmacy	**lekarnu**	*lek*-ahr-noo
the park	**park**	pahrk
the theater	**divadlo**	*dee*-vahd-loh
the tourist office	**cestovní kancelář**	*tses*-tohv-nee *kahn*-tseh-larsh

ENGLISH	CZECH	PRONOUNCED
the embassy	**velvyslanectví**	*vehl*-vee-slahn-ets-tvee
Where is the nearest telephone?	**Kde je nejbližší telefon?**	gde yeh *nay*-bleesh-ee *tel*-oh-fohn
I would like to buy . . .	**Chci koupit . . .**	khtsee *koh*-peet . . .
a stamp	**známku**	*znahm*-koo
a postcard	**pohlednici**	*poh*-hlehd-nit-seh
a map	**mapu**	*mahp*-oo

Signs

No Trespassing	**Cizím vstup zakázán**
No Parking	**Neparkovat**
Entrance	**Vchod**
Exit	**Východ**
Information	**Informace**
No Smoking	**Kouření zakázáno**
Arrivals	**Příjezd**
Departures	**Odjezd**
Toilets	**Toalety**
Danger	**Pozor, nebezpečí**

Numbers

1 **jeden** (*yeh*-den)	15 **patnáct** (*paht*-nahtst)	60 **šedesát** (*she*-deh-saht)
2 **dva** (dvah)	16 **šestnáct** (*shest*-nahtst)	70 **sedmdesát** (*seh*-duhm-deh-saht)
3 **tři** (trshee)	17 **sedmnáct** (*seh*-doom-nahtst)	80 **osmdesát** (*aw*-suhm-deh-saht)
4 **čtyři** (*chtee*-rshee)	18 **osmnáct** (*aw*-soom-nahtst)	90 **devadesát** (*deh*-vah-deh-saht)
5 **pět** (pyet)	19 **devatenáct** (*deh*-vah-teh-nahtst)	100 **sto** (staw)
6 **šest** (shest)	20 **dvacet** (*dvah*-tset)	500 **pět set** (*pyet* set)
7 **sedm** (*seh*-duhm)	30 **třicet** (*trshee*-tset)	1,000 **tisíc** (*tyee*-seets)
8 **osm** (*aw*-suhm)	40 **čtyřicet** (*chti*-rshee-tset)	
9 **devět** (*deh*-vyet)	50 **padesát** (*pah*-deh-saht)	
10 **deset** (*deh*-set)		
11 **jedenáct** (*yeh*-deh-nahtst)		
12 **dvanáct** (*dvah*-nahtst)		
13 **třináct** (*trshee*-nahtst)		
14 **čtrnáct** (*chtur*-nahtst)		

Dining

ENGLISH	CZECH	PRONOUNCED
Restaurant	**Restaurace**	*rehs*-tow-rah-tseh
Breakfast	**Snídaně**	*snee*-dah-nyeh
Lunch	**Oběd**	*oh*-byed
Dinner	**Večeře**	*veh*-chair-sheh
A table for two, please. (Lit.: There are two of us)	**Jsme dva.**	*ees*-meh dvah
Waiter	**Číšník**	*cheess*-neek
Waitress	**Servírka**	ser-*veer*-ka
I would like . . .	**Chci . . .**	khtsee . . .
a menu	jídelní lístek	*yee*-del-nee *lees*-teck
a fork	**vidličku**	*veed*-leech-koo
a knife	**nůž**	noosh
a spoon	**lžičku**	lu-*shich*-koo
a napkin	**ubrousek**	*oo*-broh-seck
a glass (of water)	**skleničku (vody)**	*sklehn*-ich-koo (vod-*deh*)
the check, please	**účet, prosím**	*oo*-cheht, *praw*-seem
Is the tip included?	**Je v tom zahrnuto spropitné?**	yeh *ftohm*-zah *hur*-noo-toh *sproh*-peet-neh?

Menu Terms: General

Soup	**Polévka**	*poh*-lehv-kah
Eggs	**Vejce**	*vayts*-eh
Meat	**Maso**	*mahs*-oh
Fish	**Ryba**	*ree*-bah
Vegetables	**Zelenina**	*zehl*-eh-nee-nah
Fruit	**Ovoce**	*oh*-voh-tseh
Desserts	**Moučníky**	*mohch*-nee-kee
Beverages	**Nápoje**	*nah*-poy-yeh
Salt	**Sůl**	sool
Pepper	**Pepř**	*peh*-prsh
Mayonnaise	**Majonéza**	*mai*-o-neza
Mustard	**Hořčice**	*hohrsh*-chee-tseh
Vinegar	**Ocet**	*oh*-tseht
Oil	**Olej**	*oh*-lay
Sugar	**Cukr**	*tsoo*-ker
Tea	**Čaj**	chye
Coffee	**Káva**	*kah*-vah
Bread	**Chléba**	*khlehb*-ah

ENGLISH	CZECH	PRONOUNCED
Butter	**Máslo**	*mahs*-loh
Wine	**Víno**	*vee*-noh
Fried	**Smažený**	*smah*-sheh-nee
Roasted	**Pečený**	*pech*-eh-nee
Boiled	**Vařený**	*vah*-rsheh-nee
Grilled	**Grilovaný**	*gree*-loh-vah-nee

Soup

Bramborová potato
Čočková lentil
Gulášová goulash

Rajaská tomato
Slepičí chicken
Zeleninová vegetable

Meat

Biftek steak
Guláš goulash
Hovězi beef
Játra liver
Jehněčí lamb
Kachna duck

Klobása sausage
Králík rabbit
Skopové mutton
Telecí veal
Telecí kotleta veal cutlet
Vepřové pork

Fish

Karp carp
Kaviár caviar
Rybí filé fish filet
Sled herring

Štika pike
Treska cod
Úhoř eel
Ústřice oysters

Eggs

Míchaná vejce scrambled
eggs
Smažená vejce fried eggs
Vařená vejce boiled eggs

Vejce na měkko soft-boiled
eggs
Vejce se slaninou bacon
and eggs
Vejce se šunkou ham and
eggs

Salad

Fazolový salát bean salad
Hlávkový salát mixed green
salad

Okurkový salát cucumber
salad
Salát z červené řepy beet
salad

Vegetables

Brambory potatoes
Celer celery
Chřest asparagus
Cibule onions
Houby mushrooms

Květák cauliflower
Mrkev carrots
Paprika peppers
Rajská jablíčka tomatoes
Zelí cabbage

Dessert

Koláč cake
Cukrovi cookies
Čokoládová zmrzlina chocolate ice cream

Jablkový závin apple strudel
Palačinky pancakes
Vanilková zmrzlina vanilla ice cream

Fruit

Citrón lemon
Hruška pears

Jablko apple
Švestky plums

Beverages

Čaj tea
Káva coffee
Mléko milk
Víno wine

cervené red
bílé white
Voda water

B. METRIC MEASURES

LENGTH

1 millimeter (mm)	=	0.04 inches (*or* less than $\frac{1}{16}$ in.)
1 centimeter (cm)	=	0.39 inches (*or* under ½ in.)
1 meter (m)	=	39 inches (*or* about 1.1 yd.)
1 kilometer (km)	=	0.62 miles (*or* about ⅔ of a mile)

To convert kilometers to miles, multiply the number of kilometers by 0.62. Also use to convert kilometers per hour (kmph) to miles per hour (m.p.h.).

To convert miles to kilometers, multiply the number of miles by 1.61. Also use to convert from m.p.h. to kmph.

CAPACITY

1 liter (l)	=	33.92 fluid ounces = 2.1 pints
	=	1.06 quarts = 0.26 U.S. gallons
1 Imperial gallon	=	1.2 U.S. gallons

To convert liters to U.S. gallons, multiply the number of liters by 0.26.

To convert U.S. gallons to liters, multiply the number of gallons by 3.79.

To convert Imperial gallons to U.S. gallons, multiply the number of Imperial gallons by 1.2.

To convert U.S. gallons to Imperial gallons, multiply the number of U.S. gallons by 0.83.

WEIGHT

1 gram (g)	=	0.035 ounces (*or* about a paperclip's weight)
1 kilogram (kg)	=	35.2 ounces
	=	2.2 pounds
1 metric ton	=	2,205 pounds (1.1 short ton)

To convert kilograms to pounds, multiply the number of kilograms by 2.2.

To convert pounds to kilograms, multiply the number of pounds by 0.45.

AREA

1 hectare (ha)	=	2.47 acres
1 square kilometer (km²)	=	247 acres = 0.39 square miles

To convert hectares to acres, multiply the number of hectares by 2.47.

ACCOMMODATIONS
In Prague

Outside Prague

RESTAURANTS
In Prague

Outside Prague

Please Send Me the Books Checked Below:

FROMMER'S COMPREHENSIVE GUIDES
(Guides listing facilities from budget to deluxe,
with emphasis on the medium-priced)

	Retail Price	Code		Retail Price	Code
☐ Acapulco/Ixtapa/Taxco 1993–94	$15.00	C120	☐ Morocco 1992–93	$18.00	C021
☐ Alaska 1994–95	$17.00	C131	☐ Nepal 1994–95	$18.00	C126
☐ Arizona 1993–94	$18.00	C101	☐ New England 1994 (Avail. 1/94)	$16.00	C137
☐ Australia 1992–93	$18.00	C002	☐ New Mexico 1993–94	$15.00	C117
☐ Austria 1993–94	$19.00	C119	☐ New York State 1994–95	$19.00	C133
☐ Bahamas 1994–95	$17.00	C121	☐ Northwest 1994–95 (Avail. 2/94)	$17.00	C140
☐ Belgium/Holland/Luxembourg 1993–94	$18.00	C106	☐ Portugal 1994–95 (Avail. 2/94)	$17.00	C141
☐ Bermuda 1994–95	$15.00	C122	☐ Puerto Rico 1993–94	$15.00	C103
☐ Brazil 1993–94	$20.00	C111	☐ Puerto Vallarta/Manzanillo/Guadalajara 1994–95 (Avail. 1/94)	$14.00	C028
☐ California 1994	$15.00	C134	☐ Scandinavia 1993–94	$19.00	C135
☐ Canada 1994–95 (Avail. 4/94)	$19.00	C145	☐ Scotland 1994–95 (Avail. 4/94)	$17.00	C146
☐ Caribbean 1994	$18.00	C123	☐ South Pacific 1994–95 (Avail. 1/94)	$20.00	C138
☐ Carolinas/Georgia 1994–95	$17.00	C128	☐ Spain 1993–94	$19.00	C115
☐ Colorado 1994–95 (Avail. 3/94)	$16.00	C143	☐ Switzerland/Liechtenstein 1994–95 (Avail. 1/94)	$19.00	C139
☐ Cruises 1993–94	$19.00	C107	☐ Thailand 1992–93	$20.00	C033
☐ Delaware/Maryland 1994–95 (Avail. 1/94)	$15.00	C136	☐ U.S.A. 1993–94	$19.00	C116
☐ England 1994	$18.00	C129	☐ Virgin Islands 1994–95	$13.00	C127
☐ Florida 1994	$18.00	C124	☐ Virginia 1994–95 (Avail. 2/94)	$14.00	C142
☐ France 1994–95	$20.00	C132	☐ Yucatán 1993–94	$18.00	C110
☐ Germany 1994	$19.00	C125			
☐ Italy 1994	$19.00	C130			
☐ Jamaica/Barbados 1993–94	$15.00	C105			
☐ Japan 1994–95 (Avail. 3/94)	$19.00	C144			

FROMMER'S $-A-DAY GUIDES
(Guides to low-cost tourist accommodations and facilities)

	Retail Price	Code		Retail Price	Code
☐ Australia on $45 1993–94	$18.00	D102	☐ Israel on $45 1993–94	$18.00	D101
☐ Costa Rica/Guatemala/Belize on $35 1993–94	$17.00	D108	☐ Mexico on $45 1994	$19.00	D116
☐ Eastern Europe on $30 1993–94	$18.00	D110	☐ New York on $70 1994–95	$16.00	D120
☐ England on $60 1994	$18.00	D112	☐ New Zealand on $45 1993–94	$18.00	D103
☐ Europe on $50 1994	$19.00	D115	☐ Scotland/Wales on $50 1992–93	$18.00	D019
☐ Greece on $45 1993–94	$19.00	D100	☐ South America on $40 1993–94	$19.00	D109
☐ Hawaii on $75 1994	$19.00	D113	☐ Turkey on $40 1992–93	$22.00	D023
☐ India on $40 1992–93	$20.00	D010	☐ Washington, D.C. on $40 1994–95 (Avail. 2/94)	$17.00	D119
☐ Ireland on $45 1994–95 (Avail. 1/94)	$17.00	D117			

FROMMER'S CITY $-A-DAY GUIDES
(Pocket-size guides to low-cost tourist accommodations and facilities)

	Retail Price	Code		Retail Price	Code
☐ Berlin on $40 1994–95	$12.00	D111	☐ Madrid on $50 1994–95 (Avail. 1/94)	$13.00	D118
☐ Copenhagen on $50 1992–93	$12.00	D003	☐ Paris on $50 1994–95	$12.00	D117
☐ London on $45 1994–95	$12.00	D114	☐ Stockholm on $50 1992–93	$13.00	D022

FROMMER'S WALKING TOURS
(With routes and detailed maps, these companion guides point out the places and pleasures that make a city unique)

	Retail Price	Code		Retail Price	Code
☐ Berlin	$12.00	W100	☐ Paris	$12.00	W103
☐ London	$12.00	W101	☐ San Francisco	$12.00	W104
☐ New York	$12.00	W102	☐ Washington, D.C.	$12.00	W105

FROMMER'S TOURING GUIDES
(Color-illustrated guides that include walking tours, cultural and historic sights, and practical information)

	Retail Price	Code		Retail Price	Code
☐ Amsterdam	$11.00	T001	☐ New York	$11.00	T008
☐ Barcelona	$14.00	T015	☐ Rome	$11.00	T010
☐ Brazil	$11.00	T003	☐ Scotland	$10.00	T011
☐ Florence	$ 9.00	T005	☐ Sicily	$15.00	T017
☐ Hong Kong/Singapore/ Macau	$11.00	T006	☐ Tokyo	$15.00	T016
☐ Kenya	$14.00	T018	☐ Turkey	$11.00	T013
☐ London	$13.00	T007	☐ Venice	$ 9.00	T014

FROMMER'S FAMILY GUIDES

	Retail Price	Code		Retail Price	Code
☐ California with Kids	$18.00	F100	☐ San Francisco with Kids (Avail. 4/94)	$17.00	F104
☐ Los Angeles with Kids (Avail. 4/94)	$17.00	F103	☐ Washington, D.C. with Kids (Avail. 2/94)	$17.00	F102
☐ New York City with Kids (Avail. 2/94)	$18.00	F101			

FROMMER'S CITY GUIDES
(Pocket-size guides to sightseeing and tourist accommodations and facilities in all price ranges)

	Retail Price	Code		Retail Price	Code
☐ Amsterdam 1993–94	$13.00	S110	☐ Montréal/Québec City 1993–94	$13.00	S125
☐ Athens 1993–94	$13.00	S114	☐ Nashville/Memphis 1994–95 (Avail. 4/94)	$13.00	S141
☐ Atlanta 1993–94	$13.00	S112	☐ New Orleans 1993–94	$13.00	S103
☐ Atlantic City/Cape May 1993–94	$13.00	S130	☐ New York 1994 (Avail. 1/94)	$13.00	S138
☐ Bangkok 1992–93	$13.00	S005	☐ Orlando 1994	$13.00	S135
☐ Barcelona/Majorca/ Minorca/Ibiza 1993–94	$13.00	S115	☐ Paris 1993–94	$13.00	S109
☐ Berlin 1993–94	$13.00	S116	☐ Philadelphia 1993–94	$13.00	S113
☐ Boston 1993–94	$13.00	S117	☐ San Diego 1993–94	$13.00	S107
☐ Budapest 1994–95 (Avail. 2/94)	$13.00	S139	☐ San Francisco 1994	$13.00	S133
☐ Chicago 1993–94	$13.00	S122	☐ Santa Fe/Taos/ Albuquerque 1993–94	$13.00	S108
☐ Denver/Boulder/ Colorado Springs 1993–94	$13.00	S131	☐ Seattle/Portland 1994–95	$13.00	S137
☐ Dublin 1993–94	$13.00	S128	☐ St. Louis/Kansas City 1993–94	$13.00	S127
☐ Hong Kong 1994–95 (Avail. 4/94)	$13.00	S140	☐ Sydney 1993–94	$13.00	S129
☐ Honolulu/Oahu 1994	$13.00	S134	☐ Tampa/St. Petersburg 1993–94	$13.00	S105
☐ Las Vegas 1993–94	$13.00	S121	☐ Tokyo 1992–93	$13.00	S039
☐ London 1994	$13.00	S132	☐ Toronto 1993–94	$13.00	S126
☐ Los Angeles 1993–94	$13.00	S123	☐ Vancouver/Victoria 1994–95 (Avail. 1/94)	$13.00	S142
☐ Madrid/Costa del Sol 1993–94	$13.00	S124	☐ Washington, D.C. 1994 (Avail. 1/94)	$13.00	S136
☐ Miami 1993–94	$13.00	S118			
☐ Minneapolis/St. Paul 1993–94	$13.00	S119			

SPECIAL EDITIONS

	Retail Price	Code		Retail Price	Code
☐ Bed & Breakfast Southwest	$16.00	P100	☐ Caribbean Hideaways	$16.00	P103
☐ Bed & Breakfast Great American Cities (Avail. 1/94)	$16.00	P104	☐ National Park Guide 1994 (Avail. 3/94)	$16.00	P105
			☐ Where to Stay U.S.A.	$15.00	P102

Please note: if the availability of a book is several months away, we may have back issues of guides to that particular destination. Call customer service at (815) 734-1104.